HERITAGE MOVEMENTS IN ASIA

Explorations in Heritage Studies

Series Editors:
Ali Mozaffari, *Deakin University*
David Charles Harvey, *Aarhus University*

Explorations in Heritage Studies responds directly to the rapid growth of heritage scholarship and recognizes the trans-disciplinary nature of research in this area, as reflected in the wide-ranging fields, such as archaeology, geography, anthropology and ethnology, digital heritage, heritage management, conservation theory, physical science, architecture, history, tourism, and planning. With a blurring of boundaries between art and science, theory and practice, culture and nature, the volumes in the series balance theoretical and empirical research, and often challenge dominant assumptions in theory and practice.

Volume 1
Politics of Scale
New Directions in Critical Heritage Studies
Edited by Tuuli Lähdesmäki, Suzie Thomas, and Yujie Zhu

Volume 2
Heritage Movements in Asia
Cultural Heritage Activism, Politics, and Identity
Edited by Ali Mozaffari and Tod Jones

HERITAGE MOVEMENTS IN ASIA

Cultural Heritage Activism, Politics, and Identity

Edited by
Ali Mozaffari and Tod Jones

NEW YORK · OXFORD
www.berghahnbooks.com

First published in 2020 by
Berghahn Books
www.berghahnbooks.com

© 2020, 2023 Ali Mozaffari and Tod Jones
First paperback edition published in 2023

All rights reserved. Except for the quotation of short passages for the purposes of criticism and review, no part of this book may be reproduced in any form or by any means, electronic or mechanical, including photocopying, recording, or any information storage and retrieval system now known or to be invented, without written permission of the publisher.

Library of Congress Cataloging-in-Publication Data

Names: Mozaffari, Ali, editor. | Jones, Tod, 1977– editor. | Berghahn Books.
Title: Heritage Movements in Asia: Cultural Heritage Activism, Politics, and Identity / edited by Ali Mozaffari and Tod Jones.
Other titles: Explorations in Heritage Studies.
Description: First Edition. | New York: Berghahn Books, 2020. | Series: Explorations in Heritage Studies; volume 2 | Includes bibliographical references and index.
Identifiers: LCCN 2019037873 (print) | LCCN 2019037874 (ebook) | ISBN 9781789204810 (Hardback) | ISBN 9781789204827 (eBook)
Subjects: LCSH: Cultural property—Asia.
Classification: LCC DS12 .A4757 2020 (print) | LCC DS12 (ebook) | DDC 363.6/9095—dc23
LC record available at https://lccn.loc.gov/2019037873
LC ebook record available at https://lccn.loc.gov/2019037874

British Library Cataloguing in Publication Data

A catalogue record for this book is available from the British Library

ISBN 978-1-78920-481-0 hardback
ISBN 978-1-80073-634-4 paperback
ISBN 978-1-78920-482-7 ebook

https://doi.org/10.3167/9781789204810

Contents

List of Illustrations	vii
Foreword *James M. Jasper*	viii
Acknowledgments	xi
Introduction. Negotiation, Strategic Action, and the Production of Heritage *Ali Mozaffari and Tod Jones*	1
Chapter 1. Understanding Heritage Activism: Learning from Social Movement Studies *Tod Jones, Ali Mozaffari, and James M. Jasper*	32
Chapter 2. "The Past Is Always New": A Framework for Understanding the Centrality of Social Media to Contemporary Heritage Movements *Tod Jones, Transpiosa Riomandha, and Hairus Salim*	56
Chapter 3. The Exemplary Foreigner: Cultural Heritage Activism in Regional China *Gary Sigley*	80
Chapter 4. Heritage Activism in Singapore *Terence Chong*	107
Chapter 5. Riverscape as Biocultural Heritage: A Local Indigenous Social Movement Contests a National Park in Nepal *Sudeep Jana Thing*	123
Chapter 6. Heritage for Whom? Caste and Contestation among Sri Lanka's Dumbara Rata Weavers *Aimée Douglas*	147

Chapter 7. Heritage Activism and the Media (Framing)
in Iran, 2005–2013   170
  Ali Mozaffari

Index   197

Illustrations

Tables

2.1. Demographic characteristics of Bol Brutu members — 68
5.1. Key events in the Sonaha social movement — 135

Figures

2.1. The restoration of a terrace beneath Candi Ijo — 70
2.2. Sculpture of an ancestor — 71
3.1. Map of the People's Republic of China — 82
5.1. Lower Karnali River delta to the west of Bardia National Park — 125
5.2. Sketch map of the river delta locating the Sonaha settlements — 126
5.3. Key players and supporters of the Sonaha social movement — 133

Foreword

James M. Jasper

In our intellectual era, we tend to see humans as agents, pursuing a variety of projects and desires, engaging with others across many personal and political settings. Our distant ancestors placed more explanatory weight on fate, fortune, and the gods; our recent ancestors on nature, tradition, history, and structure. Today, we still acknowledge external constraints like these, but we see them in relation to human efforts, not as forces in themselves. Part of today's vision derives from a humanistic compassion for others, bolstered by feminism and other movements for rights and respect. Part comes from the research techniques refined by generations of social scientists, giving us access to sociological, psychological, and even neurological details that were once invisible.

Part of our current vision involves regard for the points of view of those we study. One root of this is the anguish of anthropologists as they have struggled to respect the humanity of those they study who are apparently so different from them. More broadly, the flourishing of cultural theories across the social sciences have helped us grasp how others situate themselves in the world, how they feel and think about things, whether they inhabit Pacific Islands or high-tech laboratories. Empathy and sympathy have become research techniques. We hear more and more about emotional intelligence, which would have been considered an oxymoron only a generation ago.

This is both a more generous and a more realistic view of humans that allows us to see them at work in many ways: not only communicating and supporting each other, following rules and habits, but also blocking one another, concocting tendentious stories, twisting and breaking the rules, inventing practices, and crushing other people's dreams. We find contention across all areas of human activity, from the most intimate to the most global, alongside the most pure acts of love and caring. We know too much to fall back on abstract, theological theories of human nature as inherently aggressive or cooperative. In fact, we can decisively reject most of the either/or theories that have so often hobbled social science and history.

The book in front of you explores various sorts of human activities, projects, and engagements around heritage, itself a contested term. They are neither a romantic rebellion from below nor a narcotic offered from above to quiet the masses. A variety of players pursue their dreams and interests on this terrain. Heritage, in my view, opens several new arenas for contestation, and people bring an amazing diversity of projects and motives into those arenas.

Until recently, most scholars defined social movements as efforts of oppressed groups to throw off their chains and become members of a political system, a formulation that would exclude many or most heritage movements. Heritage movements are sometimes political movements indirectly, in the form of projects to craft useful collective identities that in turn would help a group gain political respect, along with other trappings of citizenship. Other heritage movements reflect the imagination of those who already enjoy the privileges of citizenship but nonetheless see ways in which they would like to transform the world. Elites are perfectly capable of forming social movements when they need to, to which they bring advantages in resources, social connections, cultural symbolism, and more. Advantaged groups participate in arenas in other, non-movement forms as well, but that does not prevent them from forming movements when they see some advantage to doing so.

Heritage contests look like many other types of cultural contestation, in which objects, ideas, places, and even people are subject to contentious interpretation. As we see from the related field of collective memory, the past is a rich collection of references for actively shaping our current views and positions. Heritage is distinct in what kinds of meanings are open to debate, those from a specific past, as well as in opening particular arenas in which those meanings are debated. But in most ways, heritage movements fit new visions of social movements as efforts to persuade others and to make claims on other players, especially state players.

Many heritage contests reflect disagreements over collective identities, especially—in the age of the nation-state—national identities. Some collective identities revolve around "who we will be"—religious and political groups, for instance—but national identities inevitably rely on "who we have been," often seeking deep historical roots to establish essential, inherent characteristics. Groups dig up, ransack, and invent history to support their definitions of the nation. Collective identities have been described as necessary fictions, crucial bases for political claims, yet never as solidly grounded as proponents pretend; the "past" fits this definition, as both a source for identity claims and an inaccessible "foreign country," always a bit opaque to us.

Over the years, I have come to rely on a simple language of players and arenas to describe strategic interactions, and I am gratified that some contributors have also found these terms useful. The concept of players forces us to specify who is doing what to whom, delving deeper than traditional formulations such as social movements or states. Formal organizations, factions, informal networks, and even individuals, are the usual players, with enough coherence in goals and action to cooperate and act. Arenas are the places where outcomes are worked out: the legislatures, hearings, and meeting rooms where different players engage one another. (The media are a more metaphorical use of the term arena, but there are clear contests and outcomes even here.) Arenas assemble a variety of objects, from entrances and exits to lighting and seating, alongside formal and informal rules of engagement.

Challenges remain. How do we link fine-grained micro-social analysis with big macro-level trends and outcomes? How do we trace the impact of a small group sitting around a kitchen table on national policies? How do we incorporate new insights into cultural meanings and feelings into structural factors such as capitalism or state constitutions? Ideally, we would follow long chains of interactions across many arenas, but realistically, we concentrate on a few key interactions, highlight a handful of powerful players, but nonetheless try to remain attentive to obscure, surprising, unsung players as well. Simple catalogs of all the players, as well as all the arenas, can often clarify our explanations.

Ali and Tod have already done fine work to apply social movement theories to heritage, but here they arrive at a whole new level. The first two chapters of *Heritage Movements in Asia: Cultural Heritage Activism, Politics, and Identity* lay out a theoretical vocabulary for grasping the roiling contestation at the heart of heritage construction and policy. The editors describe the many purposes to which players try to put heritage, including domestic and foreign policies, economic interests, and development, and more. I then join them in chapter 2 to try to draw on social-movement theory more explicitly. The following chapters address numerous heritage issues from a rich variety of angles, all showing the incredible diversity of contestation that makes up human cultures and politics. They examine a range of topics, from a riverscape to a boutique hotel, the influence of social media but also traditional media, in a diverse selection of countries to which "Asia" hardly does justice. These are fascinating stories, but even more, they are powerful explanations of where heritage comes from and what we do with it.

James M. Jasper teaches in the Sociology PhD program at the Graduate Center of the City University of New York. His latest books include *Protest: A Cultural Introduction to Social Movements* (2014) and *Players and Arenas* (2015). More information is available on his website, www.jamesmjasper.org.

Acknowledgments

This book has been a very long time in the making. The initial ideas about the area and the topic were conceived by the editors in late 2013 and subsequently developed through a workshop at Curtin University with Professor James M. Jasper, and a dedicated workshop convened by the editors at Curtin University in 2016. Throughout this time, we were encouraged by many of our colleagues and supported by various parts of our institutions. In particular, we would like to thank Professor Jasper, whose work on the cultural aspects of social movements we attempted to extend into the field of heritage and who has supported this project from early in its inception. We are grateful for the time and attention of our colleagues Graham Seal, Tim Winter, Shaphan Cox, and Marieke Bloembergen for their assistance and support during the various stages of preparing this volume. We acknowledge Adam Crowe's outstanding work in assisting us with the editing and formatting of the complete manuscript. We also wish to thank our contributors, as well as David Harvey and Caryn Berg (of Berghahn Books), without whose patience this collection would not have materialized.

We also wish to acknowledge our institutions, the School of Design and Built Environment, the Australia-Asia-Pacific Institute, and the Research Unit for the Study of Societies in Change at Curtin University, as well as Deakin University's Alfred Deakin Institute for Citizenship and Globalization, for their support through various small grants and for awarding Tod Jones an Alfred Deakin Visiting Fellowship in December 2016. Tod was able to complete his chapter and edit other chapters while on an Academic Study Program supported by the School of Design and Built Environment and the Humanities Office of Research and Graduate Studies at Curtin University and was assisted in his travels for collaborations and presentation by an Operational Research Support grant from the School of Design and Built Environment in 2016. The production and completion of this work was also made possible through a competitive grant (ARC-DECRA) awarded by the Australian Research Council to Ali Mozaffari (grant no. DE170100104).

Finally, we would like to thank our families. Thank you Minoo and Kate for putting up with our early mornings and late nights, and to Sepanta, Bara, Gabriel, and Owen for your patience as we finish the sentences and paragraphs that sometimes delay our attention to you.

Introduction
Negotiation, Strategic Action, and the Production of Heritage
Ali Mozaffari and Tod Jones

The structure's fate attracted much attention after the Xicheng district government announced plans to bulldoze the building to make way for public green space, prompting calls for better protection of historical architecture amid rampant urbanization . . . In response to public outcry, Wang said that the district government would enhance protection of its 184 cultural heritage sites, including 23 former residences of famous people. ("Beijing Withdraws Demolition Plan for Late Writer's Residence," *China Times*, 26 March 2012)

The race is on to salvage banks flanked by Corinthian pillars, courthouses adorned with limestone lions, and shipping headquarters decorated with dark wood and brass fixtures before they collapse of decay . . . The conservation of the buildings . . . says Thant Myint-U, the head of the Yangon Heritage Trust. "The future is all about cities," said Mr. Thant Myint-U, who is trying to convince the government that the old has value and must be preserved. "Having a beautiful downtown will bring investment and give us an advantage over cities like Chennai and Kuala Lumpur." ("In Myanmar, Racing to Save a Colonial Past," *New York Times*, 13 December 2014)

These passages represent but two examples of a growing trend in the Global South by which unofficial groups and individuals actively participate in the construction and contestation of heritage at various scales. The contents of this book analyze and attest to a growing activism under the banner of heritage in Asia, a label we shall define later in this introduction. This growing trend is concerned with a diversity of heritages, both tangible and intangible, from various historic periods, including colonial times. The first quote was about a plan to demolish the residence of the Chinese literary master Lu Xun in Beijing. The second quote illustrates a desire on the part of influential players (in this case, Thant Myint-U, a Cambridge historian and Chair of the Yangon Heritage Trust) who are attempting to preserve colonial urban heritage for what they claim to be its historical and tourism values. In both instances, activism transformed the official scope and definition of heritage.

The historian Raphael Samuel (1994: 288, 292) notes "preservationism is a cause which owes at least as much to the Left as to the Right" and has "a predilection for direct action." In other words, heritage can be used by a variety of groups across political and social spectrums. Focusing on countries in Asia, the chapters in this volume address this proposition by avoiding the pitfall of dichotomous perspectives—such as "dominant-subaltern" and "authorized-unauthorized," "experts and nonexperts"—that seem to have dominated the field in the past decade (Rico 2015). Avoiding such dichotomous positions requires approaches that consider the details of the shifting agencies of various actors or players and the circumstance as well as the settings in which they engage with heritage and one another. The chapters in this book represent instances of such approaches in different Asian settings.

The two examples at the opening of this introduction are representative of a broader development in diverse contexts hinting at the rise of heritage and its contests in the popular imagination. Developing an academic perspective on heritage activism and the characteristics it takes relates to three big concepts in social sciences: globalization, scale, and civil society (and the state). In the following, we will briefly describe our position on these concepts and their importance to understanding heritage activism, before focusing on transformations in heritage studies itself and foregrounding the methodological and epistemological implications of learning from social movements theories in advancing our understanding of heritage. As we shall discuss later, the chapters of this volume take a range of approaches to conceptualize agency and activism in heritage, using a range of disciplinary methodologies that will be detailed throughout the chapters.

Globalization

According to Malcolm Waters (2013: 5), globalization is "a social process in which the constraints of geography on economic, political, social and cultural arrangements recede, in which people become increasingly aware that they are receding and in which people act accordingly." According to some theorists, links between various actors, circulation of materials, and information intensify in this process, leading to a collapse of the effects of distances and time (Labadi and Long 2010; Waters 2013). While this may be true on one level, we believe, on another level, relationships of heritage grow out of specific material conditions in places that in turn affect the capacities and actions of human agents. Among these theorists, there is broad agreement that such transformations have occurred in waves. The latest wave began in the 1960s and intensified from the 1980s. The effects of this social process are discernible on the three areas of economy, polity, and culture, with the latter gaining the most emphasis in recent times. The result is a stronger cultural circulation.

The growth of tourism indicates the intensification of both economic and cultural circulation. According to the World Tourism Organization (UNWTO 2015: 2), global tourism has steadily grown from 25 million in 1950 to 1,133 million in 2014. These statistics also clearly show a significantly higher rate of growth in international tourism in "emerging economies" (roughly mapping onto the countries of the Global South) in comparison to the "advanced economies" (roughly mapping on the countries of the Global North) (4). However, rather than homogenization driven by centralization and harmony over all scales, globalization results in "high levels of differentiation, multi-centricity and chaos" (Waters 2013: 30). This at once chaotic and global experience, the concurrent homogenizing and diversification, is to be expected. Similarly, Anna Tsing (2005) argues globalization processes are effective only once they instigate local engagement and that leads to a diverse and messy array of outcomes within scaled material networks that connect and influence a variety of people and places. Thus, while we agree heritage, in its current use, is a universalized Western European concept (Anheier and Isar 2011; Labadi and Long 2010), we also note this does not translate into uniformity across the board. Rather, heritage is the product of two conflicting forces of homogenization at global level and diversification at the local level.

Under the circumstances, and following Tsing's (2005) formulation, heritage should be understood as an "engaged universal" (Jones et al. 2016) or a globalizing project (Labadi and Long 2010, echoing Tsing 2000)—one that, as Tim Winter (2013: 74) points out, is unfinished and "consists of [various] networks, pyramids and . . . clusters of institutions and actors who organize themselves across borders, with the deliberate aim of drawing the world together in new ways." With the proliferation of various global nongovernmental bodies (historical societies, national trusts, and international bodies including UNESCO and the Global Heritage Fund), cultural heritage is now implicated in and related to human rights, climate change, issues of development, sustainability, poverty alleviation, and urban regeneration, to name but a few. As an engaged universal, even the demands of the most official and universalizing processes of heritage—World Heritage—is susceptible to translation, transformation, and conflict through existing political and bureaucratic cultures (Jones et al. 2016). Through this process, rather than a uniform, singular "regime," multiple heritage claims are created across various scales (Bendix et al. 2012: 14). Broadly speaking, as competing actors have proliferated, there is an increasing multivocality in heritage because these interactions are crucial to the constitution of heritage. This brings us to the second issue: scale

Scale

Traditionally, scale referred to how researchers balanced the extent (boundaries) and resolution (depth of information) of their research (N. Smith 1993). The political upheavals of the 1960s led to a focus on the social construction of scale, generally at the predefined levels of household, neighborhood, city, region, nation, and globe (Brenner 1997). However, this approach allocated too much causal power to the higher-level scales (particularly the global), misrepresenting local actors as without agency, and local conditions as determined by global or national forces (Marston 2000). Another critique of this understanding of scale in the heritage context is that local actors are automatically marked as progressive but powerless and national, or global actors as powerful but conservative or repressive. These critiques have been made both about the use of scale in the social sciences (Massey 2005) and in heritage research (Harvey 2015). Richard Howitt (2003) eloquently captures the contemporary definition of scale as size (geographical scale or pattern and extent), level (vertical scale of organizations), and relation (an understanding that scale is constituted through dynamic relationships in specific contexts).

The last element, relation, is the most profound, as it points out that scale is negotiated, contingent, and political (Jones et al. 2016). A focus on relations acknowledges scales are constituted as much through messy negotiations and misunderstandings as they are through collaboration and consensus. Scale itself is not a cause; it is best thought of as an "empirical generalization" or "a concept made real by building up an understanding of complex and dynamic relationships and processes in context" (Howitt 2003: 151). Like heritage, scale gains meaning and definition only when we look at the specific sets of relations that players are trying to invoke or contest (Jones et al. 2016). The attraction of heritage is often that it seeks to articulate new scales, or sets of relations between people, institutions, and things, that in turn shift relations between levels and change geographical scales.[1] Heritage and its associated scales therefore require tools that analyze the relationships between players: the activists as well as the experts, developers, bureaucrats, lawyers, and anyone else involved in heritage creation. Scale can be applied consciously through examining its three elements, or through analysis that recognizes concepts, debates, and conflicts are negotiated and distributed and that these connections and disconnections are formative. While scale is not often explicitly invoked in this book, this approach to scale informs its analysis. This brings us to the last of the three concepts, that of civil society and, by extension, the state.

Civil Society (and the State)

Civil society is a contested and "elastic" concept that may be articulated in at least three ways: as part of society characterized by voluntary associations, a kind of society ruled by certain norms (law, civility, etc.), and a type of space for citizen interaction (Edwards 2011: 3). It is also continually being reshaped and reinterpreted by new actors in new contexts. Despite all these fluctuations, scholars argue the idea that voluntary collective action can influence the world for the better seems to have remained at its core. A cogent and helpful definition of civil society is provided by Michael Walzer (1998: 123–124, quoted in Edwards 2011: 4): "Civil society is the sphere of uncoerced human association between the individual and the state, in which people undertake collective action for normative and substantive purposes, relatively independent of government and the market." Civil society relies on diverse forms of infrastructure that takes diverse shapes including grassroots organizations, professional societies, and NGOs, and these may vary in the degree of formality. It also is the outcome of the network among these organizations resulting in "assemblages, ecologies, or 'ecosystems,' which vary widely in their details from one context to another" (Edwards 2011: 7–8). Michael Edwards (2011: 3) describes this as the "geometry of human relations" in which individuals can engage autonomously of the state. It is important to note that networking and collective action do engender a sense of identity and strengthen civil society. However, the limits and shape of civil society are determined by other issues, including "insecurity, inequality, factionalism, the structure of communications, and the extent of civil and political liberties" (10). In other words, the political culture of the society, the type of state, and the dominant traditions are all at play.

Civil society is itself an invention and a product of particular practices of government and politics. Michel Foucault traces the historical development of increasingly sophisticated "technologies" of government that have evolved to increasingly focus on the productivity of populations (and its obstructions). In liberal democracies, productivity is governed through indirect regulation that creates and protects individual freedoms important for contemporary conceptions of civil society while seeking to influence the habits and practices of populations. The shifting definitions of "what is within the competence of the state and what is not, the public versus the private" (Foucault 1991: 103), and therefore the limits and practices of civil society, is a historical phenomenon connected to changing ideas and "techniques" of government. These "techniques" of government have been and continue to be applied not just in liberal democracies but also colonies, kingdoms, and dictatorships (Hindess 2001; Philpott 2000). Association, resistance, and debate—all important elements of civil society—existed and exist within the diverse circumstances of any given society and form of state, and are limited and defined against and within them.[2] Hence, the same political practices of debate and engagement can be acceptable and even normal in one political system but outlawed in another. This diversity of norms and forms and extents of civil society is understood in relation to the concentration and exercise of power—a diffuse and unstable "ensemble of actions which induce others and follow from one another" (Foucault 1982: 217)—within the state-society relations.

Heritage is strongly implicated in political power relations. As Irene Maffi and Rami Daher (2014) point out in the context of Arabic-speaking countries, power relationships across all types of actors, boundaries, and distances are crucial for analyzing and understanding heritage. Such analytical understanding requires a concept of power able to recognize the diverse sets of relationships and actors in the making of heritage. Our volume, like theirs, relates "to meaningful objects and dynamic actions through which various categories of agents configure or reconfigure history, identity, culture and power" (Daher and Maffi 2014: 3). In our concern for heritage objects, actors, and agents, we are also mindful that various complex bodies within states constitute significant, if at times conflicting, actors in the field. While it may be true that the current regime of heritage management privileges the nation-state (Labadi and Long 2010: 9), we, following Michael Herzfeld (1991, 2014), contend the state is not a uniform body, and that it cannot enforce a perpetual monopoly over heritage.

Heritage is mobilized for various reasons, including diplomacy (Winter 2015), business ties, economic development, urban renewal, and nation-building (Bendix et al. 2012: 18). The latter is especially significant in Asia, where many countries have gained their independence in the past century and have turned to heritage to chart their historical and cultural trajectories. An interesting example of this is China's partnership with the World Bank (WB 2011), where two of its three objectives focus on heritage (and conservation) in urban renewal and development projects (Ebbe et al. 2011). In this instance, we witness the bigger role played by a central state in heritage-related processes and nation-building. However, states only rarely retain exclusive power over heritage. As heritage has proliferated, various social groups find it a useful vehicle for contesting state power (Bendix et al. 2012: 19). Therefore, even highly centralized states may be compelled to be responsive to various social and economic pressures for heritage reform. As we shall discuss, the state may be crucial for the initial production of heritage, but understanding the dynamics or even the conditions of possibility of collective action becomes a useful means to understanding heritage processes. To elaborate, it is useful to briefly examine the transformation of the field of heritage highlighting the shifts in its object of study. Despite these changes, there are still few systematic studies of the role of various stakeholders and actors—institutional or otherwise—and their processes of communication and contestation in heritage.

Heritage 1: Schematizing the Evolution of Heritage Practice

Discussing the evolution of heritage comprises two aspects: how heritage has evolved in practice and how heritage research itself has evolved from multiple disciplines. For the purposes of the argument, we will schematize approaches to heritage in three time periods: first, the period leading to the 1980s when heritage was chiefly considered a resource; second, the 1990s when heritage was the field of enquiry especially dominated by archaeologists; and third, since the 2000s when critical developments has taken place and new scholarship has emerged in understanding heritage.

Current scholarship has established that, since the nineteenth century, heritage has been central to the establishment of nation-states, at first in Europe and then, often drawing on and rereading colonial research, throughout their former colonies in Asia and North Africa (Hall 2005; Kaplan 1994; Mitchell 2001; Roces 1978). The concern for heritage and its loss was prompted by Enlightenment's transformation of the ideas of history and science, as well as social and economic changes set in motion by the Industrial Revolution, which together propelled a romantic nostalgia and the desire to preserve and resuscitate aspects of the past and the connection to nature (Lowenthal 1998; West and Ansell 2010).

In Europe and North America, activists and heritage enthusiasts initially formed societies that prompted wider, legislated protection for heritage (both natural and cultural). These societies also acted as precursors to institutionalized heritage. In a succinct summary of the development of heritage in the West, Rodney Harrison (2013a, following West and Ansell 2010) traces the creation of inventories of historic sites to 1837 in the wake of the French Revolution. There is a clear link between the production of such inventories and the concomitant perspective on the meaning of history on the one hand, and the epistemic shifts produced by the Enlightenment and the production of the encyclopedia on the other hand. Thus, heritage processes of this period were concerned with scientific knowledge production, and its main protagonists were usually those equipped with knowledge of ordering and preserving material evidence of the past (generally professional experts). Thus, in the latter part of the nineteenth century, various "wilderness societies" appeared in North America with parallels in the United Kingdom. Concurrently, protection for both natural zones and monuments were being introduced into legislation. Nevertheless, the history of legislation for protecting heritage may be traced to Napoleon and his laws for protecting artifacts, which emerged during the Napoleonic Wars.

In the early days, two factors must be borne in mind: first, most heritage organizations began in the shape of activist organizations and preservationist societies outside the state apparatus. This suggests the strong link between the development of heritage and the formation of public spheres and civic societies. Second, and especially in the Asian context (Aikawa 2004; Bloembergen and Eickhoff 2015), international events and international networks were central in establishing the machinations of heritage within the state. For example, in Iran, heritage legislation was the result of a long process beginning with European rivalries in archaeological expeditions and then a French monopoly given by the Iranian government at the latter part of the nineteenth century, and culminated in a group of elites who led the establishment of Society for National Artefacts (Heritage) (Mozaffari 2014). The German archaeologist Ernst Herzfeld and the French architect and archaeologist André Godard were instrumental to forming heritage, legislation, and institutions such as the National Museum (known as the Ancient Iran Museum, est. 1936) (Mozaffari 2007).

There has been a steady growth in state control and legislation of heritage in each country. This process is combined with the rise of international concern for heritage (the case of Aswan Dam being the exemplary "myth of origin" for World Heritage (see Wangkeo 2003) and, subsequent to that, the establishment of various national legislations and institutions following the Western models. Concurrently, there has been a steady growth and diversification of specializations of various branches of heritage and thus the corresponding bureaucratic apparatuses to manage and preserve heritage. This rise has in turn expanded the scope of heritage regimes: what initially began as a concern for artifacts and sites (e.g., in the Athens Charter of 1931; see ICOMOS 2011) is expanded to include intangible practices in 2003 and the "diversity of cultural expressions" in 2005 (UNESCO 2005).

Further to this diversification, and especially since the late 1990s, it is increasingly recognized that designation, protection, and experience of heritage needs to be an inclusive process (Jones and Shaw 2012; Millar 2006).

The scope and purpose of heritage custodianship has changed to include a diversity of players (actors) at various scales, from government and state institutions to local participants from among laypeople; heritage is thus being "democratized." Increasingly, and especially in conflict zones—given the rise of various destructive conflicts around the world and especially in the Middle East targeting heritage (e.g., Stone and Bajjaly 2008)—community engagement and capacity building have become major concerns.

In this way, it is possible to observe an almost universal pattern by which heritage processes are coming to a full circle: what began through the efforts of concerned individuals (which included experts) and societies was then gradually built into numerous legislations and state institutions (which at times absorbed the same individuals and their ideas), but throughout the twentieth century, these disparate institutions and legislations were increasingly centralized, officialized, and driven by professionals. Today, these professionals aspire to be more inclusive and recognize the diversity of stakeholders and their cultural expressions. It is noteworthy that these developments proceed from a wave of rising globalization and strategic shifts in the power balances in the world, particularly after World War II. Thus, for example, Japan's push for the recognition of intangible cultural heritage must be seen as part of the process of legitimizing non-Western cultural attitudes in the global arena, as well as its attempt to act as a cultural powerhouse in Asia (Akagawa 2014). Within the established nation-states of the present world, heritage is also implicated in and informs development processes (e.g., China's aforementioned partnership with the World Bank), cultural policies, issues of sustainable development (see, e.g., Labadi and Logan 2015; UNESCO 2017), and domestic and international relations (through diplomacy, as illustrated in recent research by Meskell 2015; Meskell and Brumann 2015; Winter 2015).

This "opening up" of heritage has coincided with rapid development in various Asian countries and concomitant economic shifts that have strained state resources and power, and contributed to social upheavals in the region. Heritage is thus further entangled in the transformation and development of public spheres, communications, and state-society relations. Political and economic shortcomings at the state level alongside the expansion of political opportunities have resulted in the growth of uncertainty, prompting people to seek further individual autonomy outside state control. If effectively organized, such cultural action can disrupt the state and undermine or displace fixed territorial boundaries (Waters 2013: 55–56). Thus, within social institutions, heritage is increasingly apparent as a significant contributor to the formation and operation of a public sphere and civil society as indicated through media and various forms of collective and individual expression. Despite these changes, as we will discuss, there are still few systematic studies of the role of various stakeholders and actors—institutional or otherwise—and their processes of communication and contestation in heritage in Asia. We now turn to the evolution of heritage research in the past decades to trace the treatment of heritage activism and social movements in heritage scholarship.

Heritage 2: Activism in Heritage Research

1980s: The Growth of a Field

Critical interest in heritage gained momentum in the 1980s with the introduction of cultural studies analysis about the growth and present-day use of heritage and history (see, e.g., Johnson et al. 1982). Implicitly or otherwise, social movements feature in the scholarship because of the cultural studies focus on the dominant subaltern class and group dynamics within their readings of history and heritage. Heritage movements generally received negative attention (Hewison 1987; Wright 1985). Often called preservationist groups, heritage movements' main aim was the conservation of one or more sites, objects, or practices due to their interpretation of its significance to present. Our purpose here is to review the treatment of heritage movements in key texts in heritage studies to analyze why heritage movements have not consistently received the attention they have in similar fields such as environmental studies or gender studies. We have chosen these authors because of their prominence, their influence on heritage research as a field (rather than within a specific discipline), and their focus on heritage broadly conceived.

The first group of texts inspired a critical approach to heritage across several disciplines (Carman and Stig Sørensen 2009; Harrison 2013a). Patrick Wright's (1985) *On Living in an Old Country* and Robert Hewison's (1987) *The Heritage Industry* provide important analyses of the entry of heritage into everyday life and its political uses. Both authors take as their primary topic the links between the growth of heritage policy and practice, and conservative class politics, arguing that national heritage in particular is a product of a conservative reaction to changing class relations (Hewison 1987: 139; Wright 1985: 24–27, 52). Unsurprisingly, given this focus, both engage extensively with the National Trust for Places of Historic Interest or Natural Beauty in England, Wales, and Northern Ireland (henceforth, the National Trust) and depict its role as freezing "the whole of social life over" (1985: 26).[3] Heritage movements are characterized as reactionary, conservative, and captured by political elites. The opportunity to study the engagement between modernity and heritage through the interaction of political and economic circumstances and the culture and social changes of the times was overlooked. This is unfortunate, as the approach of these important books constrained the possibilities for locating the growth and shifts in heritage practices in the dynamics of social movements in critical heritage scholarship.

David Lowenthal's *The Past Is a Foreign Country* is a survey of how people in different time periods, in particular the present, see, value, and understand the past. Lowenthal argues contemporary society's engagement with the past through collecting and preserving is stultifying the past and limiting creative engagement. The basis of his argument is through a survey of written texts that, according to Lowenthal (1985: xxv–xxvi), is not a systematic sampling and "are heavily weighted toward literate elites who troubled to record their views." Heritage activism is largely absent from *The Past Is a Foreign Country* because of Lowenthal's choice of source material and his textual approach. Despite their absence, Lowenthal's approach has implications for understandings of heritage activism, in particular his representation of preservation. Lowenthal views preservation as a limited engagement with the past caused by, and resulting in, an incapacity to understand and engage with it.[4] Rather than being engaged drivers of understandings of heritage and history, heritage organizations in this formulation are reactive respondents to broader social changes (feelings of loss, the role of landmarks, the linking of personal with public histories (364)). Furthermore, Lowenthal's arguments are based on a distinction between heritage and history that denigrates heritage as "domesticating the past" and reactive, reducing the creativity and capacities of its enthusiasts. While not as overt as Hewison, *The Past Is a Foreign Country* also relies on a distinction between history as critical scholarship and heritage as mindless populist entertainment that does not allow heritage activists agency in a richer formulation of social and economic change and the responses of movements.

1990s: Challenges to the Class Critique

Revisions of early critical approaches to heritage that viewed it as a limited and populist version of history came from several directions. Here we focus on scholarship from the fields of history (Raphael Samuel), geography (Greg Ashworth, Brian Graham, and John Tunbridge, who coauthored in various permutations many books and articles),[5] and anthropology (Michael Herzfeld).[6] Samuel's *Theatres of Memory* provides a critique and a counterpoint to the earlier works of the 1980s. Samuel's starting point is that history (including heritage) is a social form of knowledge—"the work ... of a thousand hands"—and therefore requires an approach that addresses the "ensemble of activities and practices in which ideas of history are embedded or a dialectic of past-present relations is rehearsed" (1994: 8). He also criticizes the treatment of heritage enthusiasts within earlier approaches, and its characterization of them as "passive consumers" of a conservative version of history, rather than as learners engaged in leisure and play who are as likely to be engaged in historical reflection and thought as the student of history (259–273).

Samuel's chapter on politics includes a set of insights that overlaps heritage and social movement theory. He notes strong connections to cities (through land use and conflict over urban space), where the gatherings of people and resources essential to contemporary social movements were and generally continue to be located. He highlights the mobilizing power of heritage.[7] Samuel also identifies the importance of the political opportunities within arenas to the expression of heritage, and the importance of national cultures, all important elements of social movements research: "It takes on quite different meanings in different national cultures, depending on the relationship of the state and civil society, the openness or otherwise of the public arena to initiatives which come from below or from the periphery" (1994: 306). Samuel locates the constant (re-)creation of heritage in the complexities of economic and social change, and assigns heritage organizations and activists a crucial role.[8] Samuel's broad approach and denial of the history-heritage division anticipated directions in heritage studies today toward analyzing the diversity of understandings and uses of heritage beyond heritage institutions and organizations, and the politics of memory and commemoration (Gentry 2014).

While writing earlier than Samuel, the anthropologist Michael Herzfeld's *A Place in History* primarily engages with ethnography rather than the debates about history that incensed Samuel. A detailed study of battle "over the future of the past" of the Cretan town of Rethemnos (1991: 5), the book hinges on the division of social time, or "the grist of everyday experience" and monumental time, defined as focusing on the past and reducing social experience to steps along a collective official history (10). The richness of *A Place in History* is its detailed account of how the residents of Rethemnos encounter and respond to the assertion of monumental time through the conservation of their Old City. Perhaps because of the social time–monumental time division, activists are absent from a book whose primary division is between residents and bureaucrats. Heritage in this formulation is an assertion of the bureaucrats into the social time of the residents and becomes defined as an external imposition that social actors adapt "to promote some of their own ideas about what tradition might be" (205), in the process recasting and shifting official concepts. There are two issues with this formulation. First, activists are absent from the formation of heritage and debates over designation, which may be the case in Rethemnos (where heritage was imposed under a military junta) but not at other scales or in many other locations. Second, heritage is defined narrowly as official, invented tradition in contradistinction to the richness of social life. Research from the Pacific certainly would contest the notion that heritage is narrow and initially imposed from the state (Rio and Hviding 2011). Contemporary heritage studies has a much wider and fuller definition of heritage that has broadened and enriched heritage research. Furthermore, as Samuel argued, much historical research and interest in heritage emanates from social life through the interests and leisure time of the public. Herzfeld (1991) avoids the limitations of his narrow definition of heritage through the complexity of his detailed analysis of state-society (in his terms, bureaucrat-resident) relationships. He recognizes bureaucrats as complex social actors, and the official language and rules of heritage are often turned around in the hurly-burly of contention. His attention to the use of heritage in contention is an important precedent for analyzing heritage activism.

Ashworth, Graham, and Tunbridge's most influential work in heritage studies, which popularized the concept in its title, is *Dissonant Heritage: The Management of the Past as a Resource in Conflict* (Tunbridge and Ashworth 1996).[9] As geographers, Ashworth, Graham, and Tunbridge step away from concerns over history to focus on how heritage shapes and changes the world at different hierarchical and spatial scales. They treated heritage as a distinct phenomenon with specific characteristics that recur across space in particular and are evolving in a linked, simultaneous way. Their clearest and often-quoted definition of heritage (Graham et al. 2000: 2) as "the contemporary use of the past" emphasizes heritage is connected to the present needs of people and that its characteristics are located in its interpretations. They argue dissonance, or the discrepancy and/or incongruity caused by a lack of agreement over what constitutes heritage, is intrinsic to heritage because of these multiple interpretations and uses. Heritage is therefore implicated in creating and maintaining collective identities through the identification of key categories of "human division" (Tunbridge and Ashworth 1996: 71) that generate dissonance: culture/ethnicity (incorporating race, religion, and language); class (in particular, industrial heritage); and key social divisions including gender, the LGBTQ movement, and disability.

While dissonance is intrinsic to heritage, they argue dissonance can be reduced through management, most often by the state. In *Dissonant Heritage*, the concern with management is developed through a division between the "producers" of heritage ("cultural institutions, governments or enterprises" (Tunbridge and Ashworth 1996: 69) and the "consumers," or the ethnic, LGBTQ, working class, disabled, or other groups whose heritage may be causing dissonance. While this is clearly a division of convenience, and they themselves advocate for consultation, it is the social movements that are being managed by the providers of resources and heritage expertise. Their attention is on the management of heritage rather than the dynamics of how a social movement uses heritage and how the characteristics of heritage are formed through the complex interactions of social movements, activism, and political elite. The creation of heritage in their model (Tunbridge and Ashworth 1996: 7) starts with the conservation agencies rather than the more complex dynamics that are inherent in their discussion of the extension of heritage in scope and volume.

2000s: The Discursive Turn and Beyond in Critical Heritage Analysis

An important shift in heritage studies occurred with the publication of Laurajane Smith's *The Uses of Heritage* because of her critical analysis of heritage management, including the concept of the authorized heritage discourse (AHD).[10] Smith used a suite of contemporary concepts (discourse, memory, place, and collective identity) to shift the focus of heritage research toward the situated experiences of people and how heritage management affected their relationship with and use of heritage. Smith's primary argument was that the AHD, defined as "a dominant Western discourse about heritage . . . that works to naturalize a range of assumptions about the nature and meaning of heritage" (2006: 4), gave the power to manage and define heritage to experts and applied an object, rather than a people centered approach, that "explicitly promotes the experience and values of elite social classes" (30). She argues the AHD and the experts who use it undermine the relationships between heritage and subaltern groups including women, ethnic groups, Indigenous groups, and the working class. A critique of *The Uses of Heritage* is the determining power that Smith gives to the AHD to define the identity and practices of heritage practitioners and the subaltern status of other groups.[11] Heritage activism comes from many places, including the inside of institutions, and experts can simultaneously be activists and community members. Furthermore, the idea of an elite tends to fuse various kinds of group advantages, as if they were tightly correlated, into a catchall notion of "power." This language makes it hard to understand how non-elites, without power, can ever exert influence in contestation (Robertson 2012). Outcomes can never be assumed in advance or easily explained on the basis of "power."

Further useful developments have been introduced through appropriating disciplinary methodologies. A recent change in archaeology that begins to address the need for nuanced understandings of the relationships and alliances in heritage work is the incorporation of ethnographic methodologies into heritage and particularly archaeological practice (Byrne 2014; Meskell 2005, 2009). Accommodations between archaeology and ethnography have pushed heritage studies toward greater reflexivity, attention to the influence of the relationship between contemporary ethical and political issues and heritage practices, and acknowledgment of the diverse and active construction of heritage by nonexpert actors (in particular, Indigenous people)

(Meskell 2009). In one of her first articles on her understanding of "archaeological ethnography," Meskell (2005: 84) writes: "My focus, however, remains squarely on contemporary culture. I want to know the ways in which archaeology works in the world. What kinds of, and what intensities of, connection exist? How is archaeology transformative in the fashioning of possible futures?" While this is an important reframing of archaeological practice that incorporates methods capable of engaging with nonexpert perspectives and locating archaeology within broader power structures, these questions and the research that followed focus first on archaeological or heritage practices and then on the extent and qualities of participation by other groups. Hence, Helen Human's (2015) excellent article on the effects of UNESCO requirements for greater participation on Turkish heritage management uses research methods required to understand local and activist groups and engages with them, but remains centered on archaeological practice within state and international institutions, so it does not address how these groups formulated and prosecuted their claims and therefore formulate and shape heritage.

In a later development, the material turn in the social sciences (Joyce and Bennett 2010) has begun to open up new approaches in heritage studies. Harrison in particular (2013a, 2013b, 2014) has been at the forefront of the application in heritage studies of concepts that question and ultimately seek to dissolve binaries like human/nonhuman and society/nature that have been at the foundation of contemporary Western science, including heritage management. After identifying that critical heritage research has not always adequately addressed the role of material "things" because of its emphasis on discursive approaches (2013a: 112–113), Harrison advocates for a dialogical model of heritage that views it as

> emerging from the relationship between people, objects, places and practices, and that does not distinguish between or prioritize what is "natural" and what is "cultural," but is instead concerned with the various ways in which humans and non-humans are linked by chains of connectivity and work together to keep the past alive in the present for the future. (2013a: 4–5)

Harrison uses Bruno Latour's (2005) actor-network theory and Charles Deleuze and Felix Guattari's (1987) concept of assemblages to address the range of objects, people, categories, lists, and relationships implicated in heritage. Harrison's attention to the range of relationships, including affect and emotions, and objects in heritage is an important reminder that heritage activists respond and use a range of material affordances in their actions and relationships with heritage. While his application of these ideas opens up heritage studies to include a range of groups of people and things, including heritage activists and their affordances, his research has tended to focus on institutions without consideration of these groups, and his application of assemblages is similarly limited (Harrison 2013b, 2014). Such work still needs to be done.

This Volume

Our schematization of the practical and scholarly aspects of heritage suggests that while activism is always present, both practice and theory can benefit from a more deliberate engagement with various forms of activism and the lessons that may be drawn from the study of social movements. Social movements are defined as "sustained, intentional efforts to foster or retard broad legal and social changes, primarily outside the normal institutional channels endorsed by authorities" (Jasper 2014: 5). This includes heritage activists, like the Iranian activists who have carefully advocated through newspapers and occasional protests for preIslamic heritage to be considered national heritage (Mozaffari 2015), or the Pacific Island social movements that have made strong appeals to heritage in their mobilizations (Rio and Hviding 2011). It also includes movements focused on other issues who have made use of heritage. For instance, environmental groups have fought for the preservation and thus created "natural heritage," and religious reform or revival movements have resacralized ancient religious sites that had become heritage. Heritage processes may vary according to cultural, national, geographical, and historical contexts, which makes comparative heritage research complex. In the field of critical heritage studies, scholars have rightly critiqued Western, expert-led approaches to heritage for their exclusion of the broader public and local perspectives (Winter and Daly 2012; L. Smith 2006). Others have focused on issues in state heritage management such as the division between nature and culture, or on the dynamics of UNESCO heritage claim making (Meskell 2015, 2009; Meskell and Brumann 2015). Still, the field seems to be dominated by a focus on (first) the perspective and actions of the state or large heritage institutions and (then) the reactions, or the extent and qualities of participation by other groups.

This volume stems from an alternative proposition: begin with the social movements that perform and maintain alternative forms of heritage and heritage practice in Asia, and work to have these practices acknowledged and/or supported by other, often larger, institutions (in particular, official institutions). As such, the book pursues both epistemological (how we research and understand heritage and social movements) and ontological (moving toward a broader consideration of heritage and its relationship to a range of players) goals. Analysis of heritage in Asia tends to rest on a set of theoretical considerations that have not been empirically tested

(Winter and Daly 2012). Extending the direction of research on heritage and communities (Smith and Waterton 2009), this study provides an alternative basis for heritage theory in the circumstances, actions, and dynamics of civil society rather than in state policies and programs and the responses of specific groups. Heritage research, while recognizing the expansion of heritage in Asia (Winter and Daly 2012), has yet to focus on the groups who have lobbied for heritage reform in Asia, or to have undertaken this sophisticated analysis of heritage politics. In examining the construction, formation, and contestation of heritage in Asia, the focus of the book is driven by geographical context, as well as methodological concerns, which, as our chapters illustrate, highlight several worthwhile themes, to which we shall return. However, in the first instance, one needs to clarify our use of the term Asia in this volume.

A Note on the Concept of Asia

Our intention here is not to outline the problems inherent in the concept of "Asia," a task others have undertaken with considerable eloquence (Lewis and Wigen 1997). Rather, in this brief passage, our intention is to orient the reader as to its logic and our use of the term. In this respect, we wish to outline the pitfalls we want to be avoided in using the term here and highlight the geographical logic of the contributions to the volume, which is undeniably also partly determined by the availability of the scholarship in the field of heritage. Deploying "Asia," we recognize the contested nature of this "metageographical" concept. While the term is deployed in multiple contexts and in various combinations, its boundaries and connotations are context-specific and just as varied. In *The Myth of Continents*, Martin Lewis and Kären Wigen present a fascinating exploration of the history of metageographical concepts such as continents, (first, second, and third) worlds, and East-West or North-South divisions. As social constructs, such taxonomic systems set up zones of identity and othering rather than empirically verifiable geographical facts on the ground. The deployment of such categories may be prompted by perceptions of or desire to instill cultural, religious, or ultimately civilizational differences. An East-West division, for example, could be traced to the old-world empires of Romans (and the Greek before them, if need be) (1997: 53) in distinction to the Persians. Then, as in many instances in the nineteenth and twentieth centuries, Romans were usually designated as the roots of European culture and civilization (Aïnalov 1961; Strzygowski 1902) and in relation to Christendom versus the others. Throughout history, such divisions (for example, farther East and hither East in Hegel) have been revised many times and their boundaries redrawn depending on global geopolitical developments. Thus, such divisions perform a political and cultural function (Hall and Page 2017; Lewis and Wigen 1997). For example, their deployment in the nineteenth century reaffirmed European colonial power and outlook. However, non-European ideologies including variations of pan-Islamism and pan-Asianism (Aydin 2007) have used the very same categories, albeit uncritically, to challenge European hegemonies (Lewis and Wigen 1997: 189).

A conventional step is to conceive of Asia as a continent. Even so, one can recognize that the notion of Asia, which has been used since the time of Homer, and Herodotus after him, designated a different place (essentially around present-day Turkey) than the landmass to which it referred in the late nineteenth century. In other words, the boundaries and meaning of the term have changed in time. Nevertheless, as we noted, the use of "Asia" (which also implies "not Europe") suggests cultural and civilizational differentiation. Building on this, our use of the term implies not uniformity but rather a gradation of cultural practices, political systems, and social structures that make for geographical and human entities that are distinguishable from non-Asia, meaning Europe, large parts of Africa, and the Americas. The recognition of cultural differences and the role they play in the propagation of historical memory but also in social norms is thus a motivation for our use of Asia (Chong 2004; Tamney 1996; Weiming 2000). However, in this usage, we are also cautious to avoid four common pitfalls in the use of metageographical concepts.

The first pitfall, which is evident from our discussion to this point, is the assumption of the immutability and "naturalness" of such metageographical divisions. We acknowledge the boundaries of "Asia" are highly fluid and fraught with political intent. We even acknowledge our inclusion of Iran as one bookend of Asia, while acceptable to many, including the World Tourism Organization, which considers Iran as part of South Asia,[12] may be surprising to others. By the same token, and following Lewis and Wigen (1997), among others, we do not subscribe to any essentialist divisions of geographical categories. Thus, we see little analytical value in the use of notions such as East versus West or North versus South in this context. Such "jigsaw puzzle" conceptions of the world are at once inaccurate and risk the naturalization and imposition of constructed hierarchies (Lewis and Wigen 1997: 10). In our opinion, such a reductionist and essentialist conceptualization constitutes the second pitfall, is to be avoided.

A corollary conception and third pitfall to be avoided is "geographical determinism," as "the belief that social and cultural differences between human groups can ultimately be traced to differences in their physical environments" (Lewis and Wigen 1997: 42). The last pitfall we wish to avoid is suggestions of Asian exceptionalism: that there is an essentially immutable "Asian" set of values that differentiate Asia from others, presumably the Europeans, in areas including cultural heritage. We do nevertheless acknowledge that even in heritage, the tacit or explicit invocation of the idea of Asia has led to productive imaginations. For example, the promotion and institutionalization of intangible heritage, especially by Japan (Aikawa 2004; UNESCO 2003), is indebted to notions of an Asian culture in contradistinction to Eurocentric conceptions of material, monumental heritage, and authenticity (Smith and Akagawa 2008). In this respect, heritage is also an instrument of cultural diplomacy within Asia (Akagawa 2014).

Other economic and infrastructure developments propelled by powers such as China and India have created new international dynamics in within the continent, which may result in concomitant cultural and heritage components. A significant example in this regard is China's Belt and Road Initiative. In constructing major "economic cooperation corridors," China invokes and reinvents the historic notion of the Silk Road in both land and maritime contexts. The initiative's areas of emphasis include development policies, infrastructure, investment and trade, financial cooperation, and social and cultural exchange (Wade 2016). The already-apparent result of this—also contested by other powers such as India—is a greater connectivity with tangible movements of people, technologies, and materials that results in reconceptualizing the notion of an Asian continent with China as its major powerhouse (Habib and Faulknor 2017; Winter 2016). Considering all these transformations, our conception of Asia in this volume refers to a "more or less discrete" landmass (Lewis and Wigen 1997: 35). Here, Asia is neither determined nor dominated by any singular civilization, religion, language, or political culture and social norms.

Within this broad and loose definition of Asia, our chapters address various regions—"more or less boundable areas united by broad social and cultural features"—that are conceptualized based on "real patterns in the world that precede to understand them," and their identities are amplified through globalization (Lewis and Wigen 1997: 14). We therefore use the term Asia to refer to a large and diverse region that has, through political, economic, and academic processes, become defined in contradistinction to other diverse regions, primarily Europe but also Africa and the Americas, and we use contemporary geographical groupings while acknowledging their historical contingency and mutability. As such, our chapters address the social aspects of heritage construction ranging from East Asia to South, Southeast, and finally West Asia. Despite our efforts, we could not find contributors from the Central Asian region, which remains a fascinating area for future investigation.

Chapters in This Book

Heritage studies is an umbrella field, a trans-field that brings together various disciplines ranging from history to sociology and anthropology. While the chapters in this book exemplify various forms of individual or collective activism in heritage, not all borrow explicitly from social movements theories and terminologies. This unevenness, we feel, is justified by disciplinary multiplicity in heritage studies itself, and contributes to building a variety of approaches to understanding activism and social movements in heritage that are required to address different circumstances.

In chapter 1, Tod Jones, Ali Mozaffari, and James Jasper illustrate the methodological implications of approaching the question of activism and movements in heritage through the lens of social movements theories. We use heritage research and exemplar to demonstrate how heritage is produced through the activities and occasional protests by activists with various agenda. As we have already mentioned in this introduction, there is a methodological weakness, if not a gap, in understanding and conceptualizing activism in heritage studies. This is also apparent in the shortage of terminologies that can sufficiently or systematically categorize with various analytical concepts required for understanding heritage activism. Therefore, our chapter explicitly borrows from and experiments with terminologies and concepts such as "players" and "arenas," developed by James Jasper, from the field of social movements. Our chapter introduces a different perspective into the reading and understanding of heritage politics and civil society. Exploring the relationship between heritage and activism also pertains to the formation or "geometry," as well as the limits, of civil society and the public sphere. In this respect, the role of various forms of media in relation to heritage activism becomes significant. However, heritage studies has yet to fully incorporate this aspect into its theoretical and methodological repertoire. Chapters 2 and 7 in this collection go some way to initiate this this aspect of heritage research.

In chapter 2, Tod Jones, Transpiosa Riomandha, and Hairus Salim examine the role of social media—in this instance, Facebook—in forming new identity groups and redefining heritage in Indonesia. Acknowledging the nascent research in the relationship between social media and heritage activism, the authors provide an engaging account of the relationship between social media and heritage by focusing on one particular heritage group: Bol Brutu. Engaging with Indonesian archaeological sites through social media combined with trips to sites and other activities, the group promotes creative and entertaining engagement with material remains, and through this, shifts their members' heritage practices. The authors highlight the importance of intermodality and recognizing the continuum of online-offline activities of heritage activists—a fact insufficiently examined in current heritage activism and heritage and digital media literature. It would be erroneous to imagine social media detached from the vast network of connections, exchanges, and knowledges on which it rests, and concurrently, it helps make and promote heritage. Bol Brutu exemplifies this relationship in the specific historical, cultural, and political context of Indonesia. However, as the authors tell us, the group's existence is underpinned by practices of travel to, and movement in and around, heritage sites. This combination of social media (with all their affordances) and on-site practices creates a focus around which social class, cosmopolitanism, and new conceptions and practices of heritage coalesce. Importantly, the chapter shows that not all heritage activism is driven by oppositional politics against a reductionist conception of a "state." Rather, there are complexities and nuances in the production of heritage and social class that may be discerned through a careful attention to the activists and their modes of internal and external communication.

While speaking of Asia, we are mindful of the significant variations in the shape and extent of the civil society and the potential dominance of the state apparatuses in the daily affairs of the citizens. As Gary Sigley shows in chapter 3, the tensions between this and the globalization of heritage, as evidenced through rising tourism, illustrates an interesting dynamic in China. The strong hand of the various factions within the state suggest there is only limited potential for explicit social activism that may upset the authorities in various locations. While China seeks to expand its tourism market and increase its prestige through the inscription of World Heritage Sites, the political opportunities for activism in various forms of heritage are bound to be limited by the willingness of state apparatuses. Nevertheless, Sigley points out the limited albeit expanding nature of the public sphere in China. Rising wealth in Chinese society and the opening of borders to foreign visitors has stimulated domestic and international tourism. China is thus playing an increasingly strong globalizing role just as it engages with global demands, movements, and pressures, including in tourism. Focusing on the commercial tourism activities of the US citizen Brian Linden and his family in China's city of Dali, Sigley illustrates how one individual's understanding of cultural and linguistic nuance can help him pave the way for both his commercial gain and the presentation of a different Chinese cultural experience to his clientele. The chapter illustrates the importance of particular actors to understandings of heritage and how their institutional and subject positions (in this case, as a foreigner in a nation-state that controls the limits of political speech) shape their activism and understandings of heritage.

Singapore provides an interesting comparison with China. A state with strong central control, but more open than China, Singapore affords greater opportunities for heritage activism. In chapter 4, Terence Chong offers a short and engaging account of the development of middle-class heritage activism in Singapore understood as a corporatist, centralized state. It integrated the development of heritage with the shifting political, economic, and social conditions of Singapore. Chong demonstrates how the political modalities of Singapore condition heritage activism and heritage activists are able to pick at the seams of these modalities through their use of local, national, and international narratives and networks. Chong's chapter shows the delicacies of heritage activism that seeks to engage with and collaborate with the state. In such instances—as is the case in several other countries, including Iran—activist groups and individuals draw on their personal networks and engage in "backroom activism" to realize their goals. Through such activism, activists engage in a politics of scale. Like their Iranian counterparts, they use international listings and covenants to pressure the state over heritage regulation (as Chong notes, "calibrating local practices to international norms"). Chong shows the media are also used to pressure the state in decision-making about heritage matters, a clear indication of the role of civil society players in the formation of heritage. Here too the rise of heritage and its concomitant activism is linked to the growth of the middle class and identity politics in Singapore.

In chapter 5, Sudeep Jana Thing writes about a local Indigenous movement in a Nepalese national park, providing an interesting contrast with Chong's nationwide Singaporean activism. Thing establishes the concept of biocultural heritage—a recent international concept that is itself the product of international NGOs and organizations—and then applies it to the Sonaha minority and their relationship to a riverscape that is now within a national park. Applying a lens of political ecology to contests over natural resource management, the chapter examines the activities of Indigenous ethnic social movements and other players in various arenas. The author argues biocultural heritage is shaped through the political opportunities, circumstances, and rifts within the Indigenous ethnic Sonaha social movement. He also suggests this type of heritage is a useful concept for empowering minority ethnic groups in their relations with the state. Thing clearly demonstrates Indigenous social movements are crucial for understanding the articulation of biocultural/cultural landscape heritage and that the political opportunities the state provides for Indigenous recognition and rights are therefore linked to the emergence of such heritage, however it is termed.

In chapter 6, Aimée Douglas turns her attention to Sri Lanka's Dumbara Rata weavers to critically examine the relationship between various parties and their contests over heritage and traditional knowledge in a village impacted by the global pressures of a changing market economy. As modernity and globalization have increased the demand for "authentic" crafts of the weavers, the ownership of the knowledge of its production has become a source of social and class contention in that region. Presenting a detailed and fascinating ethnographic account of the relevant events in the village, Douglas shows how market forces (modern and global) shift communal and class identities (local and traditional) and how this results in claims and counterclaims over the authenticity and ownership of traditional production. In this displacement, both local activists, who enter the contest to protect their class interests, and officials engage. This engagement is beginning to change the nature of the caste and the old order that dominated interactions and relations of production surrounding Dumbara Rata. Here the scale of activism is local and within the community of the village but also involves players representing the state.

In the final chapter, Ali Mozaffari examines the relationship between heritage activism and the media in Iran. Through a close reading of media statements issued by activists in two provinces (the capital of Tehran and the southern provincial city of Ahwaz), the chapter traces some of the characteristics of heritage activism in Iran. The media releases examined here relate to two specific events: one related to a dam near the World Heritage Site of Pasargadae, and the other related to metro lines in Ahwaz. While concentrating on specific sites, both cases have national repercussions for defining collective identity and heritage, illustrating the interdependence of heritage and scale. The chapter shows heritage activism—rather like all forms of activism—goes through cycles of escalation and de-escalation. Also, activists adapt their tactics to the political environment around them, which is to say the shape and characteristics of civil society are in a constant process of change and evolution. Working with the concept of framing in social movements, the chapter shows representations (in this case, words and speech) function as frames in the construction and sustenance of heritage activism both at local and national scales. Like some other examples in this book, Iran has "strong" state apparatuses, and activists tend to be cautious in their challenges. Similar to their Singaporean peers, in addition to occasional protests, they tend to draw on their networks to persuade various factions within the government toward their goals. This suggests activism, at times, takes the form of cooperation or critical engagement with state institutions.

In its totality, the volume, which covers several subregions within Asia, suggests interesting peculiarities around activism and contestation of heritage in Asia. First, we can see the political structure of the state determines the limits of the public sphere and thus the very possibility and tone of activism. Understanding the nature, shape, and even the possibility of heritage activism in a given context thus relies on many other analyses, namely the cultural and political history of the given context; the diversity, depth, and machinations of social institutions; and the availability and spread of various forms of technology, especially communication technologies. It follows that not all heritage contests and activism is resolved through conflict. In this sense, understanding heritage and its dissonances and contestations may deviate from the core concerns of many social movement theories. Second, although controlled, media and, increasingly, social media play a significant role in shaping imaginations and practices of heritage. They help recruit, legitimize, and promote a point of view but also, through framing, turn emotional concerns into persuasive arguments. Third, the appearance of heritage activism is a symptom of and a prompt for social change. Fourth, in any given context, activists employ a range of strategies to advance their cause. Finally, the role of individual players in heritage activism should not be discounted. Many movements begin with and are sustained through the actions of a few or even one committed individual.

As many of Asian societies experience modernization within a postcolonial condition, traditional social dynamics are reconfigured not only by an often insular and controlling cultural nationalism and the global exchange of ideas and capital, but also by social movements who reconfigure these forces through their activism and circumstances. The change in heritage is also intimately related to shifts in class consciousness and identity (such as the rise of the middle class in its broadest definition). These characteristics distinguish the Asian heritage scene from much of what takes place where heritage has a longer history of institutionalization, such as Europe and North America. As this introduction has shown, the significance of activism in heritage should be understood as a constituting element of the rise of heritage in Asia—a phenomenon that is occurring right now, driven by increasingly sophisticated and politically astute individuals operating in and across groups who are pursuing their interests and making brave decisions to influence and direct powerful and, in some places, repressive regimes.

Acknowledgments

The research for and production of this introduction was made possible in part thanks to a grant awarded by the Australian Research Council (grant no. DE170100104) to Ali Mozaffari.

Ali Mozaffari is a fellow of the Australian Research Council with the Alfred Deakin Institute at Deakin University. Through his research, he seeks to understand the uses of the past in contemporary discourses of heritage and built environment in Iran and West Asia. His areas of interest include heritage and social movements, liminality and heritage, and development and heritage in late-twentieth century Iranian architecture. His publications include *Forming National Identity in Iran: The Idea of Homeland Derived from Ancient Persian and Islamic Imaginations of Place* (2014) and *World Heritage in Iran: Perspectives on Pasargadae* (2016), and "Picturing Pasargadae: Visual Representation and the Ambiguities of Heritage in Iran" (*Iranian Studies*, 2017).

Tod Jones is Associate Professor in Geography in the School of Design and Built Environment at Curtin University. His research interests are cultural and political geographies in Australia and Indonesia, in particular bringing contemporary geography approaches to cultural economy and heritage issues. His current projects are on Australian Aboriginal heritage and urban planning, social movements and heritage, and applying a sustainable livelihoods approach to assess heritage initiatives. His most recent book is *Culture, Power, and Authoritarianism in the Indonesian State: Cultural Policy across the Twentieth Century to the Reform Era* (2013). His research has been published in numerous journals, including the *International Journal of Heritage Studies*, the *Journal of Arts, Law, Management and Society*, the *International Journal of Cultural Policy*, and *Indonesia*, and he edited volume 125 of the online magazine *Inside Indonesia* in 2016 on heritage politics and issues in Indonesia.

NOTES

1. For a recent collection of essays dedicated to the exploration of heritage and scale, see Lähdesmäki et al. (2019).
2. For an example of the cultural policy continuities and breaks across different political periods in Indonesia, see Jones (2013).
3. The National Trust's history is viewed through the lens of its conservative political affiliations in the 1980s. For instance, Wright (1985: 51) characterizes the goals of the National Trust's three founders, Octavia Hill, Robert Hunter, and Hardwicke Rawnsley, as "saving beauty spots" and focuses on its role in shaping national heritage in a way that accorded with the goals of the conservative establishment. For instance, he writes: "One doesn't have to take a completely negative view of the National Trust to see that the inalienability of the Trust's property can be regarded (and also stages) as a vindication of property relations" (52). Both Wright (1985: 48–56) and Hewison (1987: 54–58) focus on the National Trust's role in the preservation of the English country house, characterized as a process through which English landscape, the political elite, and conservative ideals coalesced to produce a "dominant" version of English heritage. Reading the National Trust through Frankfurt School theories of modernity and mass culture (explicitly in Wright 1985: 1–32, implicitly in Hewison 1987, although he does acknowledge his debt to Wright's ideas) leads to issues with the characterization and analysis of heritage movements.

4. For instance, Lowenthal (1985: 405) writes: "Preservation can fairly be charged with segregating the past. Consciousness of the past as a separate realm arouses the urge to save it; doing so then further sunders it from the present."
5. As the permutations of Ashworth, Graham, and Tunbridge changed between publications, we are keeping them in alphabetical order here and providing longer citations to indicate order in a specific publication where necessary.
6. There were also challenges from archaeology through public archaeology (Carman and Stig Sørensen 2009; Skeates et al. 2012) and in museums through the new museology (Vergo 1989).
7. Samuel (1994: 292) writes: "The cry of 'heritage in danger' has proved by far the most potent of mobilizing forces—and of networking—in environmental campaigns."
8. Samuel's nuanced treatment of the National Trust notes the activities of two of its founders in defending the land rights of villagers and commoners (Robert Hunter), and defense of open space against private property (Octavia Hill) (1994: 296–297). He records that the National Trust welcomed the Labour government after World War II in Britain (288) and that the preservation of country houses was thought be a Labour cause in the 1930s (297).
9. They also contributed earlier books on heritage management including *Heritage Planning* (Ashworth 1991) and *The Tourist-Historic City* (Ashworth and Tunbridge 2000), and prominent later books such as *A Geography of Heritage* (Graham et al. 2000) and *Pluralising Pasts: Heritage, Identity and Place in Multicultural Societies* (Ashworth et al. 2007).
10. Harrison (2013a: 110–12) labels this the "discursive turn" in heritage studies.
11. While Smith (2006: 299) provides provisos about her "strong characterization of a discourse" when she writes about the AHD, these do not temper her statements about experts.
12. This is also noted by Hall and Page (2017). For the UNWTO, see UNWTO (2019).

REFERENCES

Aikawa, Noriko. 2004. "An Historical Overview of the Preparation of the UNESCO International Convention for the Safeguarding of the Intangible Cultural Heritage." *Museum International* 56 (1–2): 137–149. https://doi.org/10.1111/j.1350-0775.2004.00468.x.

Aĭnalov, D. V. 1961. *The Hellenistic Origins of Byzantine Art*. Trans. Elizabeth Sobolevitch and Serge Sobolevitch. New Brunswick, NJ: Rutgers University Press.

Akagawa, Natsuko. 2014. *Heritage Conservation and Japan's Cultural Diplomacy: Heritage, National Identity and National Interest*. London: Routledge.

Anheier, Helmut K., and Yudhishthir Raj Isar. 2011. *Cultures and Globalization: Heritage, Memory and Identity*. London: Sage.

Ashworth, Gregory J., Brian Graham, and John E. Tunbridge. *Pluralising Pasts: Heritage, Identity and Place in Multicultural Societies*. London: Pluto Press.

Aydin, Cemil. 2007. *The Politics of Anti-Westernism in Asia: Visions of World Order in Pan-Islamic and Pan-Asian Thought*. New York: Columbia University Press.

Bendix, Regina F., Aditya Eggert, and Arnika Peselmann. 2012. *Heritage Regimes and the State*. Göttingen: Universitätsverlag Göttingen.

Bloembergen, Marieke, and Martijn Eickhoff. 2015. "Save Borobudur! The Moral Dynamics of Heritage Formation in Indonesia across Orders and Borders, 1930s–1980s." In *Cultural Heritage as Civilizing Mission: From Decay to Recovery*, ed. Michael Fasler, 83–199. New York: Springer.

Brenner, Neil. 1997. "State Territorial Restructuring and the Production of Spatial Scale: Urban and Regional Planning in the Federal Republic of Germany, 1960–1990." *Political Geography* 16 (4): 273–306. https://doi.org/10.1016/S0962-6298(96)00003-0.

Byrne, Denis Richard. 2014. *Counterheritage: Critical Perspectives on Heritage Conservation in Asia*. London: Routledge.

Carman, John, and Marie Louise Stig Sørensen. 2009. "Heritage Studies: An Outline." In *Heritage Studies Methods and Approaches*, ed. Marie Louise Stig Sørensen and John Carman, 32–52. London: Routledge.

Chong, Alan. 2004. "Singaporean Foreign Policy and the Asian Values Debate, 1992–2000: Reflections on an Experiment in Soft Power." *Pacific Review* 17 (1): 95–133. https://doi.org/10.1080/0951274042000182438.

Daher Rami, and Irene Maffi. 2014. "Introduction." In *The Politics and Practices of Cultural Heritage in the Middle East: Positioning the Material Past in Contemporary Societies*, ed. Rami Daher and Irene Maffi, 1–54. London: I.B. Tauris.

Deleuze, Gilles, and Félix Guattari. 1987. *A Thousand Plateaus: Capitalism and Schizophrenia*. Trans. Brian Massumi. Minneapolis: University of Minnesota Press.

Ebbe, Katrinka, Guido Licciardi, and Axel Baeumler. 2011. *Conserving the Past as a Foundation for the Future: China-World Bank Partnership on Cultural Heritage Conservation*. Washington, DC: World Bank.

Edwards, Michael. 2011. "Introduction: Civil Society and the Geometry of Human Relations." In *The Oxford Handbook of Civil Society*, ed. Michael Edwards, 3–14. Oxford: Oxford University Press.

Foucault, Michel. 1982. "The Subject and Power." *Critical Inquiry* 8 (4): 777–795. https://doi.org/10.1086/448181.

———. 1991. *The Foucault Effect: Studies in Governmentality*. Chicago: University of Chicago Press.

Gentry, Kynan. 2014. "'The Pathos of Conservation': Raphael Samuel and the Politics of Heritage." *International Journal of Heritage Studies* 21 (6): 561–576. https://doi.org/10.1080/13527258.2014.953192.

Graham, Brian, Gregory J. Ashworth, and John E. Tunbridge. 2000. *A Geography of Heritage: Power, Culture and Economy*. London: Taylor & Francis.

Habib, Benjamin, and Viktor Faulknor. 2017. "The Belt and Road Initiative: China's Vision for Globalisation, Beijing-Style." *The Conversation*, 17 May. http://theconversation.com/the-belt-and-road-initiative-chinas-vision-for-globalisation-beijing-style-77705.

Hall, C. Michael, and Stephen J. Page. 2017. "Introduction: Tourism in Asia: Region and Context." In *The Routledge Handbook of Tourism in Asia*, ed. C. Michael Hall and Stephen J. Page, 3–24. New York: Routledge.

Hall, Stuart. 2005. "Whose Heritage? Un-Settling 'the Heritage,' Re-Imagining the Post-Nation." In *The Politics of Heritage: The Legacies of "Race,"* ed. Jo Littler and Roshi Naidoo, 23–34 London: Routledge.

Harrison, Rodney. 2013a. *Heritage: Critical Approaches*. London: Routledge.

———. 2013b. "Reassembling Ethnographic Museum Collections." In *Reassembling the Collection: Ethnographic Museums and Indigenous Agency*, ed. Rodney Harrison, Sarah Byrne, and Anne Clarke, 3–18. Santa Fe: School for Advanced Research Press.

———. 2014. "Observing, Collecting and Governing 'Ourselves' and 'Others': Mass-Observation's Fieldwork *Agencements*." *History and Anthropology* 25 (2): 227–245. https://doi.org/10.1080/02757206.2014.882835.

Harvey, David C. 2015. "Heritage and Scale: Settings, Boundaries and Relations." *International Journal of Heritage Studies* 21 (6): 577–593. https://doi.org/10.1080/13527258.2014.955812.

Hewison, Robert. 1987. *The Heritage Industry: Britain in a Climate of Decline*. London: Methuen.

Herzfeld, Michael. 1991. *A Place in History: Social and Monumental Time in a Cretan Town*. Princeton, NJ: Princeton University Press.

———. 2014. *Cultural Intimacy: Social Poetics in the Nation-State*. London: Routledge.

Hindess, Barry. 2001. "The Liberal Government of Unfreedom." *Alternatives* 26 (2): 93–111. https://doi.org/10.1177/030437540102600201.

Howitt, R. 2003. "Scale." In *A Companion to Political Geography*, ed. John Agnew, Katharyne Mitchell, and Gerard Toal, 132–157. Hoboken, NJ: Blackwell Publishing.

Human, Helen. 2015. "Democratising World Heritage: The Policies and Practices of Community Involvement in Turkey." *Journal of Social Archaeology* 15 (2): 160–183. https://doi.org/10.1177/1469605314566557.

ICOMOS (International Council on Monuments and Sites). "The Athens Charter for the Restoration of Historic Monuments—1931." 11 November. https://www.icomos.org/en/charters-and-texts/179-articles-en-francais/ressources/charters-and-standards/167-the-athens-charter-for-the-restoration-of-historic-monuments.

Jasper, James M. 2014. *Protest: A Cultural Introduction to Social Movements*. Hoboken, NJ: John Wiley & Sons.

Johnson, Richard, Gregor McLennan, Bill Schwarz, and David Sutton. 1982. *Making Histories: Studies in History-Writing and Politics*. London: Hutchinson.

Jones, Roy, and Brian Shaw. 2012. "Thinking Locally, Acting Globally? Stakeholder Conflicts over UNESCO World Heritage Inscription in Western Australia." *Journal of Heritage Tourism* 7 (1): 83–96. https://doi.org/10.1080/1743873X.2011.632482.

Jones, Tod. 2013. *Culture, Power, and Authoritarianism in the Indonesian State: Cultural Policy across the Twentieth Century to the Reform Era*. Leiden: Brill.

Jones, Tod, Roy Jones, and Michael Hughes. 2016. "Heritage Designation and Scale: A World Heritage Case Study of the Ningaloo Coast." *International Journal of Heritage Studies* 22 (3): 242–260. https://doi.org/10.1080/13527258.2015.1120226.

Joyce, Patrick, and Tony Bennett. 2010. "Material Powers Introduction." In *Material Powers: Cultural Studies, History and the Material Turn*, ed. Tony Bennett and Patrick Joyce, 1–21. London: Routledge.

Kaplan, Flora Edouwaye S. 1994. *Museums and the Making of "Ourselves": The Role of Objects in National Identity*. Leicester: University Press Leicester.

Labadi, Sophia, and William Logan. 2015. *Urban Heritage, Development and Sustainability: International Frameworks, National and Local Governance*. London: Routledge.

Labadi, Sophia, and Colin Long. 2010. *Heritage and Globalization*. London: Taylor & Francis.

Lähdesmäki, Tuuli, Suzie Thomas, and Yujie Zhu, eds. 2019. *Politics of Scale: New Directions in Critical Heritage Studies*. New York: Berghahn Books.
Latour, Bruno. 2005. *Reassembling the Social: An Introduction to Actor-Network-Theory*. Oxford: Oxford University Press.
Lowenthal, David. 1985. *The Past Is a Foreign Country*. Cambridge: Cambridge University Press.
———. 1998. *The Heritage Crusade and the Spoils of History*. Cambridge: Cambridge University Press.
Lewis, Martin W., and Kären Wigen. 1997. *The Myth of Continents: A Critique of Metageography*. Berkeley: University of California Press.
Maffi, Irene, and Rami Daher. 2014. *The Politics and Practices of Cultural Heritage in the Middle East: Positioning the Material Past in Contemporary Societies*. London: I.B. Tauris.
Marston, Sallie A. 2000. "The Social Construction of Scale." *Progress in Human Geography* 24 (2): 219–242. https://doi.org/10.1191/030913200674086272.
Massey, Doreen B. 2005. *For Space*. London: Sage.
Meskell, Lynn. 2005. "Archaeological Ethnography: Conversations around Kruger National Park." *Archaeologies* 1 (1): 81–100. https://doi.org/10.1007/s11759-005-0010-x.
———. 2009. *Cosmopolitan Archaeologies*. Durham, NC: Duke University Press.
———. 2015. "Transacting UNESCO World Heritage: Gifts and Exchanges on a Global Stage." *Social Anthropology* 23 (1): 3–21. https://doi.org/10.1111/1469-8676.12100.
Meskell, Lynn, and Christoph Brumann. 2015. "UNESCO and New World Orders." In *Global Heritage: A Reader*, ed. Lynn Meskell, 22–42. Chichester: Wiley-Blackwell.
Millar, Sue. 2006. "Stakeholders and Community Participation." In *Managing World Heritage Sites*, ed. Anna Leask and Alan Fyall, 37–54. Amsterdam: Elsevier.
Mitchell, Timothy. 2001. "Making the Nation: The Politics of Heritage in Egypt." In *Consuming Tradition, Manufacturing Heritage: Global Norms and Urban Forms in the Age of Tourism*, ed. Nezar AlSayyad, 212–239. London: Routledge.
Mozaffari, Ali. 2007. "Modernity and Identity, the National Museum of Iran." In *Museum Revolutions: How Museums Change and Are Changed*, ed. Simon J. Knell, Suzanne MacLeod, and Sheila Watson, 87–104. London: Routledge.
———. 2014. *Forming National Identity in Iran: The Idea of Homeland Derived from Ancient Persian and Islamic Imaginations of Place*. London: I.B. Tauris.
———. 2015. "The Heritage 'NGO': A Case Study on the Role of Grass Roots Heritage Societies in Iran and Their Perception of Cultural Heritage." *International Journal of Heritage Studies* 21 (9): 1–19. https://doi.org/10.1080/13527258.2015.1028961.
Perlez, Jane. 2014. "In Myanmar, Racing to Save a Colonial Past." *New York Times*, 13 December.
Philpott, Simon. 2000. *Rethinking Indonesia: Postcolonial Theory, Authoritarianism and Identity*. New York: Springer.
Rico, Trinidad. 2015. "After Words: A De-dichotomization in Heritage Discourse." In *Heritage Keywords*, ed. Kathryn Lafrenz Samuels and Trinidad Rico, 285–292. Boulder: University Press of Colorado.
Rio, Knut M., and Edvard Hviding. 2011. "Introduction: Pacific Made: Social Movements between Cultural Heritage and the State." In *Made in Oceania: Social Movements,*

Cultural Heritage and the State in the Pacific, ed. Knut M. Rio and Edvard Hviding, 5–30. Wantage: Sean Kingston Publishing.

Robertson, Iain J. M. 2012. "Introduction: Heritage from Below." In *Heritage from Below*, ed. Iain J. M. Robertson, 1–27. Farnham: Ashgate Publishing.

Roces, Alfredo R. 1978. *Filipino Heritage: The Making of a Nation*. Manila: Lahing Pilipino Publisher.

Samuel, Raphael. 1994. *Theatres of Memory: Past and Present in Contemporary Culture*. London: Verso.

Skeates, Robin, Carol McDavid, and John Carman. 2012. *The Oxford Handbook of Public Archaeology*. Oxford: Oxford University Press.

Smith, Laurajane. 2006. *Uses of Heritage*. London: Routledge.

Smith, Laurajane, and Natsuko Akagawa. 2008. *Intangible Heritage*. London: Taylor & Francis.

Smith, Laurajane, and Emma Waterton. 2009. *Heritage, Communities and Archaeology*. London: Duckworth.

Smith, Neil. 1993. "Homeless/Global: Scaling Places." In *Mapping the Futures: Local Cultures, Global Change*, ed. Jon Bird, Barry Curtis, Tim Putnam, George Robertson, and Lisa Tickner, 87–119. London: Routledge.

Stone, Peter G., and Joanne Farchakh Bajjaly. 2008. *The Destruction of Cultural Heritage in Iraq*. Woodbridge: Boydell & Brewer.

Strzygowski, Josef. 1902. "Orient Oder Rom." *Klio: Beiträge Zur Alten Geschichte* 2 (2): 105–124. https://doi.org/10.1524/klio.1902.2.2.105.

Tamney, Joseph B. 1996. *The Struggle Over Singapore's Soul: Western Modernization and Asian Culture*. Berlin: De Gruyter.

Tsing, Anna L. 2000. "The Global Situation." *Cultural Anthropology* 15 (3): 327–360. https://doi.org/10.1525/can.2000.15.3.327.

———. 2005. *Friction: An Ethnography of Global Connection*. Princeton, NJ: Princeton University Press.

Tunbridge, John E., and Gregory J. Ashworth. 1996. *Dissonant Heritage: The Management of the Past as a Resource in Conflict*. Chichester: John Wiley & Sons.

UNESCO. "Convention for the Safeguarding of the Intangible Cultural Heritage." Paris, 17 October. https://ich.unesco.org/en/convention.

———. 2005. "Convention on the Protection and Promotion of the Diversity of Cultural Expressions." Paris, 20 October. http://portal.unesco.org/en/ev.php-URL_ID=31038&URL_DO=DO_TOPIC&URL_SECTION=201.html.

———. 2017. "World Heritage and Sustainable Development." New York, 22 May. http://whc.unesco.org/en/sustainabledevelopment.

UNWTO (World Tourism Organization). 2015. *UNWTO Tourism Highlights, 2015 Edition*. Madrid: UNWTO.

———. 2019. "Member States." Accessed 18 June. http://asiapacific.unwto.org/members/states.

Vergo, Peter. 1989. *The New Museology*. London: Reaktion.

Wade, Geoff. 2016. "China's 'One Belt, One Road' Initiative." Foreign Affairs, Defence and Security: Parliament of Australia. http://www.aph.gov.au/About_Parliament/Parliamentary_Departments/Parliamentary_Library/pubs/BriefingBook45p/ChinasRoad.

Walzer, Michael. 1998. "The Idea of Civil Society: A Path to Social Reconstruction." In *Community Works: The Revival of Civil Society in America*, ed. E. J. Dionne, 123–144. Washington, DC: Brookings Institution Press.

Wangkeo, Kanchana. 2003. "Monumental Challenges: The Lawfulness of Destroying Cultural Heritage during Peacetime." *Yale Journal of International Law* 28 (1): 183–274. http://digitalcommons.law.yale.edu/yjil/vol28/iss1/6.

Waters, Malcolm. 2013. *Globalization: Key Ideas*. 2nd ed. London: Taylor & Francis.

Weiming, Tu. 2000. "Multiple Modernities: A Preliminary Inquiry into the Implications of the East Asian Modernity." In *Culture Matters: How Values Shape Human Progress*, ed. Lawrence E. Harrison and Samuel P. Huntington, 256–267. New York: Basic Books.

West, Susie, and Jacqueline Ansell. 2010. "A History of Heritage." In *Understanding Heritage in Practice*, ed. Susie West, 7–46. Manchester: Manchester University Press.

Winter, Tim. 2013. "Clarifying the Critical in Critical Heritage Studies." *International Journal of Heritage Studies* 19 (6): 532–545. https://doi.org/10.1080/13527258.2012.720997.

———. 2015. "Heritage Diplomacy." *International Journal of Heritage Studies* 21 (10): 997–1015. https://doi.org/10.1080/13527258.2015.1041412.

———. 2016. "One Belt, One Road, One Heritage: Cultural Diplomacy and the Silk Road." *Diplomat*, 29 March. https://thediplomat.com/2016/03/one-belt-one-road-one-heritage-cultural-diplomacy-and-the-silk-road/.

Winter, Tim, and Patrick Daly. 2012. "Heritage in Asia: converging forces, conflicting values." In *Routledge Handbook of Heritage in Asia*, ed. Patrick Daly and Tim Winter, 1–35. Hoboken: Taylor and Francis.

WB (World Bank). 2011. "Conserving the Past as a Foundation for the Future: China–World Bank Partnership." 6 December. http://www.worldbank.org/en/news/feature/2011/12/06/conserving-past-as-foundation-for-future.

Wright, Patrick. 1985. *On Living in an Old Country: The National Past in Contemporary Britain*. London: Verso.

 CHAPTER 1

Understanding Heritage Activism
Learning from Social Movement Studies
Tod Jones, Ali Mozaffari, and James M. Jasper

The introduction of this volume located heritage activism in both heritage practice and heritage research. It argued that social movements have always been important to the generation of heritage and are now increasingly central to how researchers define heritage due to the recognition of the importance of resident and other nonexpert practitioners to its creation and upkeep. These shifts are apparent if we look at the changing definitions of heritage. Before the 1970s, heritage was defined as "individual inheritance" rather than practices and things related to the history or identity (Graham et al. 2000: 1). After challenges from activist groups in the 1960s and 1970s, the definition of heritage diversified and, in recent decades, was recast as the "contemporary use of the past" (Graham et al. 2000: 2), a "cultural process" (Smith 2006: 44), and, more recently, a "relational dialogue" (Harrison 2013: 213). The redefinition of heritage suggests a growing focus on the social and material relations and networks that are in a mutual relationship with heritage. These include different groups, species, and things and networks they use to maintain and interact with heritage (Harrison 2013, 2015). It is now understood that heritage has multiple meanings because of the multiplicity underpinning its conception and that this often causes conflict and contests (Silverman 2011; Tunbridge and Ashworth 1996). The centrality of conflict to much heritage is because of the way social movements use heritage in their activism.

Social movement studies has a long history of analyzing contestation and can provide numerous perspectives and concepts that may prove useful to heritage scholars. Social movements are defined as "sustained, intentional efforts to foster or retard broad legal and social changes, primarily outside the normal institutional channels endorsed by authorities" (Jasper 2014: 5). The study of social movements necessarily includes understanding other individuals and groups, as well as the broader social-political setting, as these influence the direction and path of social movements. This is a field that originally emerged in sociology in the late 1960s and 1970s but now includes participants in psychology, political science, anthropology, and other disciplines (Klandermans and Roggeband 2007).

Complementing the introduction, which located activism in the history and study of heritage, this chapter focuses on social movement studies to explore new ways of approaching heritage activists and movements. We begin by explaining our use of the language and concepts of social movements and then identify how this approach assists analysis of contemporary heritage. Heritage researchers are just beginning to explore the field of social movements (Jones et al. 2017; Message 2015; Mozaffari 2015), and our hope is to suggest its most useful current approaches. The second half of this chapter deploys examples of existing heritage research from the perspective of social movements, next to examples from within this volume, to demonstrate our approach and tools for understanding the dynamics of heritage contests and heritage formation. The outcomes of contention shape heritage both in its strategic use (what is heritage) and its material form (what becomes heritage). Building on our earlier work (Jones et al. 2017), we argue our approach expands the disciplinary and methodological aspects of heritage research through analyzing heritage politics, strengthening approaches to heritage that allow for the consideration of the range of interactions between micro-politics and macrostructures, and illustrating the role of social movements in shaping and spreading of heritage, even when they are not successful in achieving their goals. In conclusion, we reflect on the potentials of a social movements approach to furthering research in heritage studies.

Social Movements Research

Early social movement theories generally took psychological approaches that focused on individual behavior, such as grievance theories and crowd theory (Klapp 1969). These theories tended to be anti-protest. In the 1970s, competing structuralist theories emphasized institutional constraints, in particular the resources available to different groups (resource mobilization theory; McCarthy and Zald 1977) and the structural openings of the polity (political opportunity structure; Kriesi et al. 1995; McAdam 1995). While providing important insights into the influence of different types of political systems and organization on social movements, these theories struggled to understand persuasion, or the way groups use a variety of means to influence decisions at the micro-political level, and the reasons people's decisions do not always flow with structural forces (Jasper 2014: 15–38). Kylie Message (2015: 260) notes the application of social movement approaches, particularly in cultural fields such as heritage and museums, "need to overcome constrained structuralist forms of analysis." Contemporary social movements approaches are now addressing the micropolitics of emotion and affect (Woods et al. 2012), as well as the range of objects and meanings deployed to understand agency (Waitt et al. 2014) in addition to the structuralist constraints and influences on groups advocating for and against change.

This chapter employs and explains an interactionist perspective on social movements that uses the language of strategic players and arenas (Jasper and Duyvendak 2015) and incorporates emotions (Jasper 1998, 2014). Considering heritage in terms of players and arenas and their strategic interactions employs a nuanced understanding of heritage and its contestation that takes into account the role of negotiation, as well as a variety of means and methods of persuasion, which may not always result in overt conflict. Players are those who engage in strategic action with some shared goals and sense of identity (Jasper 2015: 10). Players may be simple—individuals—or compound—groups of affiliated individuals or organizations or even whole societies that engage in action. Either way, players are evolving, mutually constituted entities that have multiple, concurrent, shifting, and at times preconscious goals, and use various means and strategies in pursuing them. The multiplicity of goals for each player suggests the role of a player must be determined through empirical investigations rather than deduced from preconceived theories (Jasper 2015: 14). Players' goals and priorities shift because of internal conflicts and external opportunities.

Arenas are places in which rules (formal and informal) and resources facilitate and govern players' interactions, with decisions and outcomes at stake. The rules that constitute an arena can be challenged, ignored, or replaced, in which case a new arena may emerge. Like players, arenas may be formal and institutionalized (courts) or informal and amorphous (public opinion); they may comprise players only, or players and spectators; and they may be related to or affect one another (such as the mood and morale of players and their decisions). Arenas, while related to structural forces, are transformable rather than fixed, and they create and contain cultural meanings. They are often filled with meaningful physical objects that influence action. For instance, room size and layout, amplification devices, other technologies, and seating arrangements can all influence how contention unfolds.

Not all actions occur in arenas; some are intended to influence arenas from the outside by sending messages to various players. For example, the primary purpose of a protest march is not to make movement decisions but to put other players on notice and to prepare participants for further action. These are staging areas or pre-arenas for what occurs in arenas. On the other hand, each compound player also forms its own arenas, such as when it needs to make decisions about its own actions. A protest group or a university faculty meets to decide what it will say or do in other arenas—when meeting in this way it is itself forming an arena.

Social Movements in Heritage Research

Most critical heritage theorists deploy causal factors we find in the field of social movements, not least because scholars have begun to acknowledge heritage activism as organized forces that fit almost any definition of social movement (Mozaffari 2015, 2016). Social movements are increasingly recognized as important actors in heritage contests (De Cesari and Herzfeld 2015; Herzfeld 2015; Rio and Hviding 2011). Iain Robertson (2012a: 15) directly acknowledges the relationship between social movements' circumstances, goals, and strategies and the formation of heritage: "Certain expressions of a sense of inheritance from the past, therefore, would appear to have the capacity to function as a resource for social movements and also as the dynamic product of these movements." Heritage is invoked as both a "creative force that engages people in diverse courses of action toward new political contexts" (Rio and Hviding 2011: 25), and a discourse of neoliberal economic and spatial transformation that displaces existing communities that social movements can also use in their resistance (De Cesari and Herzfeld 2015). Both are accurate and indicate the key issue of how social and economic structures interact with agency in the production of heritage. While some social movements theories (particularly those based on resource mobilization) have been critiqued for having a structuralist bias (Gerbaudo and Treré 2015; Jasper 2014), heritage studies has been critiqued for making assumptions about the structural positions of different actors (e.g., Harvey's 2015 critique of assumptions about local people, and De Cesari and Herzfeld's 2015 critique of NGOs). Both critiques of instrumentalism require a similar solution: concepts and methods that focus on and explain the perspectives, options, and decisions of all the different players involved in a heritage conflict. The allocation of heritage as a creative force, effect of a limiting structure, or anything else should be situation-specific and use empirical evidence to draw careful and constrained conclusions.

Some heritage scholarship relies implicitly or explicitly on a language of "elites" (Smith 2006), which often captures what Marxists called the ruling class. The idea of an elite tends to fuse various kinds of group advantages, as if they were tightly correlated, into a catchall notion of "power." This language makes it hard to understand how non-elites, without power, can ever exert influence in contestation (Robertson 2012b). The concepts of players and arenas recognizes that elites are not the only players in an arena, even while it shows that some players have more resources, especially money, so that they usually win. But outcomes can never be assumed in advance, or easily explained on the basis of "power." Clever strategic choices can sometimes compensate for a lack of resources.

Rodney Harrison's (2013: 13–41) location of heritage within contemporary debates about structure and agency moves beyond bipolar models like dominant-subaltern and local-global. Drawing in particular from Latour (2004, 2005) and Deleuze and Guattari (1987), Harrison argues for an actor-network approach to heritage that conceives of agency over heritage as distributed through specific "assemblages" (DeLanda 2006; Deleuze and Guattari 1987) of people, technologies, and things. As Latour clarifies, this is to suggest not that the latter exercise agency in the way humans do but that they are participants in actions and as such have a range of influences and functions (2005: 72). Both our approach to social movements[1] and actor-network theory (ANT) seek to overcome macro-micro divisions and the undue explanatory power given to structure in social movement theory and social sciences more generally. However, an approach framed through players and arenas and ANT have important differences.

First, there is a difference between actors and players. For Latour (2005), an actor is not the source of action but part of an ensemble that carries out the action, and this includes both human and nonhuman (animals and objects). In our approach, however, the term players excludes nonhuman actors—things—on their own, but it takes into account how players are influenced by and make use of things such as places, arenas, resources, emotions, affect, and objects. Second, an arena is a locus of social action where materials, players, and norms associated with the arena shape contention and its outcomes. This is quite different to an actor-network, which assists with tracing a relation that is understood only temporally with the passage of each actor and ultimately "social fluid" through it. While arenas are focused on understanding contention, actor-networks draw attention to the distinctive kinds of effects that material objects and processes exert as a consequence of the positions they occupy within specifically configured networks of relations (Joyce and Bennett 2010).

Focusing on players and arenas identifies the linked causal mechanisms of action and inaction at the observable level of individuals and their interactions (Jasper and Duyvendak 2015). A gain in one arena may lead to either a gain or a loss in another arena, linking them together. The approach we advocate is geared toward analyzing interactions and activities with the greatest capacity (whether realized or latent) to generate or resist society-wide shifts (sea changes) in how heritage is understood and treated. Things—

material objects—are important in contests over heritage inasmuch as they are part of, facilitate, and afford certain experiences and interactions. Players in heritage contests make specific claims, devise certain strategies to achieve their goals, and attempt to persuade others to recognize and join their cause. These are the characteristics of the realm of social movements. Players' claims may be interpretations or valuations of what the past has left us, but they also imply claims to a kind of ownership of and the right to influence a group's heritage. They are necessarily political because they contest others' claims. This process of claims and counterclaims, strategic actions, and political persuasion form the core of social movements studies.

Heritage and Social Movements

We have argued there is a case for drawing on a particular approach to social movement concepts in heritage research. To pursue this line of argumentation systematically requires a focus on particular issues and may be directed by specific questions (Jones et al. 2017). In the following sections, we refer to existing and emerging scholarship to elicit the particular perspective that underpin a social movements approach to heritage as we see it. While using exemplars presents social movement analysis in action, it also presents a problem: the breadth of a social movements approach to heritage cannot be captured in a single example, as each example highlights parts of the approach. Our solution is to present and explore empirical directions and tasks through an engagement with both our and other people's heritage research to identify the important currents and questions in the literature. The division of the empirical directions into themes helps to clarify the social movements approach we are advocating.

Players

Given that players are the essential component of social movements, understanding heritage activism begins with identifying and cataloging the various players, noting they may be individuals or compound players, unofficial or official. Understanding their constitution, networks, and resources is crucial to understanding the dynamics and outcomes of heritage contests and therefore what the category of heritage includes. It is important to start by cataloging the players, potential and activated, in as much detail as possible. Cataloging should include individuals as well as compound players such as NGOs, private companies, and government agencies. Players will differ significantly. In particular, it is important to understand the different resources they have at their disposal, their allies, and their personal skills and capacities. The extent of their organizational knowledge and capabilities will also influence their effectiveness.

Raphael Samuel's (1994: 295–259) writing on the National Trust for Places of Historic Interest or Natural Beauty in England, Wales, and Northern Ireland—which at the time was accused of being a conservative institution that acted in the interests of rich gentry (Hewison 1987; Wright 1985)—contains a useful example of players. Samuel looked to the three players who founded the National Trust, and identified a shared basis in a commitment to public access and Christian socialism that remains important today. Robert Hunter was a lawyer who had been fighting common rights cases for about thirty years and had worked on commons preservation with John Stuart Mill. Octavia Hill had a career in social housing, was a defender of public access to open space, and was a disciple of John Ruskin, the leading advocate of social commitment in the arts in the second half of the nineteenth century. Canon Rawnsley, like Hill and Hunter, was influenced by Christian socialism and a follower of Ruskin. They prosecuted their ideals through their organizations, social networks, writings, and political lobbying.

Octavia Hill's public profile, public speaking, and advocacy in the media was particularly important (Hall 2016). She had built a public profile through her work advocating for social housing and women and children's rights and education. Although not exceedingly wealthy, her commitment to social reform, public access, and Christian socialism provided a strong network and platform for advocacy of heritage (Darley 2016). She was a credible advocate for public access to and preservation of heritage sites. Her organizational capacity and allies, many of whom were lawyers and social reformers, helped establish an organizational structure that has endured. She continues to be an effective player for the National Trust today because of her public commitments and her achievements.[2] Indeed, Hill's strain of activism continues to inform the National Trust's understanding of its role and actions. The strategies of Hill, such as claims for public access and education, and her use of the media remain the favored strategies of the National Trust.

Individuals who regularly influence the path of contestation become central to a cause or movement, through either their symbolism to the public or becoming a symbol for a group, tactic, place, or moral position. Significant figures such as Hill tend to remain important as symbols after they pass away, and their importance can shift. The ongoing controversy over the British imperialist and founder of the British South Africa Company, Cecil Rhodes, and the focus on his statues in Cape Town and at Oxford University in the Rhodes Must Fall movement is a recent example of how social movements can use past figures as villains to prosecute a case for reforms (Knudsen and Andersen 2019).

The Indonesian nationalist Sukarno is another important figure. Sukarno was the most publicly prominent Indonesian nationalist leader during the last few decades of the Dutch colonial period, the Japanese interregnum from 1942 to 1945, and as Indonesia's first president from 1945 until 1965. Sukarno was an incredible orator[3] and over several years enunciated many nationalist concepts and slogans that remain important today. Sukarno's terms and principles were central to government policy from 1955 until 1965, when he was forced to resign by the Indonesian military (Jones 2013). Many of his terms were related to Indonesia's shared national heritage and could not be discarded by the military dictatorship of General Suharto. Instead, Sukarno's place in nationalist history was rewritten, and his terms were redefined.[4] The resources the military dictatorship were able to deploy once they had control of the state were substantial and included the state cultural institutions that managed heritage.

Katharine McGregor's (2003) study of the National Monument History Museum (Monas Museum) is an interesting study in how historical players are reinterpreted between regimes. Monas Museum consists of a series of historical dioramas depicting key nationalist historical events. Conceived during a period when Sukarno was in power, the dioramas were reviewed during the early Suharto period and became an early representation of the new government's perspective on history. Sukarno's role in history shifted from the early plans to the finished dioramas. An important change was an attempt to reduce the connection between Sukarno and the creation of the Pancasila, or the five unifying principles of the Indonesian nation-state. The Monas Museum emphasized there were three creators of the Pancasila and shifted the date of its creation from Sukarno's public announcement. From a revolutionary program under Sukarno, Pancasila came to exemplify a conservative approach to social change and political reform that was embedded into the education system and bureaucracy. The most prominent Indonesian nationalist of the twentieth century was transformed into one of many founding fathers, alongside many military men, and his radical politics and principles were repressed and reinterpreted as he became a nationalist symbol for an authoritarian regime. However, like in his lifetime, Sukarno's radicalism, complexity, and broad popularity prevent a singular interpretation, and he remains a potent figure for different causes.

Heritage activism includes both activists, like Octavia Hill, who advocate for the preservation of heritage, and the use of heritage by activists who are advocating for or against social change. The skills, resources, and networks of key players like Hill and Sukarno are crucial to how effectively they articulate and advocate for heritage. While we have focused on individuals, compound players are also very important, in particular state agencies, community groups, and businesses. Sudeep Jana Thing's chapter in this volume indicates how internal conflict within a player (in Thing's case, the organization advocating for Sonaha rights in Nepal) can prevent it from taking action. Ali Mozaffari's chapter indicates how particular agencies were able to assert expertize in support of their advocacy for the Sivand Dam near the tomb of Cyrus the Great in Iran and how heritage activists contested their authority. The choices of different players have ongoing implications for how heritage is conceived. To understand these choices, we need to understand the arenas within which these choices are made.

Arenas

Contestation unfolds in real (e.g., courtrooms) or metaphoric (e.g., newspapers or social media) places, resulting in arenas for social action. Arenas are bundles of rules and resources that allow or encourage particular interactions to take place, and where something is at stake (Jasper 2015). The rules in arenas can be formal (as in a court) or informal and flexible (as at a dinner party), or somewhere between (like at a town hall meeting). It is important to understand how different individuals and groups get access to arenas (like a nomination to a town planning committee, a recommendation from a friend, or through a local government election to a council). However, access and resources are not the only determinants of who wins in different arenas. Events that unfold in arenas, some of which are pivotal to heritage movements, can be influenced by arenas' physical settings; possibilities for entrances, exits, and audiences; access to direct proceedings and set agendas; and the technologies that regulate (decorum) and disseminate interactions (media). Arenas are physical, visceral places[5] that influence the outcomes of contention.

The World Heritage Committee (WHC) is a much-observed arena in heritage studies. It has strong rules about regulation, membership, and the process of nominating and deciding on inscription onto the World Heritage List (Bertacchini et al. 2015). Assessments of applications for World Heritage designation are undertaken at arm's length from the WHC by the International Centre for the Study of the Preservation and Restoration of Cultural Property, the International Council on Monuments and Sites, or the International Union for Conservation of Nature, and its operations are overseen by the World Heritage Office within UNESCO. Access to the WHC is open only to nation-states that are signatories to UNESCO's Convention concerning the Protection of World Cultural and Natural Heritage, and appointed to the WHC during UNESCO's General Assembly.

Despite small changes in the rules governing the WHC's operations at that time, a major change occurred in 2009 when a new group of nation-states, including China, Brazil, and Egypt, became members. The relationships between the BRICS (Brazil, Russia, India, China, South Africa) and some other members strengthened a trend toward politicized decision making, and it became increasingly common for the WHC to vote against the advice of the expert groups (Meskell and Brumann 2015). The debates and voting became increasingly and obviously political, revealing the priorities of the nation-state delegates. For instance, the Historic District of Panama—two archaeological sites that date back to 1519 and 1671, respectively, that were the launching point for Spanish colonization of the Western parts of Latin America, and a historic neighborhood—were in the process of being encircled by a new highway when the World Heritage Committee met in 2012 in Saint Petersburg to discuss putting the area on the list of World Heritage in Danger. At this meeting, a series of photographs were shown of a viaduct that was under construction to support the highway and were surreally ignored by their spokesperson. Representatives from the World Heritage Centre, because of the conventions of diplomacy, are unable to challenge or contradict the state party (Meskell 2014: 232). The highway was routed through an archaeological site that would destroy Spanish relics. At a later meeting in 2013, the South African ambassador requested numerous pictures, before calling seventeenth-century buildings "unsightly villages" and claiming the viaduct improved the view, a perspective supported by India and Qatar (233). After a long debate, and after the issue was sent to a subcommittee, a decision was made to not revoke or change the listing but to instead request boundary modifications and revisit the listing in two years. These interactions and practices are now webcast globally, which appears to have little impact on the committee's operations (Meskell 2015).

The case of the Historic District of Panama also indicates the importance of linked arenas. The politicization of UNESCO increases the importance of other, linked political arenas and decisions. A coalition of eleven civic groups in Panama had demanded a halt to construction. On the other side, a Brazilian company had been contracted to build the third stage of the highway and was integrated into the government delegation that represented Panama and a UNESCO session in 2013 (Meskell 2014). Trade-offs across arenas have become increasingly public and acceptable despite poor conservation outcomes (Meskell 2015), including Qatar and South Africa finalizing trade agreements with Panama after their vocal support in the WHC (Meskell et al. 2014). There are also transactions with individual players; individual representatives receive gifts from different nations seeking favor from delegates, and there are numerous receptions and side events (Meskell 2015).

Social movements will often use contention in public arenas to draw attention to their cause and strengthen their group. During the public consultation period for the prospective World Heritage listing of the Ningaloo

Coast in Western Australia, coastal campers who felt threatened by changes to tenure arrangements were organized by station owners to travel in convoy to town-hall-style meetings where they read prepared questions to Western Australian officials (Jones et al. 2016). The physical structure of town-hall format facilitated questions from the floor, which were then used to put pressure on the officials who stood in front of them, and supporters of inscription who felt the rising tension. Protestors asked questions surrounded by their friends and supporters, and bureaucrats' responses stoked anger further. Opponents of the Ningaloo World Heritage listing found this format so useful that they arranged an unofficial public meeting with a sympathetic politician after the consultation period had closed.

A few chapters in this book, as well as recent research, indicate the importance of both media and social media as arenas for contention and decision-making. Mozaffari's chapter on Iran indicates how heritage activists are able to contest official decisions and perspectives in news media despite strong state controls over behavior and expression. It is possible to debate within the rules of political expression in Iran, and influence public opinion. This chapter is also an important reminder that the political system restricts opportunities for activism more in some parts of Asia than others. Heritage activists in Iran must be more careful in their newspaper articles than is the case in other countries with more open public spheres and political systems. Social media is increasingly important for heritage movements. Tod Jones, Transpiosa Riomandha, and Hairus Salim's chapter on a contemporary heritage group in Indonesia indicates how the rules and structures of social media shape interactions and debates, and Terence Chong's chapter demonstrates it is also important for heritage activists in Singapore. Online heritage arenas are often combined with offline activities and make much use of evocative images and videos (see also Gregory 2014; Knudsen and Andersen 2019). As Jones, Riomandha, and Salim argue, social media constitutes a fundamental shift in engagement in heritage activism and how heritage sites are engaged with, visited, and ultimately constituted. The alignments of online and offline arenas have already become very important to activism. The settings and material and immaterial structures that shape heritage contests are both online and offline.

As we can see, arenas have different characteristics and serve different (although not fixed) objectives, and at times with unpredictable results. While there is usually logic in choosing arenas, neither the logic nor the timing are linear, and players usually operate in several arenas concurrently. A common way of forcing players into a different arena in heritage is through court challenges and appeals against planning decisions. Entering a new strategic arena always raises the engagement dilemma: the outcomes are always uncertain, and even the strongest player can never fully control what happens.

Thinking-Feeling Processes and Making and Sustaining Activists

Thinking-feeling processes are important to players' actions and responses, including their commitment to particular causes. They have always been important to social movements (Jasper 2014). In recent heritage and museum-studies literature, thinking-feeling processes fall under the broad rubric of emotions and affect and are influenced by a growing interest in the area, particularly in sociology and anthropology. Although valuable, this interest has not translated into a systematic identification and study of emotions and affect—thinking-feeling processes—in heritage movements. However, there are some useful grounding propositions we can glean from a selective reading of the scholarship for the purposes of our discussion.

Iain Robertson's (2015) article on the Scottish black houses, following his trajectory of research on "heritage from below," analyzes the history and memory of land rights, dispossessions, and linguistic displacements (from Gaelic to English) in the Scottish highlands and islands. There, black house ruins function as an allegory that mediates quotidian practices and memories of past dispossessions, and as such, it expresses "the heritage of the marginalized" (as opposed to official tourist heritage of the same edifice) and a history of connection with the landscape. This heritage from below is always grasped multisensorially, with individuals engaging in a "spatial dance" between past and present. This kind of heritage and the identity work it performs are not necessarily about direct political action but about preserving identities through historically rooted practices that includes memories of social movement activities and political protests.

Activists can use emotions and affect to reject heritage and in doing so reject identities and historical legacies. The Rhodes Must Fall movement in South Africa began when a student activist, Chumani Maxwele, threw human feces on a statue of Rhodes at the University of Cape Town on 15 March 2015. Britta Timm Knudsen and Casper Andersen (2019) identify how the affective reaction of disgust that people feel on viewing or hearing about shit on the statue aligns with the disgust that students thought should be accorded the legacy and images of Rhodes on campus. Indeed, Maxwele said at the time: "As black students we are disgusted by the fact that this statue still stands here today as it is a symbol of white supremacy" (Goodrich and Bombardella 2016: 7). The act of throwing human feces began a broader movement that aimed to challenge the policies and politics of tertiary education in University of Cape Town specifically and South Africa more generally and had an aligned movement at Oxford questioning Rhodes's legacies there. The valued heritage of past regimes and opposition groups is an emotive focus for action, such as the Taliban's destruction of the Seated Buddha of Jahan Abad in the Swat Valley (De Nardi 2018).

In their chapter "The Elephant in the Room: Heritage, Affect, and Emotion," Laurajane Smith and Gary Campbell (2015) argue for the significance of the study of affect and emotions to a critical understanding of heritage. Following William Reddy (2001) and Andrew Sayer (2007), they point out, "emotions are socially, culturally, discursively, and politically mediated" evaluative judgments "of matters that are understood as affecting our well-being" (2015: 448, 451). Thus, they correctly emphasize the significance of context broadly understood in analyzing the role of emotions and that emotions are in turn consequential in reshaping contexts, an observation also made in Robertson's (2015) reading of the black house ruins. In other words, emotions are the result of both structural aspects of a specific context as well as the agency of the feeling individual(s). Thus, the background, social status, educational level, and other characteristics of the individual too are pertinent in emotional engagements with heritage. Here, emotions are central to the things that underpin heritage: memory, commemoration, remembering, affect, and identity making.

Smith and Campbell (2015) emphasize the relationship between thinking (judgments and evaluations) and cognitive emotive processes that become significant when social movements energize through collective actions and articulating identities. Encounters with heritage involve complex, multilevel emotions that cannot be essentialized to simplistic categories such as deep versus shallow or progressive versus conservative. Thus, museums and heritage sites are characterized as places of feeling and "arenas" for managing emotions (2015: 445). In our understanding, museums and heritage sites often form pre-arenas for collective action, meaning places that instigate and energize thinking-feeling processes, intergroup discussions, and potential forms of mobilization. Without outlining a robust or systematic approach, one that allows for a critical reading of heritage production and collective action, their chapter is nonetheless a genuine call to the examination of the role of emotions in heritage contexts pertaining to issues such as social justice.

Already, a common thread is emerging between Robertson (2015) and Smith and Campbell (2015). This thread calls multiple modes of emotions to be taken seriously as the basis for heritage formation and thus containing analytical value. It also suggests the significance of place and of embodied or bodily and multisensorial engagement with material surroundings in giving rise to thinking-feeling processes and heritage itself. We have elsewhere considered such processes and their connection to heritage in relation to the World Heritage Site of Pasargadae in Iran in the context of recruiting and sustaining activists. At a gathering at Pasargadae, activists held hands and sang nationalist songs while being observed by the security apparatus in an action that both consolidated the group and sent a message to opponents and potential supporters (Jones et al. 2017). Emotion and affect are often important for these essential tasks (Jasper 2014). In this volume, chapters engage with such processes in various ways. One of those ways is the consideration of social media platforms as pre-arenas for heritage mobilization and action.

For example, in chapter 2, "The Past Is Always New," Jones, Riomandha, and Salim examine the activities of a successful online platform, Bol Brutu, in Indonesia. The group, whose founders and most of its members are from an educated "middle class," engages with and represents what they term marginal heritage, meaning a heritage that falls outside the purview of state preservation practices. Similar to what Smith and Campbell (2015) note, here the interest began through site visitation, and thus a direct sensory experience of place, but was then expanded through a Facebook platform. Their mode of practice, which is centered on imaginative, creative, and fun engagements with sites facilitates an affective affiliation with artifacts and sites for platform members while simultaneously raising awareness in Indonesia about heritages in the margin. The emotions that are activated from such sites are not necessarily that of outrage and protest but also include care, respect, and affinity. Their activism straddles online-offline modes, thus bridging the discursive and visual (photographs) on one hand and the experiential through site visitations on the other. The act of walking on sites is itself a mode of acquiring knowledge (Ingold 2011) but also reinforces scaled connections between people, place, the past, and the future (similar to the case of black house ruins). However, the sensibilities that propel the activity and the activities themselves are always context-specific. Thinking-feeling processes are therefore also important for maintaining the interest, commitment, and energy of movement members.

In a contrasting case, in chapter 4, Chong discusses the case of Bukit Brown Cemetery in Singapore, part of the largest Chinese burial grounds outside China, which was earmarked for residential development in 2011. While the emotive aspects of this place would become clear to the Chinese population of Singapore, it also propelled careful planning and protest organization on the part of Singapore Heritage Society and other civil society groups, to avert destruction. Here, the cemetery was at once an emotional resource and a pre-arena for staging protests and for putting heritage on the national agenda.

In sum, a starting point for understanding thinking-feeling processes in heritage movements is to be specific about the tactics people use, the kind of mood or excitement that is aroused and the causes for that, and the detailed consideration of how bodies are engaged collectively and in what spaces and spatial configurations. Thinking-feeling processes are essential to any social movement because of the way they consolidate and maintain the movement and draw in new supporters. Heritage sites, objects, and traditions are particularly useful because of their symbolism and historical connections, and therefore the possibilities for evoking responses and emotions through its strategic use.

Narratives

Culturally rooted narratives are essential tools of communication, persuasion, and meaning making in any movement (Polletta 2006). The body of literature that presently forms the corpus of scholarship in critical heritage studies is replete with implicit or explicit claims and counterclaims about identity, memory, and the past in present. Indeed, this was arguably at the root of the idea of dissonance in heritage—dissonance being "the mismatch between heritage and people, in space and time" (Graham et al. 2000: 89). At the core of any dissonant heritage are divergent, at times conflicting, ideas of the past and the identities they sustain. Claims and narratives about heritage work across local (subnational), national, and transnational levels. Such claims are raised in relation to significant places, individuals (historic heroes), events, and artifacts. Here we focus on the relationship between the narratives of heritage activists, the broader identity narratives within which these claims are made (such as national, religious, or ethnic narratives) and how these shape the claims of activists about heritage.

Examining the evolution of the National Museum of Iran, Mozaffari (2014) demonstrates how successive state ideologies have sought authentication through heritage and how this directly affects the displays and narratives of the museum. Specifically, he speaks of two identity narratives, one associated with Shiism (the official religion of Iran) and the other with the Persianate (pre-Islamic) within heritage displays and sites. The World Heritage Site of Pasargadae has been the focus of conflicting narratives and activist political agendas, and continues to be a symbol for activist groups with a range of agendas within and outside Iran (Jones et al. 2017; Mozaffari 2017). The site of Pasargadae has served as an object of nostalgia and the symbol of the fall from imperial glory, but it has also been mobilized by many to counter the official cultural preferences and identity proclamations of the Islamic Republic, in short the primacy of Islamism. However, some of the slogans chanted on the same site have become contentious at both regional and subnational scales (drawing criticism from Arab neighbors, as well as some ethno-nationalist and irredentist groups within Iran) (Mozaffari 2017). Yet again, some groups from within the state establishment, as well as most people, take the site as a symbol of national unity and identity, a claim corroborated by massive participations in New Year celebrations around the Tomb of Cyrus the Great.

Narratives perform a similar, albeit perhaps less confrontational, function in other forms of heritage activism around Asia. Chong's chapter clearly demonstrates how heritage activism has served to rewrite the position and history of ethnic groups—for example, the Chinese—within the grand narrative of nationhood in Singapore. The result of activism has not been a radical rewriting of the story of the nation, which was already culturally diverse and multiethnic. Rather, it was introducing a nuance in the framing of ethnic groups (e.g., the Chinese) through their heritage within the meta-narrative of the nation. At a different scale but culturally no less significant is the case taken up by Aimée Douglas in chapter 6. Referring to the traditional craft of Dumbara Rata, she shows how the implementation of state-driven modernizing processes—heritage protection policies working in tandem with commercialization of handicrafts—have resulted in the emergence of new subjectivities that destabilize presumed cultural norms and social relations. Caste and lineage-based ownership of production knowledge has come into conflict with the development of national heritage, resulting in the destabilization of age-old cultural narratives and assumptions in the social system in a village.

Narratives clearly have a significant role in the formation of heritage and heritage movements. We recommend a systematic consideration of narratives, a detailed (as much as possible) understanding of the claims and counterclaims of contending groups, attention to the metaphors and allegories they use, and consideration of how heritage movement narratives are positioned relative to powerful meta-narratives (e.g., national, ethnic, religious) within which situated claims are positioned.

Collective Identities

Many heritage movements encompass strategies that redefine existing identities and actions to create and shape new identities as a driver of the proliferation of heritage (Tunbridge and Ashworth 1996). Collective identities are shaped and concretely expressed as a result of the convergence senses of time and place—in all their multitudinous forms. In their seminal work *A Geography of Heritage*, Brian Graham et al. (2000: 75–95) argue challenges to the Western grand narratives of heritage were driven by diversifying collective identities, and their expression through the increasing creation, consumption, and use of heritage. The Rhodes Must Fall movement is one example of how heritage is used to contest and critique existing collective identities (Knudsen and Andersen 2019). Throughout this book, there are multiple examples of how collective identities are constituted and contested through heritage processes. Thing's chapter on the Sonaha ethnic movement in Nepal is an example of how collective identity and heritage are expressed through collective action. Jones, Riomandha, and Salim's chapter analyzes how a social movement's engagement with heritage can be a way to creatively explore collective identities. It can equally be a way to consolidate conservative identities and reject change (Harvey 2015).

Recent scholarship demonstrates the role of non-state actors, such as NGOs, in challenging or renegotiating collective identities. For example, Mozaffari's work (2015, this volume) shows the role of grassroots heritage societies in challenging the Iranian state identities in relation to the country's pre-Islamic past, which has deeper historical roots than Islam. The Iranian NGOs frame and express wider sentiments within the society in relation to Iran's past with reference to particular characters and sites such as the World Heritage Site of Pasargadae and expressed through various forms of media, as well as celebrations and performances on sites (see also Jones et al. 2017; Mozaffari 2016, 2017). In a series of studies, De Cesari (2010a, 2010b) shows heritage is also mobilized as a form of resistance to produce and maintain a collective identity even in the absence of a state or under the conditions of occupation. In the absence of a state, she argues (2010a: 630) "NGOs supported by international funding" have taken on the task of preserving a Palestinian past and identity. A significant part of that identity is a response to and rejection of Israeli occupation. The memorial referent for this identity is the 1948 mass exodus of Palestinians from their homes, known as the Nakba, forced by Israeli army. In a specific case, the organization and content of the Palestinian art *biennales* becomes the vehicle for creatively merging folklore, art, and heritage, combining resistance with nation-building in the absence of a state (De Cesari 2010a).

These examples show the various ways, historical depths, and scales in which collective identities are made and contested—that there are various mediums of expression for identity claims. While we have not gone into a detailed analysis of claim making, our discussion demonstrates how heritage relates to the group claims over collective identities. Further analysis would look at the scales through which these narratives are constructed, including the characters constructed and emotions evoked, and the tensions that exist between contested identities.

Patterns of Contention

Considerations of heritage and social movements need to be grounded in both space and time. Patterns of contention shift over time, and this can relate to the sequence of events, as well as the internal politics of the different players involved. The Rhodes Must Fall movement began with and was enlivened by acts of activist vandalism and artistic expression. The statue was covered in various materials more than once, and a performance artist posed with feathers on the empty plinth. Other important elements were University of Cape Town meetings, protests, and criticisms of events and attitudes within the social movement. This included an incident of sexual harassment at a Rhodes Must Fall protest, and subsequent critiques and protests at the gender politics and leadership of the movement (Knudsen and Andersen 2019: 245).

The importance of these patterns, shaped both by politics and events external and internal to social movements, are common to many examples of heritage movements. External events of protest and contention enliven movements and engage their members, and internal events can prevent action or energize participants. As we have discussed elsewhere, in the case of the Iranian heritage activists actions over Pasargadae, there was a four-month hiatus because of a disagreement between two key leaders following a disagreement over who should consult with officials during a protest at the parliament house (Jones et al. 2017). In our example, as in many other social movements, activist strategies change in time and across locations, with due consideration to what is possible and plausible on the ground, and to the members of their movement.

No social movement lasts forever, and only a few last beyond the life of their issue. Maintaining the unity and energy of a social movement requires constant hard work and energy. The Sonaha groups in Thing's chapter struggle to maintain cohesion over time in the face of the opportunities for different villages to gain access to resources in the National Park. The Indonesian group in Jones, Riomandha, and Salim's chapter was beginning to wind down at the time of the analysis, as demonstrated by its declining online activity, and they now rarely undertake trips (while Facebook is still used to share photographs and have discussions). While the method we recommend provides tools to zoom in and analyze key events and moments of contention, analysis also requires the bigger picture of who is winning over time and why, the effects on the internal politics and events of different compound players, and whether claims grow more or less radical in reaction to other players' responses. While an event may be important to an activist movement, its place in and importance to the broader escalating or de-escalating spiral of activity needs to be explained in order to understand its significance.

Discussion and Conclusion

Understanding heritage as a "cultural process" unavoidably includes activism and contentious politics, which are the provinces of social movements research. Social movements research demonstrates that collective identity is an open performance driven by the contingencies of social interactions. An approach to heritage that cognizant of scholarship in social movements encompasses a good dose of ethnographic methods but is more than ethnographic fieldwork, particularly because a social movements perspective can highlight the dynamics of group decision-making and the relationship between internal and external pressures, encompassing activist and other interest groups' formulation and use of heritage. This approach transcends a tendency within heritage studies to divide people and groups into elite and subaltern, and make political assumptions based on structuralist positions (local/national, NGOs / private organizations), essentializing collective identity through a structural perspective. We have advocated for a nonessentialist approach that affords different groups the agency to shape heritage while recognizing their different structural constraints and opportunities. Importantly, from the interactions of players, the boundary between the official and unofficial is clearly porous. Heritage movements come not only from above or below but from many directions.

The concept of players requires a nuanced understanding of the variety of positions and rifts within the state and civil society, the geometries of the public sphere, and the porous boundary between state and society. We seek to avoid simplistic divisions into stakeholder or interest groups. The details and contingencies of the micropolitics of arenas are worthy of careful analysis, as we showed through our discussion of the World Heritage forum. Despite the influence of online broadcasting of sessions that was intended to increase transparency, and despite the obvious ridiculousness of some of the claims by WHC members, political expediency bulwarked by the conventions of diplomacy has continued to win the day. This can be contrasted with the effect of hurling human feces onto the statue of Rhodes at the University of Cape Town. Heritage was crucial to the thinking-feeling processes that energized activists, and conveyed their attitudes and demands to other players and moved the struggles into university committees, including those across the Atlantic at Oxford University. The strength of a social-movement approach is its attention to the details of social interactions within their broader structural context, right down to the micropolitics of a moment and out to a compound player's resources and strategic decisions.

Approaching heritage activism in this way draws attention to how resources and power in their various forms (structural forces) influence interactions in place and time, and how strategies and circumstances can overcome deficiencies in resources and political power. Analysis of heritage movements and activism needs to capture the contingencies of different moments and locate those moments in the entwined process of shaping heritage and players' pursuit of goals. This chapter, and indeed this book, contribute to what we hope will become a nuanced and powerful set of tools for analyzing the dynamics of contention and interaction, which have been the drivers of the proliferation of heritage. These analytical tools should enable a detailed account the social relations that constitute one of the most important dimensions of the heritage process.

Acknowledgments

The research for and production of this chapter was made possible in part thanks to grant awarded by the Australian Research Council (grant no. DE170100104) to Ali Mozaffari.

Tod Jones is Associate Professor in Geography in the School of Design and Built Environment at Curtin University. His research interests are cultural and political geographies in Australia and Indonesia, in particular bringing contemporary geography approaches to cultural economy and heritage issues. His current projects are on Australian Aboriginal heritage and urban planning, social movements and heritage, and applying a sustainable livelihoods approach to assess heritage initiatives. His most recent book is *Culture, Power, and Authoritarianism in the Indonesian State: Cultural Policy across the Twentieth Century to the Reform Era* (2013). His research has been published in numerous journals, including the *International Journal of Heritage Studies*, the *Journal of Arts, Law, Management and Society*, the *International Journal of Cultural Policy*, and *Indonesia*, and he edited volume 125 of the online magazine *Inside Indonesia* in 2016 on heritage politics and issues in Indonesia.

Ali Mozaffari is a fellow of the Australian Research Council with the Alfred Deakin Institute at Deakin University. Through his research, he seeks to understand the uses of the past in contemporary discourses of heritage and built environment in Iran and West Asia. His areas of interest include heritage and social movements, liminality and heritage, and development and heritage in late-twentieth century Iranian architecture. His publications include *Forming National Identity in Iran: The Idea of Homeland Derived from Ancient Persian and Islamic Imaginations of Place* (2014) and *World Heritage in Iran: Perspectives on Pasargadae* (2016), and "Picturing Pasargadae: Visual Representation and the Ambiguities of Heritage in Iran" (*Iranian Studies*, 2017).

James M. Jasper teaches in the Sociology PhD program at the Graduate Center of the City University of New York. His latest books include *Protest:*

A Cultural Introduction to Social Movements (2014) and *Players and Arenas* (2015). More information is available on his website, www.jamesmjasper.org.

NOTES

1. For a longer account of the approach we are advocating, see Jasper (2014).
2. For instance, the National Trust for England, Wales, and Northern (2019) website has a page devoted to her life and legacy.
3. For instance, Sukarno famously used his 1930 trial by the Dutch colonial government to make a series of nationalist speeches now called Indonesia Accuses (Soekarno 1975).
4. For instance, Bowen (1986) demonstrates how the term *gotong royong* (self-help), which facilitated popular participation under Sukarno, became a way of legitimating top-down programs under Suharto.
5. We include social media here in that Facebook and Instagram are services that organize and display images and comments in a specific order. The screen itself shapes the interactions, and people view this in specific, distributed locations.

REFERENCES

Bertacchini, Enrico, Claudio Liuzza, and Lynn Meskell. 2015. "Shifting the Balance of Power in the UNESCO World Heritage Committee: An Empirical Assessment." *International Journal of Cultural Policy* 23 (3): 1–21. https://doi.org/10.1080/10286632.2015.1048243.

Bowen, J. R. 1986. "On the Political Construction of Tradition: Gotong royong in Indonesia." *Journal of Asian Studies* 45 (3): 545–561.

Darley, Gillian. 2016. "Octavia Hill: Lessons in Campaigning." In *"Nobler Imaginaries and Mightier Struggles": Octavia Hill, Social Activism and the Remaking of British Society*, ed. Elizabeth Baigent and Ben Cowell, 72–44. London: Institute of Historical Research.

De Cesari, Chiara. 2010a. "Creative Heritage: Palestinian Heritage NGOs and Defiant Arts of Government." *American Anthropologist* 112 (4): 625–637.

———. 2010b. "World Heritage and Mosaic Universalism: A View from Palestine." *Journal of Social Archaeology* 10 (3): 299–324.

De Cesari, Chiara, and Michael Herzfeld. 2015. "Urban Heritage and Social Movements." In *Global Heritage: A Reader*, ed. Lynn Meskell, 171–195. Chichester: Wiley-Blackwell.

DeLanda, Manuel. 2006. *A New Philosophy of Society: Assemblage Theory and Social Complexity*. London: Continuum.

Deleuze, Gilles, and Félix Guattari. 1987. *A Thousand Plateaus: Capitalism and Schizophrenia*. Trans. Brian Massumi. Minneapolis: University of Minnesota Press.

De Nardi, Sarah. 2018. "Everyday Heritage Activism in Swat Valley: Ethnographic Reflections on a Politics of Hope." *Heritage & Society* 10 (3): 237–258. https://doi.org/10.1080/2159032X.2018.1556831.

Gerbaudo, Paolo, and Emiliano Treré. 2015. "In Search of the 'We' of Social Media Activism: Introduction to the Special Issue on Social Media and Protest Identities." *Information, Communication & Society* 18 (8): 865–871. https://doi.org/10.1080/1369118X.2015.1043319.

Goodrich, Andre, and Pia Bombardella. 2016. "What Are Statues Good For? Winning the Battle or Losing the Battleground?" *Koers* 81 (3): 1–10. https://doi.org/10.19108/KOERS.81.3.2272.

Graham, Brian, Gregory J. Ashworth, and John E. Tunbridge. 2000. *A Geography of Heritage: Power, Culture and Economy*. London: Taylor & Francis.

Gregory, Jenny. 2014. "Connecting with the Past Through Social Media: The 'Beautiful Buildings and Cool Places Perth Has Lost' Facebook Group." *International Journal of Heritage Studies* 21 (1): 22–45. https://doi.org/10.1080/13527258.2014.884015.

Hall, Melanie. 2016. "Octavia Hill and the National Trust." In *"Nobler Imaginaries and Mightier Struggles": Octavia Hill, Social Activism and the Remaking of British Society*, ed. Elizabeth Baigent and Ben Cowell, 209–240. London: Institute of Historical Research.

Harrison, Rodney. 2013. *Heritage: Critical Approaches*. London: Routledge.

———. 2015. "Heritage and Globalization." In *The Palgrave Handbook of Contemporary Heritage Research*, ed. Emma Waterton and Steve Watson, 297–312. London: Palgrave Macmillan.

Harvey, David C. 2015. "Heritage and Scale: Settings, Boundaries and Relations." *International Journal of Heritage Studies* 21 (6): 577–593. https://doi.org/10.1080/13527258.2014.955812.

Herzfeld, Michael. 2015. "Heritage and the Right to the City: When Securing the Past Creates Insecurity in the Present." *Heritage & Society* 8 (1): 3–23. https://doi.org/10.1179/2159032X15Z.00000000035.

Hewison, Robert. 1987. *The Heritage Industry: Britain in a Climate of Decline*. London: Methuen.

Ingold, Tim. 2011. *Being Alive: Essays on Movement, Knowledge and Description*. London: Routledge.

Jasper, James M. 1998. "The Emotions of Protest: Affective and Reactive Emotions in and around Social Movements." *Sociological Forum* 13 (3): 397–424. https://doi.org/10.1023/A:1022175308081.

———. 2014. *Protest: A Cultural Introduction to Social Movements*. Chichester: John Wiley & Sons.

———. 2015. "Introduction. Playing the Game." In Jasper and Duyvendak 2015: xxx–xxx.

Jasper, James M., and Jan Willem Duyvendak, eds. 2015. *Players and Arenas: The Interactive Dynamics of Protest*. Amsterdam: Amsterdam University Press.

Jones, Tod. 2013. *Culture, Power, and Authoritarianism in the Indonesian State: Cultural Policy across the Twentieth Century to the Reform Era*. Leiden: Brill.

Jones, Tod, Roy Jones, and Michael Hughes. 2016. "Heritage Designation and Scale: A World Heritage Case Study of the Ningaloo Coast." *International Journal of Heritage Studies* 22 (3): 242–260. https://doi.org/10.1080/13527258.2015.1120226.

Jones, Tod, Ali Mozaffari, and James M. Jasper. 2017. "Heritage Contests: What Can We Learn from Social Movements?" *Heritage & Society* 10 (1): 1–25.

Joyce, Patrick, and Tony Bennett. 2010. "Material Powers Introduction." In *Material Powers: Cultural Studies, History and the Material Turn*, ed. Tony Bennet and Patrick Joyce, 1–21. London: Routledge.

Klandermans, Bert, and Conny M. Roggeband, eds. 2007. *The Handbook of Social Movements across Disciplines*. New York: Springer.

Klapp, Orrin Edgar. 1969. *Collective Search for Identity*. New York: Holt, Rinehart & Winston.

Knudsen, Britta Timm, and Casper Andersen. 2019. "Affective Politics and Colonial Heritage, Rhodes Must Fall at UCT and Oxford." *International Journal of Heritage Studies* 25 (3): 239–258. https://doi.org/10.1080/13527258.2018.1481134.

Kriesi, Hanspeter, Ruud Koopmans, Jan Willem Duyvendak, and Marco G. Giugni. 1995. *New Social Movements in Western Europe: A Comparative Analysis*. Minneapolis: University of Minnesota Press.

Latour, Bruno. 2004. *Politics of Nature: How to Bring the Sciences into Democracy*. Trans. C. Porter. Cambridge, MA: Harvard University Press.

———. 2005. *Reassembling the Social: An Introduction to Actor-Network-Theory*. Oxford: Oxford University Press.

McAdam, Doug. 1995. *Political Process and the Development of Black Insurgency, 1930–1970*. Chicago: University of Chicago Press.

McCarthy, John D., and Mayer N. Zald. 1977. "Resource Mobilization and Social Movements: A Partial Theory." *American Journal of Sociology* 82 (6): 1212–1241. https://doi.org/10.1086/226464.

McGregor, Katharine E. 2003. "Representing the Indonesian Past: The National Monument History Museum from Guided Democracy to the New Order." *Indonesia* 75 (1): 91–122.

Meskell, Lynn. 2014. "States of Conservation: Protection, Politics, and Pacting within UNESCO's World Heritage Committee." *Anthropological Quarterly* 87 (1): 217–243. https://doi.org/10.1353/anq.2014.0009.

———. 2015. "Transacting UNESCO World Heritage: Gifts and Exchanges on a Global Stage." *Social Anthropology* 23 (1): 3–21. https://doi.org/10.1111/1469-8676.12100.

Meskell, Lynn, and Christoph Brumann. 2015. "UNESCO and New World Orders." In *Global Heritage: A Reader*, ed. Lynn Meskell, 22–42. Chichester: Wiley-Blackwell.

Meskell, Lynn, Claudia Liuzza, Enrico Bertacchini, and Donatella Saccone. 2014. "Multilateralism and UNESCO World Heritage: Decision-Making, States Parties and Political Processes." *International Journal of Heritage Studies* 21 (5): 423–440. https://doi.org/10.1080/13527258.2014.945614.

Message, Kylie. 2015. "Contentious Politics and Museums as Contact Zones." In *The International Handbooks of Museum Studies*, ed. Andrea Witcomb and Kylie Message, 253–282. Chichester: Wiley-Blackwell.

Mozaffari, Ali. 2014. *Forming National Identity in Iran: The Idea of Homeland Derived from Ancient Persian and Islamic Imaginations of Place*. London: I.B. Tauris.

———. 2015. "The Heritage 'NGO': A Case Study on the Role of Grass Roots Heritage Societies in Iran and Their Perception of Cultural Heritage." *International Journal of Heritage Studies* 21 (9): 1–19. https://doi.org/10.1080/13527258.2015.1028961.

———. 2016. "Open Letter to the President Elect: An Example of Heritage Activism through the Media in Iran." In *Indian Ocean Futures: Communities, Sustainability and Security*, ed. Thor Kerr and John Stephens, 15–33. Newcastle: Cambridge Scholars Publishing.

———. 2017. "Picturing Pasargadae: Visual Representation and the Ambiguities of Heritage in Iran." *Iranian Studies* 50 (4): 601–634.

National Trust for England, Wales, and Northern Ireland. 2019. "Octavia Hill: Her Life and Legacy." Accessed 18 June. https://www.nationaltrust.org.uk/features/octavia-hill---her-life-and-legacy.

Polletta, Francesca. 2006. *It Was Like a Fever: Storytelling in Protest and Politics*. Chicago: University of Chicago Press.

Reddy, William M. 2001. *The Navigation of Feeling: A Framework for the History of Emotions*. Cambridge: Cambridge University Press.

Rio, Knut M., and Edvard Hviding. 2011. "Introduction: Pacific Made: Social Movements between Cultural Heritage and the State." In *Made in Oceania: Social Movements, Cultural Heritage and the State in the Pacific*, ed. Knut M. Rio and Edvard Hviding, 5–30. Wantage: Sean Kingston Publishing.

Robertson, Iain J. M., ed. 2012a. *Heritage from Below, Heritage, Culture and Identity*. Farnham: Ashgate Publishing.

———.2012b. "Introduction: Heritage from Below." In Robertson 2012a: 1–27.

———. 2015. "Hardscrabble Heritage: The Ruined Blackhouse and Crofting Landscape as Heritage from Below." *Landscape Research* 40 (8): 993–1009. https://doi.org/10.1080/01426397.2015.1074986.

Samuel, Raphael. 1994. *Theatres of Memory: Past and Present in Contemporary Culture*. London: Verso.

Sayer, Andrew. 2007. "Class, Moral Worth and Recognition." In *(Mis)recognition, Social Inequality and Social Justice: Nancy Fraser and Pierre Bourdieu*, ed. Terry Lovell, 88–102. London: Routledge.

Silverman, Helaine, ed. 2011. *Contested Cultural Heritage: Religion, Nationalism, Erasure, and Exclusion in a Global World*. New York: Springer.

Smith, Laurajane. 2006. *Uses of Heritage*. London: Routledge.

Smith, Laurajane, and Gary Campbell. 2015. "The Elephant in the Room: Heritage, Affect, and Emotion." In *A Companion to Heritage Studies*, ed. W. Logan, M.N. Craith and U. Kockel, 443–460. Chichester: Wiley-Blackwell.

Soekarno. 1975. *Indonesia Accuses! Soekarno's Defence Oration in the Political Trial of 1930*. Ed and trans. Roger K. Paget. New York: Oxford University Press.

Tunbridge, John E., and Gregory J. Ashworth. 1996. *Dissonant Heritage: The Management of the Past as a Resource in Conflict*. Chichester: John Wiley.

Waitt, Gordon, Ella Ryan, and Carol Farbotko. 2014. "A Visceral Politics of Sound." *Antipode* 46 (1): 283–300. https://doi.org/10.1111/anti.12032.

Woods, Michael, Jon Anderson, Steven Guilbert, and Suzie Watkin. 2012. "'The Country (Side) Is Angry': Emotion and Explanation in Protest Mobilization." *Social and Cultural Geography* 13 (6): 567–585. https://doi.org/10.1080/14649365.2012.704643.

Wright, Patrick. 1985. *On Living in an Old Country: The National Past in Contemporary Britain*. London: Verso.

CHAPTER 2

"The Past Is Always New"
A Framework for Understanding the Centrality of Social Media to Contemporary Heritage Movements

Tod Jones, Transpiosa Riomandha, and Hairus Salim

In a blog post published in July 2014, the heritage and online media commentator Elanto Wijoyono provided an overview of the formation of contemporary heritage groups in Indonesia. During the 1990s, heritage groups formed around conservation issues in several cities, which then formed regional and national networks in the 2000s. The next wave of heritage organizations is different in character, organization, and patterns of activity. Since the late 2000s, many heritage networks have formed on social media and have fostered, in Wijoyono's (2014) judgment, a more dynamic and creative engagement with heritage online than either the place-based groups or the state. Heritage groups that engage extensively using social media are widespread but little researched (Gregory 2015), although their role in heritage conflicts is strongly evident (Liew et al. 2013). Most of the research on heritage and social media has focused on institutional use of social media and the question of participation, rather than evolving heritage practices within and around social media.

Social media is now broadly recognized as very important to contemporary social movements, most notably the Occupy movement (Gaby and Caren 2012; Thorson et al. 2013) and the Arab Spring (Lim 2012; Srinivasan 2013), although analysts are still debating exactly why and how social media is important and influential (Gerbaudo and Treré 2015; Lim 2014; Padawangi et al. 2014). Social movement research on social media has been prolific but has tended to bring old questions to quickly changing cyber-social landscapes (Gerbaudo and Treré 2015), ignoring the realm of communications and overlapping practices that includes engagement with heritage.

The purpose of this chapter is to establish a framework for understanding how social media is changing heritage movements through examining their practices, their networks, and their engagements with heritage. Because of the increasing spread and ubiquity of social media, this chapter therefore addresses a global sea change in how people understand and use heritage. Developing this framework requires two bodies of literature—research on social movements and social media and research on heritage and social media—to be critically interrogated and brought together. We begin this chapter with a critical discussion of research assessing the relationships between social movements and social media. Next, we turn to recent heritage research on social media to establish the extent and insights of this research into online heritage movements and practices. The rest of the chapter critically applies the resulting framework to a case study of the heritage movement in Indonesia's shift online through a study of Bol Brutu, a heritage group that began in 2009 and is continuing its activities ten years later.

Following the definition of social movement used by James M. Jasper (2014: 5), heritage movements are defined here as sustained, intentional efforts to foster or retard changes to and engagement with heritage, primarily outside the normal institutional channels endorsed by authorities. An argument that runs throughout this chapter is that we require a broad definition of social, and heritage, movements if we are to capture the groups that contribute to and influence tidal shifts in social engagements and understandings of phenomena like heritage. It is not enough to focus on groups that lobby for political change (including for state preservation of heritage) to the exclusion of groups that open up new popular heritage practices. Hence, following Wijoyono, we argue Bol Brutu constitutes a case study that demonstrates how groups engaging with social media are able to shift their members' heritage practices through a dynamic and creative engagement with, in their case, archaeological sites. The statement of Transpiosa "Cuk" Riomandha, a Bol Brutu cofounder and still one of its most active members, that "the past is always new" highlights in Bol Brutu's unique and fun sensibility that heritage movements create possibilities and potentials, both for group members and for the broader communities and networks they enliven.

Social Movements and Social Media

Debates about the importance of social movements' use of social media, defined here as digital technologies that allow the creation and sharing of ideas, information, and other forms of expression through virtual networks, have been polarizing in both the mass media and academic journals. Much of this debate hinges on the extent to which social media can be thought to impact political opportunity structures, defined as the dimensions of the political environment that "provide incentives for people to undertake collective action by affecting their expectations for success or failure" (Tarrow 1994: 85). While one group of observers emphasized how social media augment new forms of participation and organization (Rheingold 2002), the skeptical view is that online activism is superficial and banal and does not increase political opportunities in a meaningful way, leading to terms like "slacktivism" and "clicktivism." Research working within this framework has focused on various aspects of the framing of issues (Snow et al. 1986) through social media that render those issues meaningful and shape action. In particular, it has sought to understand the extent to which these frames are shaped by the practices and platforms of social media and the extent to which they manage to disperse into mainstream media (Lim 2013; Molaei 2015; Weiss 2014). The dominant criterion of success is the achievement of a sizable mass movement that results in either physical protests (Abbott 2013; Lim 2013, 2014; Padawangi et al. 2014; Weiss 2014) or democratic debate (Hendriks et al. 2016).

Using these criteria for success, social movement research has identified a set of characteristics across the use of social media. Case studies have demonstrated that in many cases social media promotes weak ties (acquaintances and distant friendships, less binding) rather than strong ties (between close friends and family members) (Coretti and Pica 2015; Lim 2013). The structure of social media is comparatively transparent (the actions of other social media observers can be easily observed) and horizontal, but not necessarily democratic (Coretti and Pica 2015). Social media platforms therefore support networks where people access information and can be organized but are less likely to be strongly committed to a cause. However, this is not always the case (on blogs in Kyrgyzstan, see Srinivasan and Fish 2011), and these networks can become quickly politicized (on Egypt, see Lim 2012). According to Merlyna Lim (2013: 636), social media needs to "embrace the principles of the contemporary culture of consumption" to be successful. Lim (2013, 2014) argues social media communication requires content that can be enjoyed without too much time or deep reflection, makes use of simplified and sensational stories, and fits with mainstream narratives. Hence, social media privileges short, quick communications and the use of visual media (photographs, memes, videos).

Despite these characteristics, social media still provides digital affordances, as it is "remixed and mixable" and therefore a realm of social identity creation and evolution (Papacharissi 2011: 305). However, such affordances are subject to the hierarchical power structures that make the ethics and decisions of administrators very important to determining the protocols of online communications their social movements use (Coretti and Pica 2015).

Differences between technologies allow different interactions, and therefore differences in online participation (Srinivasan 2013). Lorenzo Coretti and Daniele Pica (2015: 963) write that Facebook, Bol Brutu's preferred social media platform, is "more than a communication tool [and plays] a vital role in influencing [the Italian social movement Popolo Viola's] structure, leadership communication flows and collective identity," in particular because of the high level of control it grants administrators. Similarly, Carolyn Hendriks et al. (2016) found the Facebook pages associated with opposed sides in a mining dispute to be highly scripted and policed. Technological affordances are also subject to the techno-materiality of their networks (Lim 2013); they are limited by both geographic location (urban areas are privileged) and economics (class considerations), particularly in developing countries.

Social movements research on social media, while establishing important parameters and insights, are insufficient for analyzing heritage movements, or even most use of social media by social movements, because of two issues with this body of work. The first issue is based on a critique from what can broadly be termed cultural approaches to social movements:[1] social movements research has tended toward techno-determinism that derives the logics of political action from the structure of the medium and often do not "account for the historical and cultural configurations of protest activities that ultimately shape the content and meaning of social media activism" (Gerbaudo and Treré 2015: 870). Paolo Gerbaudo and Emiliano Treré's (2015: 868) critique of social movements research, while aimed at approaches based around resource mobilization theory[2] that privilege material affordances and organizational structures, has implications for the research reviewed here. Their contention is that processes of collective (and, we would add, individual) identification remain central to social movements and that these "processes of collective identification reflect the technological affordances of social media, the cultural values associated with their use and the prevailing forms of social experience in a digital era." The identities and practices of these groups, online and offline, are shifted by the interactivity of social media. While scholars like Lim (2013) recognize the importance of these connections,[3] they do not consider the internal dynamics or relationships within the movements or, in other words, questions of collective identity and identity work as they operate in online-offline environments.

Our second critique of this body of research addresses the ubiquitous and normative judgments of what constitutes success for online social movements, which for many of these researchers is size, physical protests, and their capacity for their issue frames to move into the mainstream media (Abbott 2013; Lim 2013, 2014; Molaei 2015; Padawangi et al. 2014; Weiss 2014). For instance, Meredith Weiss (2014: 104–105) draws a strong distinction between online activism that results in concrete political action and "online engagement that is too thoughtless or shallow to foment changes in behavior, let alone identity." Such a set of criteria and distinction ignores the presence and importance of most online social movement activities and networks and their relationships to political change. Social media is inevitably viewed as ephemeral when judged using these criteria, as only a tiny proportion of communications translate into "real" activism. This perspective ignores Gerbaudo and Treré's (2015) argument that social media is a shift in social movements that affects all their practices and collective identities. Furthermore, the line between "shallow" and "real" movement practices is impossible to draw and indicates a narrow definition of social movements. Finally, "weak" ties are still political and can still have political effects including enabling creativity and empowerment. Weiss (2014: 94–95) acknowledges this with regard to LGBTQ movements when she writes, "these communities would almost certainly be less cohesive and empowered if it were not for new media activism."

While much of the work reviewed has attempted to understand how online activities can translate to large-scale political activism, there are scholars who have more closely assessed the different networks within broader social movements, as well as the relationship between different modes of interaction. Ramesh Srinivasan (2013: 50) makes the judgment that "the debate on social media and revolutions . . . tends to lack cultural, social and political context." Srinivasan argues the interfaces between different networks, online and offline, are crucial to understanding events. A broader and more nuanced approach also needs to be brought to what Lim (2014) labels intermodality, or the relationship between digital media and spaces of protest. As space is determined by relationships and is defined by multiplicity (Massey 2005), online activity can change space in multiple ways, from online representations and discussions to visits, political activities, or the locations of servers, computers, and satellites. The capacity to move from digital interactions to face-to-face interactions is not essential to social movements but enhances engagements and enriches the members of a social movement group.

Anna Tsing's work on environmental movements in Indonesia similarly draws attention to the broader lineages of movements and the importance of location in the contingencies of social movement formation. While the genealogies of movements are important and link to questions of political opportunities and resources, their sustained existence stems from their articulation of the desires and perspectives of their members that arises from the myriad of interactions between members across platforms. For Tsing (2005: 122), studying the "energizing connections to the world" essential for social movements and their exotic distinctiveness "models the inextricability of interconnection and location." They offer opportunities for members to craft themselves simultaneously with other actions, one of which is political activity. Hence, the identity work of social movements (Jasper 2015) has a range of implications beyond political activism that may be global in spread and claim but are always specific and particular in practice. Hence, the linked online and offline activities of social movements should be researched not only for their potential to contribute to political action but also because of the ways they make worlds through empowering a multiplicity of particular ways of being in them.

Heritage and Social Media

While digital heritage has been a topic of research interest in heritage studies for some time (Cameron and Kenderdine 2007; Din and Wu 2015; Giaccardi 2012), the focus of most of these studies has been museums' use of digital tools and platforms. Where social media has been a focus of research, it is often examined for the ways the interactions it enables support "democratic" or public-centered heritage activities, generally administered by large institutions (Aigner 2016; Purkis 2016; Silberman and Purser 2012; Taylor and Gibson 2016). Assessments here divide between research that argues high quality public participation in digital curation of such projects is possible and happening (Purkis 2016; Silberman and Purser 2012) and research that argues the structural and institutional forces behind such projects undermine public engagement and control (Aigner 2016; Blackburn 2013; Taylor and Gibson 2016). Neil Silberman and Margaret Pursar's (2012: 26) chapter on digital memory communities clearly establishes the stakes and reveals the dichotomy within digital research in heritage studies. They contend "the creative value of digital heritage lies ... in its power to stimulate unique, community-based reflection on past, present and future identities" and that collective memory "is a prerequisite for collective social action and cohesive, dynamic communities." The dichotomy is between expert-scripted, individual-oriented, online communication—controlled social media that is not "mixable" (Papacharissi 2011: 305)—and interactive, community-based, reflective expression about past, present, and future identities.

While aware that the stakes of social media are more than its contribution to mass political action as tends to be the case in social movements research, the scripted-interactive dichotomy begins to disintegrate when we turn to social media use that large institutions do not manage. Considering the issues raised in the previous section, several factors affect the characteristics of communities of social media users and their use of heritage: the types of communication favored in social media use; their techno-materiality that places great importance on the role of administrator; and, most importantly, the social, political, and cultural context of online users who are always constrained by political and social structures or may themselves support undemocratic or chauvinist practices. Most online heritage groups curate themselves using the digital affordances online platforms—in particular, Facebook (Gregory 2015; Liew et al. 2013)—make available to them, and their practices vary with their specific backgrounds, purpose, and circumstances, as two recent studies make clear.

Kai Khiun Liew, Natalie Pang, and Brenda Chan (2013) examine the role of social media in the conservation politics of Singapore, in particular in contests over the conservation of a railway line and cemetery. Liew et al. expertly assess the affordances and characteristics of social media (its emphasis on simple, short narratives and slogans) for heritage activism and draw attention to the way online heritage groups reterritorialize previously neglected and forbidden spaces through the creation of online archives that frame these spaces through alternative historical narratives. They are also aware of the importance of intermodality, both between different online groups[4] and the connections to site visits, new information, and protest activities. While making a convincing case for the overall character of contemporary heritage activism, they do not examine internal group dynamics or indeed any individuals involved in the group, instead presenting online heritage activism as a decisive break with "book" heritage activism, despite the presence of the same groups in both categories. Furthermore, the differences between the Facebook groups are not discussed in any detail. There is a need for greater attention to the social and cultural specifics of these groups if we want to explore their appeals to their members and how their members respond.

In contrast to this focus on the structural forces shaping how social media influences heritage politics, Jenny Gregory focuses her attention on the online interactions of the "Beautiful Buildings and Cool Places Perth Has Lost" Facebook group that posts pictures of absent heritage previously located in Perth, Western Australia. Gregory (2015: 42) demonstrates this group became an "emotional community" within the broader place-based social movement for conservation in Perth and generated social networks and trust that could be transformed into political action through sharing information on heritage issues and protests online. Like Liew et al. (2013), Gregory's article indicates the importance of the online archive of audiovisual materials, their relationship to framing heritage issues as well as creating emotional attachments, and information sharing on current heritage conflicts for contemporary heritage practices outside of official institutions and channels. However, Gregory does not consider questions of intermodality apart from the sharing of information online. Additionally, the absence of detailed information on the participants (neither article undertakes a survey of online group members, although Gregory gleans what she can from their posts) reduces the capacity of both articles to assess the more intimate relations between group members, heritage politics, and the neglected or absent heritage. Analysis of online-offline heritage movements (most heritage movements today) clearly requires a more robust and thorough analytical framework to build on these interesting and useful beginnings.

Background: Infrastructure for and Genealogies of Indonesia's Online-Offline Heritage Movements

Indonesian's use of the internet, including social media, has grown remarkably since 2000. The number of people estimated to be using the internet increased from 0.93 percent in 2000 to 21.98 percent in 2015.[5] However, in a population estimated to be 252 million in 2014 (BPS 2019), the number of mobile phone subscriptions was 325 million in the same year (more than the entire population of Indonesia), so internet use is likely to be far greater (ITU 2019). Indonesians have adapted quickly to social media use and now make up the fourth largest group of Facebook users by country.[6] The internet has been a tool of political activism since its inception. It was both an avenue for dissenting voices and publications in the last years of the Suharto regime, and students communicated through internet cafes to organize the 1998 protests that forced Suharto to resign (Hill and Sen 2005). Since the advent of free elections in 1999, the internet has been used in ethnoreligious conflict in the Moluccas and by the Islamic fundamentalist movement (Lim 2005), and has been used both to pressure politicians to address specific issues and by politicians to communicate with voters (Lim 2013; Molaei 2015). Hence, there is a history of use of social media by political activists, but the most popular Facebook pages in Indonesia are those of celebrities, indicating that most uses of the internet are not directly linked to political issues. Lim (2013) differentiates older people's use of social media to maintain their existing networks with younger (under thirty) users who pursue different groups, interests, issues, and conversations. Nonetheless, social media constitutes a growing set of overlapping networks within which new ideas flow and connections occur.

Bol Brutu is a product of these overlapping networks. It started with a group of friends from Yogyakarta who traveled around Java looking at the smaller, more marginal archaeological sites (temples, graves, old structures). After a trip on 10 October 2009 to Purworejo, where they visited Klenteng Purworejo (a Chinese shrine) and the church and cemetery of the Javanese evangelist Kyai Sadrach, they posted photos on Facebook and attracted a large number of comments and interest in their activities. Early in 2010, they formed a Facebook group and called it Bol Brutu. Bol Brutu is an abbreviation of Gerombolan Pemburu Batu, which, keeping the playfulness of the Indonesian language, can be translated into English as the Stone Hunters Gang. With increasing followers on Facebook, their activities started to be covered by the mass media including local television, radio, and newspapers. Yogyakarta is a national center for the arts and education, and their friends were painters, photographers, and writers. They began to produce works while at the archaeological sites. The group has continued to organize trips to marginal heritage sites across Indonesia, and to record and comment on their and others' journeys using their Facebook page. They have also organized four exhibitions of Bol Brutu pictures in five locations including Surabaya and Bali. Making use of a fun and creative engagement with heritage, travel, and food, Bol Brutu has sustained its activities over seven years and now has members residing across Indonesia and overseas.

While social media is a relatively new social practice, the genealogies of social movements in Indonesia have a much longer history. Tsing's (2005) genealogy of nature-loving groups in Indonesia identifies four lineages we consider here as they are relevant to Bol Brutu. The first lineage, nationalist anti-politics, stems from the Suharto government's response to the politicized youth of the early years of independence that assisted to bring down the Sukarno government in 1965. Following student protests during the visit of the Japanese prime minister in 1974, the Suharto regime clamped down hard on student political activities, preventing any form of political activities outside state-controlled activities during short periods before tightly controlled elections (Mackie and MacIntyre 1994). Police monitored the activities of all groups, student or otherwise, from the 1970s until Suharto's resignation in 1998. Heritage during this time became a target of state development, with the success of the reconstruction of Borobudur leading to investments in other areas and the spread of an archaeological bureaucracy across Indonesia that began with the colonial period. Heritage sites became linked to Suharto's emphasis on national harmony and state-led development as the expert-managed symbols of a glorious past. While there were limited opportunities for political protest for the duration of the Suharto regime, this changed in 1998 with the opening of the press and free elections. Politics shifted again in 2002 with political and economic decentralization that allowed lower levels of government to appoint their own leaders (Aspinall and Fealy 2003).

Tsing's second lineage is middle-class urban distinction that constitutes nature as an object to be explored, studied, and admired in contrast to rural Indonesians who made use of the same resources and locations, raising the issue of the background and location of online heritage groups and how they perceive and use heritage. Tsing's third lineage invokes concerns with space that are apparent in online heritage groups we reviewed earlier: the adventure geographies of nature-loving groups, or their relationships to the perceived peripheries they visit. The final lineage is youthful consumerism, or the use of expensive equipment and the entry of adventure photography into commercial youth culture in Indonesia.

While these four lineages form a guide to our considerations of Bol Brutu and allow us to use nature-loving groups as a point of comparison, archaeology in Indonesia has its own postcolonial lineages that require examination and bring postcolonial baggage. The archaeological service in Indonesia arose from colonial preoccupations and concerns that have ongoing implications for both the content and management of heritage in Indonesia. Archaeological attention has focused on Hindu and Buddhist archaeological sites driven by a global focus on Greater India that emerged in the colonial research of the nineteenth and early twentieth centuries and continues to have resonance in the focus of art museums, tourism, and UNESCO initiatives (Bloembergen and Eickhoff 2013, 2015). Like the colonial states that preceded them, postcolonial states have continued to use heritage to tie themselves to their populations and have justified their existence through their "expert" management of internationally recognized heritage sites. Furthermore, the exchange of and assistance with heritage creates postcolonial networks "of academic and political interdependencies and reciprocal obligations" (Bloembergen and Eickhoff 2015: 95). These uses of heritage broadly fit within Denis Byrne's (2009, 2014) argument for the privileging of Western, rationalist heritage practices in Southeast Asia over the widespread practices of popular religion that bring an alternative set of relationships to heritage. The practices of Javanese spirituality (*kejawén*) are widespread (Chambert-Loir and Reid 2002) and have their own set of political affiliations and uses (Pemberton 1994).

Methods

We use a case-study approach (Baxter 2010) of a single heritage group that makes great use of social media in order to examine the social media use within a heritage movement. Hence, we need to articulate what are specific characteristics and more general phenomena, noting the importance of cultural specificity (of both this group and their uses of heritage) and spreading interconnections (Tsing 2005: 121–123) that both empower individual members and shape the dynamics of the group. We used a mixed methods approach for this project to address three important aspects of groups that use social media. First, we examined the cultural, social, and political context of the group and their constituents, in particular the genealogies of the group due to the backgrounds of group members, and analysis of broader social and political shifts in Indonesia. Second, we analyzed the identity work and dynamics of the group through interviews and survey data that exist across a range of online and offline platforms in a range of locations. Third, we analyzed online posts, survey results, and interview data to assess the resulting understandings and expressions of heritage that, in the case of this chapter, are made through social media as a subset of a range of heritage interactions of group members.

Importantly, two of the three authors have been engaged with Bol Brutu since its inception, and one is a key player in Bol Brutu's online and offline activities. The process of forming relationships between the international and local authors, and formulating the chapter took place over two years, which itself has been a negotiation with reflections and leanings for all the authors. The involvement of key Bol Brutu members in authorship was crucial for there to be sufficient trust for data collection directly from Bol Brutu members, and it provides the basis for reflections on shifts in group dynamics over time, as well as information on site visits over many years. Long-term and intimate participation in Bol Brutu activities and interactions is a central element of our methodology.

We conducted key informant interviews with eight Bol Brutu members in 2014 and 2016 on Bol Brutu's history and activities. These interviews were supplemented with emails and follow-up conversations in late 2016. In addition to interviews, we conducted an online survey of Bol Brutu members using Qualtrics software. The questions were in Indonesian and distributed through a link on the Bol Brutu Facebook page, as well as through the personal contacts of the authors. Of the one hundred responses, thirteen were excluded because of missing data, and one was excluded because the answers indicated the respondent was not a member of Bol Brutu, leaving a sample of eighty-six responses. While the number of Facebook members of Bol Brutu is 1,860,[7] the number of members who have posted is 422. Using these members as the sample size, the standard error is 9.44 with a confidence interval of 0.95. The survey data were inputted into SPSS software for statistical analysis. The final source of data is the Facebook posts themselves, analyzed for the dynamics of the posting (who are the popular members and the rhythm of use of the site), as well as their content (type of post, topic, and interaction between posts). The Facebook activities were analyzed using software developed to analyze Facebook groups.[8]

Bol Brutu

Political opportunities are important to all social movements, and Bol Brutu is no exception. The resignation of Suharto in 1998 and reinstatement of the parliamentary system were followed by an explosion in new organizations and groups after the draconian regulations and periodic crackdowns on gatherings of Indonesians (Jones 2013). While the Special Region of Yogyakarta was loosely policed compared to other provinces and special regions, even Yogyakartans found themselves in a new climate of freedom of association that accompanied rapid growth in media organizations and greater political freedoms. For heritage movements, opportunities relate not only to political reform but also to changes in heritage management. While new heritage legislation that encouraged greater public participation was passed in 2010, the implementing legislation at the national level has stalled, although it is being enacted through regulations at lower levels of government. The changing political climate and decentralization has fed into a related ongoing debate within archaeology about public participation in site management,[9] and a direction in 2011 to local caretakers (*juru pelihara*) of smaller archaeological sites to facilitate greater public access (although Bol Brutu could already access many of these sites through their personal networks before 2011). While greater opportunities for organization preceded then interacted with the opening up of archaeological sites and the growth of social media, this did not open up access to all sites for Bol Brutu. Founding member Cuk Riomandha said in an interview with Tod Jones (Yogyakarta, 3 September 2014): "If we do our activities at sites that are already commercial, like Prambanan, Ratu Boko, Borobudur, for instance, we will have problems with the staff." Bol Brutu's activities are oriented toward "marginal" sites.[10]

Our survey of Bol Brutu participants revealed some interesting characteristics that distinguish them from Tsing's (2005) student-oriented, nature-loving groups (see Table 2.1). Bol Brutu members tend to be older, with almost half aged between thirty-one and forty-five and almost 80 percent aged over thirty-one. Members tend to live in urban areas, with their spread reflecting the group's origins in Yogyakarta (41 percent). Bol Brutu members tend to be highly educated, with more than 75 percent having a bachelor's degree and 22 percent a graduate degree. When asked about engagement with Bol Brutu before and after graduation, there appears to be little change in involvement. Another indication that Bol Brutu is not a student group is that only 5 percent of respondents are students, with many more working in higher education, the private sector, arts and culture, and the media. Three quarters of members are Javanese, reflecting the group's origins in Central Java. Bol Brutu is a community of educated, urban professionals with a diversity of gender and religion.[11]

Bol Brutu's founding and still most active members made it very clear during an interview that the group is not political or engaged in advocacy, although reports of heritage controversies and notices of public debates and events critical of heritage management are often posted on the Bol Brutu

Table 2.1. Demographic characteristics of Bol Brutu members

Variables	Percent	Variables	Percent
Sex (n = 83)		Employment (n = 80)	
Male	63	Higher education	31
Female	37	Private sector	21
Age (n = 82)		Arts and culture	14
18–30	22	Media	13
31–45	49	Civil servant	6
46–60	28	Student	5
61+	1	Ethnicity (n = 84)	
Home Area (n = 85)		Javanese	76
Yogyakarta	41	Religion (n = 85)	
Surabaya	12	Islam	71
Magelang	8	Catholicism	13
Jakarta	5	Protestantism	7
Sleman	5	Hinduism	6
Other	29	Buddhism	2
Level of Education (n = 84)		Other	1
Junior high school	4		
Senior high school	6		
University student	5		
Bachelor degree	56		
Masters degree	14		
Doctoral degree	8		
Other	7		

Facebook page. In this sense, they are like Tsing's nature lovers in that their appeal is to an educated urban constituency that is seeking personal fulfillment within an Indonesian cosmopolitanism. The most regular interaction between members is on Facebook, which provides many affordances for these interactions that shape engagement with heritage and other members. While Facebook has a flat structure and is transparent in that all group members can see posts, it is shaped by the principles of its administrators, who have a high degree of control, and still requires identity work from key members in order to generate and retain an ongoing dynamics of interaction. Bol Brutu has a small group of administrators (approximately ten) who remove posts that constitute advertising, are inappropriate, or are too far outside the interests of Bol Brutu members. However, they rely mostly on the continuous use of the page to draw attention to popular posts and interesting conversations: "If Bol Brutu lives, it lives on social media. Where is Bol Brutu's office? On Facebook" (interview, Yogyakarta, 3 September 2014). Site visits, meals, and other Bol Brutu activities including exhibitions are organized and promoted through social media.

The key to continuous activity on Bol Brutu's Facebook group is regular posts and the promotion of events. Of the survey respondents in 2016, 59 percent looked every week, and 21 percent posted a picture in the past month. Posts are responded to with comments and "likes" (when a Facebook user indicates they like a comment or post by another user). A small group of key players are central to generating and participating in comments and posts through both their popularity and their regular activity. Our survey indicated 40 percent looked for the posts of a particular person, and two-thirds of those people looked for one player, Cuk Riomandha, while others also looked for Kris Budiman. Cuk and Kris are the two key people in terms of both posts (Cuk has made the most posts, followed by Kris) and comments (Kris followed by Cuk).[12] As administrators and founding members, Cuk, Kris, and some other key members[13] undertake the identity work of posting, eliciting posts, and commenting, as well as organizing offline activities. It is also worth noting that the number of posts is declining annually. From an average of 3.9 original posts per day in 2014, this figure reduced to 2.3 in 2015 and 1.2 in 2016. This can be attributed to the use of alternative online platforms like WhatsApp, Facebook Messenger, and Instagram by long-term members. It is worth noting that other activities have remained regular or, in the case of exhibitions, increased in 2016.

The form of identity work in Bol Brutu is best understood through a consideration of what attracts and interests members. When asked to provide one word to describe Bol Brutu, the most popular was "unique," reflecting the different perspective that Bol Brutu brought to its engagement with landscapes. The second most popular was *blusukan*, a Javanese word meaning wayfaring or a rambling walk. Both these words point to the creative and adventurous approach Bol Brutu brings to heritage that are evident in their posts and comments. Like other online heritage groups (Gregory 2015; Liew et al. 2013), sharing photographs is central to their online communications—68 percent (n = 80) of respondents interested in pictures compared with 5 percent in commentary and 10 percent in all posts)—but these photos are not just of heritage sites or artifacts. The most common posts are of marginal, pre-Islamic heritage sites, in particular temples and stupas, but also often including selfies and pictures of fellow travelers.

The most popular posts contain an element of wonder or debate about an aspect of heritage. For instance, the most liked post (which was also disliked) was of a reconstructed temple that clearly differentiated old and new materials in a jarring style (see Figure 2.1), followed by numerous opinions about the reconstruction. Bol Brutu members debated the effect of using cement blocks alongside the original stone, the archaeologist involved, where else it occurred, and if it followed contemporary principles of archaeology. The second most popular post was of a smiling face on a statue of an "ances-

Figure 2.1. The restoration of a terrace beneath Candi Ijo. Photograph courtesy of Transpiosa Riomandha, 26 March 2016.

tor" in Sri Baduga Museum (see Figure 2.2), with the caption: "It's nice to realize that our ancestors are friendly, humorous. His life must have been happy." The posts then turned to simplicity in art, and how this can express happiness.

Popular posts are not just of sites but also of Bol Brutu activities and events involving popular members. The comments on these posts are also short and entertaining. For instance, a shot of the stout Cuk giving a presentation was quickly followed by the comment "a true enlarger" and then "a large truth teller." Play and fun here are important to both the identity of the group and their engagement with heritage. Flows of attention are directed online through new posts and conversations with and between key members more likely to draw more people and engagement. The posts themselves are short and entertaining, using Indonesian and Javanese slang, and play off each other. Combining humor with the interest in archaeological sites and activities is important for evoking responses and exploring a range of perspectives on a site or activity. Facebook affords a group of like-minded people a steady stream of archaeological pictures with entertaining comments.

A Framework for Understanding the Centrality of Social Media • 71

Figure 2.2. Sculpture of an ancestor. Photograph courtesy of Kris Budiman, 25 January 2016.

Intermodality is clearly important to the dynamics of Bol Brutu. It is most accurate to describe this, and indeed most other, heritage groups as online-offline rather than online. Bol Brutu began with a trip, and trips remain central to their activities and communications. Trips are arranged using social media, and Bol Brutu members have journeyed as a group many times around Java, as well as to Bali.[14] These are not the same as pilgrimages of Javanese spiritualism where ancestors or powerful beings are approached for interventions (although some Bol Brutu members are adherents, and others are Hindu and undertake a different set of rituals). Bol Brutu members typically seek inspiration from visits to archaeological sites and undertake activities like photography, writing poetry, and painting, which is an approach to heritage within a modern Indonesian sensibility (what Hildred Geertz (1963) termed the metropolitan superculture of Indonesia). However, it is important to note this is not a scientific or strictly rational engagement with sites. Bol Brutu celebrates feelings and emotional connections across time and space. Enjoying food together is also important to both trips and gatherings, and photographs of meals are also on Facebook, indicating that visceral experiences are recognized and celebrated alongside discussions about archaeology and history. A small inner group of Bol Brutu members organized the four exhibitions that used photographs from site visits, and put together catalogs for sale. The exhibitions had a higher level of participation from respondents (69 percent) than the trips (53 percent), although the trips dominate social media posts and discussions. Members of this inner group have also given presentations on issues like the heritage of mosques through recording and researching the use of local and earlier symbols and architecture, Buddhist temples around Yogyakarta, and a study of graves across Indonesia. In addition to Bol Brutu activities, there is a steady stream of notices of heritage activities posted onto Bol Brutu's Facebook page.

Similar to observations of online heritage activity in Singapore (Liew et al. 2013), offline activities and exchanges interact with online photographs and discussions to reterritorialize neglected and forgotten spaces within a contemporary urban sensibility. There are parallels here with Tsing's (2005) nature lovers because of the time urban groups committed to organizing and undertaking trips to often (but not exclusively) rural locations. Similarly, the choices and interactions of the visitors require interrogation. Both groups have a romantic approach to categories of things (nature and heritage) that have colonial legacies. Bol Brutu's focus on pre-Islamic heritage is a legacy of colonial archaeology that privileged Greater India over Islamic structures in particular at the time and still is privileged over Dutch colonial heritage (Bloembergen and Eickhoff 2013). However, they are not following the positivist and object-focused approach that defines official archaeological approaches in Southeast Asia (Byrne 2014) but instead bringing a different cosmopolitan engagement and sensibility to pre-Islamic heritage. Tsing (2005: 13–8) also notes the urban distinctions that nature lovers made to differentiate themselves from rural village dwellers who resided in the areas they visited. Bol Brutu's engagement with residents at the archaeological sites they visit are quite different. The site caretakers, who receive a small payment from the state, are treated with great respect, and their photographs with Bol Brutu members often appear on the website.[15] Bol Brutu members position themselves as a respectful guest in these places, and members will always talk with the caretakers and residents and ask permission before approaching a heritage site. This speaks to the forward-looking cosmopolitanism that heritage opens up for Bol Brutu members: 83 percent (n = 81) of our survey respondents indicated Bol Brutu had changed the way they appreciate heritage.

Conclusion

History, and heritage, is indeed the work of "a thousand different hands" (Samuel 1994: 8), now increasingly using PDAs and computers. We have argued in this chapter that social media is not just a communication tool but, through its affordances, also constitutes a shift in what heritage and heritage groups are and can be. To recognize and understand this shift requires a broad definition of social movements and heritage movements. They are not just groups advocating for change and seeking political outcomes but also groups that construct new consensus and open up new ways of engaging with and understanding heritage. Heritage cannot be separated here from the flows of attention, people, and information that social media is entangled with, but is properly understood as constituted through these flows. Social movements are therefore essential to the ongoing constitution of heritage and not just or primarily because of their political influence. However, as Raphael Samuel (1994: 288–312) also observed, heritage is used in very different ways and for different purposes by conservative and progressive groups and can quickly switch political poles. In this case, we need to differentiate the dynamics and structures of online social movements that influence all groups, and the specific ways Bol Brutu has entwined itself with these structures to become the group it is.

An important structural influence on heritage movements today is the affordances of social media organization. For instance, Facebook has a flat structure, has transparency through its use of posts, directs attention and creates networks through likes and comments, and is strongly hierarchical in the power it gives to administrators. While most social media allow near-constant communication, each platform needs to be examined for the specific affordances it opens up for a group. However, it is not enough to focus on the platform or online interactions. Understanding heritage groups requires an understanding of the specific social, political, and geographical context within which social movements act and interact. Political opportunity structures, including access to and management of heritage, are important to analysis. Analysis should also identify and interrogate the characteristics of group members. Once the context and background of the movement are understood, it is then possible to understand how groups form in concert with social media technologies that allow for self-curation and organization.

There also appears to be a set of similar characteristics between online-offline heritage groups across different cultures and political contexts. Photographs and images appear to be very important for their operation, and their use should constitute a focus of future research on heritage groups. Much like social movements more broadly (Jasper 2014), key people undertake identity work both on social media sites and offline to keep members engaged and interact with nonmembers for the group. Online engagement in the case of Bol Brutu was generating posts and comments within an urban cosmopolitan sensibility that opened up fun, new ways of understanding and seeing Indonesia's pre-Islamic heritage. While fun and "unique" perspectives are essential for Bol Brutu, heritage groups' use of social media can open up or close engagement with heritage. Cosmopolitan engagement is a characteristic of Bol Brutu rather than a feature of heritage movements.

Finally, these groups are most effective when they are online-offline, so it is important to pay attention to the full range of their engagements and activities. This broader perspective indicates how engagement with social media can open up flows of information, people, and resources, leading to flows of people and resources that shape landscapes. Flows of attention directed through online interactions often translate into the movement of people into peripheral and forgotten sites, beginning new engagements and interactions. Urban-rural interactions generated through these flows are worthy of further attention. Social media also shifts engagements at the sites. It directs attention and introduces new practices (e.g., the selfie) and priorities. Social movements research in its current iteration would prioritize offline, political activities. However, offline activities are incomprehensible without recognizing social media; they are parts of the same heritage practice, and they open up both new ways of being in the world and new understandings of heritage. To paraphrase Tsing (2005: 154), the personal force of heritage, and its appearance as an object of reflection, depends on both localization and its cosmopolitan referents. Social media will be a connection between these two poles for the foreseeable future.

Acknowledgments

We would like to acknowledge that ideas in this chapter were shaped through Tod Jones's collaborations with Ali Mozaffari over many years. We would also like to thank Kris Budiman for permission to use his photographs, and Bol Brutu members for their involvement in the survey. Funding for a workshop to develop these ideas was provided by the Australia-Asia-Pacific Institute at Curtin University, and the Research Unit for the Study of Societies in Change contributed to activities essential to the development of this chapter.

Tod Jones is Associate Professor in Geography in the School of Design and Built Environment at Curtin University. His research interests are cultural and political geographies in Australia and Indonesia, in particular bringing contemporary geography approaches to cultural economy and heritage issues. His current projects are on Australian Aboriginal heritage and urban planning, social movements and heritage, and applying a sustainable livelihoods approach to assess heritage initiatives. His most recent book is *Culture, Power, and Authoritarianism in the Indonesian State: Cultural Policy across the Twentieth Century to the Reform Era* (2013). His research has been published in numerous journals, including the *International Journal of Heritage Studies*, the *Journal of Arts, Law, Management and Society*, the *International Journal of Cultural Policy*, and *Indonesia*, and he edited volume 125 of the online magazine *Inside Indonesia* in 2016 on heritage politics and issues in Indonesia.

Transpiosa Riomandha is an anthropologist and ethno-photographer who is actively involved with Bol Brutu and LIKE Indonesia.

Hairus Salim is an author and intellectual who lives in Yogyakarta, Indonesia. He is Director of the Institute for the Study of Islam and Society and a founding member of Bol Brutu.

NOTES

1. See Jasper's (2014) account of cultural approaches to social movements and its differences to structural accounts.
2. Beginning with the work of McCarthy and Zald (1977), resource mobilization theory examines a social movements resources and social movements' ability to use them to explain their success.

3. Lim (2013: 637) writes: "The social impacts of the internet and social media ... should be understood as a result of the organic interaction between technology and social, political, and cultural structures and relationships."
4. Liew et al. (2013: 612) write: "the multiplicity of platforms and the multiplication of attention and interests here becomes essential for the re-evaluation of the otherwise neglected sites, giving them history, presence, relevance and future."
5. According to Indonesian Bureau of Statistics data compiled by the UN specialized agency for information and communication technologies (ITU 2019).
6. Indonesian users of Facebook totaled 77 million in May 2016, according to data sourced from Socialbakers.com (Statista 2019).
7. This is the number for 10 November 2016, when we closed the survey.
8. Two analysis tools were used: Sociograph (http://sociograph.io) and Grytics (https://grytics.com). Both tools enable data to be downloaded to Excel, where we analyzed it.
9. See the archaeologist Daud Tanudirjo's (2016) article in *Inside Indonesia* about this shift in the broader context of the discipline in Indonesia.
10. Respondents in interviews used "marginal," a term that has entered the Indonesian language from English and reflects the social science background of many of our respondents who have university educations.
11. While 71 percent of respondents were Islamic, this reflects the larger proportion of followers of Islam in Indonesia. A more important observation is that there is a mixture of religions.
12. Cuk has generated more than seven thousand comments on his posts and eleven thousand likes, and Kris has generated more than six thousand comments and three thousand likes.
13. These are Putu Sutawijaya, Ninuk Retno Raras, Apriadi Ujiarso, Feintje Likawati, and Linggar Saputra Wayan. All these users were assigned a composite score from Sociograph, taking into account activity and other member responses, of more than ten thousand.
14. Individually, Bol Brutu members have journeyed to many places including overseas.
15. This includes a photographic montage of caretakers and residents' portraits set to music by Riomandha to pay respects and acknowledge the local people who care for and guard historic sites. Riomandha (2012) says: "They are beloved people for Bol Brutu."

REFERENCES

Abbott, Jason. 2013. "Introduction: Assessing the Social and Political Impact of the Internet and New Social Media in Asia." *Journal of Contemporary Asia* 43 (4): 579–590. https://doi.org/10.1080/00472336.2013.785698.

Aigner, Anita. 2016. "Heritage-Making 'From Below': The Politics of Exhibiting Architectural Heritage on the Internet—A Case Study." *International Journal of Heritage Studies* 22 (3): 181–199. https://doi.org/10.1080/13527258.2015.1107615.

Aspinall, Edward, and Greg Fealy. 2003. "Introduction: Decentralisation, Democratisation and the Rise of the Local." In *Local Power and Politics in Indonesia: Decentral-*

isation and Democratisation, ed. Edward Aspinall and Greg Fealy, 1–11. Singapore: Institute of Southeast Asian Studies.

BPS (Badan Pusat Statistik). 2019. "Perkiraan Penduduk Beberapa Negara, 2000–2014." Accessed 18 June. https://www.bps.go.id/linkTableDinamis/view/id/960.

Baxter, Jamie. 2010. "Case Studies in Qualitative Research." In *Qualitative Research Methods in Human Geography*, ed. Iain Hay, 81–98. Melbourne: Oxford University Press.

Blackburn, Kevin. 2013. "The 'Democratization' of Memories of Singapore's Past." *Bijdragen tot de Taal-, Land- en Volkenkunde* 169 (4): 431–456. https://doi.org/10.1163/22134379-12340064.

Bloembergen, Marieke, and Martijn Eickhoff. 2013. "Exchange and the Protection of Java's Antiquities: A Transnational Approach to the Problem of Heritage in Colonial Java." *The Journal of Asian Studies* 72 (4): 893–916. https://doi.org/10.1017/S0021911813001599.

———. 2015. "Save Borobudur! The Moral Dynamics of Heritage Formation in Indonesia across Orders and Borders, 1930s–1980s." In *Cultural Heritage as Civilizing Mission*, ed. Michael Fasler, 83–119. New York: Springer.

Byrne, Denis Richard. 2009. "Archaeology and the Fortress of Rationality." In *Cosmopolitan Archaeologies*, ed. Lynn Meskell, 68–88. Durham, NC: Duke University Press.

———. 2014. *Counterheritage: Critical Perspectives on Heritage Conservation in Asia*. London: Routledge.

Cameron, Fiona, and Sarah Kenderdine, eds. 2007. *Theorizing Digital Cultural Heritage: A Critical Discourse*. Cambridge, MA: MIT Press.

Chambert-Loir, Henri, and Anthony Reid, eds. 2002. *The Potent Dead: Ancestors, Saints and Heroes in Contemporary Indonesia*. Crows Nest: Allen & Unwin.

Coretti, Lorenzo, and Daniele Pica. 2015. "The Rise and Fall of Collective Identity in Networked Movements: Communication Protocols, Facebook, and the Anti-Berlusconi Protest." *Information, Communication & Society* 18 (8): 951–967. https://doi.org/10.1080/1369118X.2015.1043317.

Din, Herminia, and Steven Wu, eds. 2015. *Digital Heritage and Culture: Strategy and Implementation*. Hackensack, NJ: World Scientific.

Gaby, Sarah, and Neal Caren. 2012. "Occupy Online: How Cute Old Men and Malcolm X Recruited 400,000 US Users to OWS on Facebook." *Social Movement Studies* 11 (3–4): 367–374. https://doi.org/10.1080/14742837.2012.708858.

Geertz, Hildred. 1963. *Indonesian cultures and communities*. New Haven: Southeast Asia Studies, Yale University.

Gerbaudo, Paolo, and Emiliano Treré. 2015. "In Search of the 'We' of Social Media Activism: Introduction to the Special Issue on Social Media and Protest Identities." *Information, Communication & Society* 18 (8): 865–871. https://doi.org/10.1080/1369118X.2015.1043319.

Giaccardi, Elisa. 2012. *Heritage and Social Media: Understanding Heritage in a Participatory Culture*. London: Routledge.

Gregory, Jenny. 2015. "Connecting with the Past Through Social Media: The 'Beautiful Buildings and Cool Places Perth Has Lost' Facebook Group." *International Journal of Heritage Studies* 21 (1): 22–45. https://doi.org/10.1080/13527258.2014.884015.

Hendriks, Carolyn M., Sonya Duus and Selen A. Ercan. 2016. "Performing Politics on Social Media: The Dramaturgy of an Environmental Controversy on Facebook." *En-*

vironmental Politics 25 (6): 1102–1125. https://doi.org/10.1080/09644016.2016.11 96967.
Hill, David T., and Krishna Sen. 2005. *The Internet in Indonesia's New Democracy*. New York: Routledge.
ITU (International Telecommunication Union). 2019. "Statistics." Accessed 18 June. https://www.itu.int/en/ITU-D/Statistics/Pages/stat/default.aspx.
Jasper, James M. 2014. Protest: *A Cultural Introduction to Social Movements*. Chichester: John Wiley & Sons.
———. 2015. "Introduction: The Identity Dilemma, Social Movements and Contested Identity." In *The Identity Dilemma: Social Movements and Collective Identity*, ed. Aidan McGarry and James M. Jasper, 1–17. Philadelphia: Temple University Press.
Jones, Tod. 2013. *Culture, Power, and Authoritarianism in the Indonesian State: Cultural Policy across the Twentieth Century to the Reform Era*. Leiden: BRILL.
Liew, Kai Khiun, Natalie Pang, and Brenda Chan. 2013. "New Media and New Politics with Old Cemeteries and Disused Railways: Advocacy Goes Digital in Singapore." *Asian Journal of Communication* 23 (6): 605–619. https://doi.org/10.1080/01292 986.2013.790911.
Lim, Merlyna. 2005. "Archipelago Online: The Internet and Political Activism in Indonesia." PhD dissertation, University of Twente.
———. 2012. "Clicks, Cabs, and Coffee Houses: Social Media and Oppositional Movements in Egypt, 2004–2011." *Journal of Communication* 62 (2): 231–248. https:// doi.org/10.1111/j.1460-2466.2012.01628.x.
———. 2013. "Many Clicks but Little Sticks: Social Media Activism in Indonesia." *Journal of Contemporary Asia* 43 (4): 636–657. https://doi.org/10.1080/00472336.2013 .769386.
———. 2014. "Seeing Spatially: People, Networks and Movements in Digital and Urban Spaces." *International Development Planning Review* 36 (1): 51–72. https:// doi.org/10.3828/idpr.2014.4.
Mackie, Jamie, and Andrew MacIntyre. 1994. "Politics." In *Indonesia's New Order: The Dynamics of Socio-cultural Change*, ed. Hal Hill, 1–53 Sydney: Allen & Unwin.
Massey, Doreen B. 2005. *For Space*. London: Sage.
McCarthy, John, and Mayer N. Zald. 1977. "Resource Mobilization and Social Movements: A Partial Theory." *American Journal of Sociology* 82 (6): 1212–41. https:// doi.org/10.1086/226464.
Molaei, Hamideh. 2015. "Discursive Opportunity Structure and the Contribution of Social Media to the Success of Social Movements in Indonesia." *Information, Communication & Society* 18 (1): 94–108. https://doi.org/10.1080/1369118X.2014.934388.
Padawangi, Rita, Peter Marolt, and Mike Douglass. 2014. "Introduction to the Special Issue: Insurgencies, Social Media and the Public City in Asia." *International Development Planning Review* 36 (1): 3–13. https://doi.org/10.3828/idpr.2014.1.
Papacharissi, Zizi. 2011. "Conclusion: A Networked Self." In *A Networked Self: Identity, Community and Culture on Social Network Sites*, ed. Zizi Papacharissi, 304–338. New York: Routledge.
Pemberton, John. 1994. *On the Subject of "Java."* Ithaca, NY: Cornell University Press.
Purkis, Harriet. 2016. "Making Digital Heritage about People's Life Stories." *International Journal of Heritage Studies* 23 (5): 1–11. https://doi.org/10.1080/13527258.2016 .1190392.

Rheingold, Howard. 2002. *Smart Mobs: The Next Social Revolution*. Cambridge, MA: Perseus Publishing.
Riomandha, Cuk. 2012. "HOW BRUTU ARE YOU?... The Alias." Video, 4:53. Published 6 February. https://www.youtube.com/watch?v=BGkHvyHQ4Fw&feature=share.
Samuel, Raphael. 1994. *Theatres of Memory: Past and Present in Contemporary Culture*. London: Verso.
Silberman, Neil, and Margaret Purser. 2012. "Collective Memory as Affirmation: People-Centered Cultural Heritage in a Digital Age." In Giaccardi 2012: 13–29.
Snow, David A., E. Burke. Rochford Jr., Steven K. Worden, and Robert D. Benford. 1986. "Frame Alignment Processes, Micromobilization, and Movement Participation." *American Sociological Review* 51 (4): 464–481.
Srinivasan, Ramesh. 2013. "Bridges Between Cultural and Digital Worlds in Revolutionary Egypt." *The Information Society* 29 (1): 49–60. https://doi.org/10.1080/01972243.2012.739594.
Srinivasan, Ramesh, and Adam Fish. 2011. "Revolutionary Tactics, Media Ecologies, and Repressive States." *Public Culture* 23 (3): 505–510. https://doi.org/10.1215/08992363-1336381.
Statista. 2019. "Countries with the Most Facebook Users 2019." Last edited 29 April. https://www.statista.com/statistics/268136/top-15-countries-based-on-number-of-facebook-users.
Tanudirjo, Daud Aris. 2016. "Shifting Sands." *Inside Indonesia* 125. http://www.insideindonesia.org/shifting-sands.
Tarrow, Sidney G. 1994. *Power in Movement*. New York: Cambridge University Press.
Taylor, Joel, and Laura K. Gibson. 2016. "Digitisation, Digital Interaction and Social Media: Embedded Barriers to Democratic Heritage." *International Journal of Heritage Studies* 23 (5): 1–13. https://doi.org/10.1080/13527258.2016.1171245.
Thorson, Kjerstin, Kevin Driscoll, Brian Ekdale, Stephanie Edgerly, Liana Gamber Thompson, Andrew Schrock, Lana Swartz, Emily K. Vraga, and Chris Wells. 2013. "Youtube, Twitter and the Occupy Movement: Connecting Content and Circulation Practices." *Information Communication & Society* 16 (3): 421–451. https://doi.org/10.1080/1369118x.2012.756051.
Tsing, Anna L. 2005. *Friction: An Ethnography of Global Connection*. Princeton, NJ: Princeton University Press.
Weiss, Meredith L. 2014. "New Media, New Activism: Trends and Trajectories in Malaysia, Singapore and Indonesia." *International Development Planning Review* 36 (1): 91–109. https://doi.org/10.3828/idpr.2014.6.
Wijoyono, Elanto. 2014. "(Konservasi) Pusaka dalam Genggaman." Elantowow, 1 July. https://elantowow.wordpress.com/2014/07/01/konservasi-pusaka-dalam-genggaman.

 CHAPTER 3

The Exemplary Foreigner
Cultural Heritage Activism in Regional China
Gary Sigley

Introduction: Players and Arenas in China's Cultural Heritage Field

The People's Republic of China (PRC) is the world's most populous nation. It is also one of the most diverse in terms of geography, ethnicity, and culture. The peoples who have over time inhabited the space we now associate with "China" have created a vast treasure trove of material and nonmaterial culture, which collectively makes for a rich human cultural heritage. This has been recognized by the Chinese government through the formal designation of cultural heritage, both tangible (such as the Imperial Palace, the Great Wall, and the Grand Canal) and intangible heritage (such as Peking opera and the Dragon Boat Festival) and handicrafts (such as paper cutting). Some, such as these examples, are internationally recognized through UNESCO's Intangible Cultural Heritage program. Nonetheless, official recognition, regardless of whether it is tangible or intangible heritage, is always framed in terms of a specific national narrative. Cultural heritage from this view is part and parcel of legitimizing the party-state's "Chinese Dream," a process that has gone through various periods with differing ideological emphases. Yet, although the party-state is often able to assert its hegemonic ambitions, the designation of cultural heritage never goes completely uncontested.

As the PRC continues its economic and social transformation, both the party-state and society in general have "rediscovered" China's cultural heritage. This rediscovery, in contrast to the sustained critique and attack on "traditional culture" during the Maoist period (1949–1978), takes several forms. First, from the perspective of the party-state, the construction of a unified sense of China's cultural heritage works toward solidifying a form of cultural nationalism and the shaping of a common identity during a period of rapid social transformation. In this sense, as social values and structures undergo change, traditional culture, insofar as it supports the status quo, can be deployed as a stabilizing force. Second, cultural heritage, both tangible and intangible, is now identified as a resource that can be deployed to promote economic development, especially in the burgeoning domestic tourism and leisure industry (see, e.g., the approach taken by Tunbridge and Ashworth 1996). Third, cultural heritage can serve a pedagogic function that seeks to educate the citizenry in the value of heritage and in the progress that has been made in the reform era (post-1978), thereby legitimizing the party-state's form of cultural nationalism. Fourth, from a grassroots societal perspective, cultural heritage is embraced as a means of strengthening local identity and a sense of place.[1] This can work with government and commercial forces, but it can also be posed against them. As I shall explore, while there is more to be said of cultural heritage in the context of a rapidly changing China, these four approaches capture much of what is happening.

Into this milieu has emerged a growing field of cultural heritage activism. Ali Mozaffari (2015: 2) defines heritage activism as that which "comprises collective challenges by people with a common purpose and solidarity to protect and conserve heritage as a conveyor and basis for collective identity, through sustained interactions with elites, opponents and authorities." This activism also takes many forms and, I would argue, includes both people and institutions. The party-state is not a monolithic entity but is instead made up of diverse forces and agencies. In this case, while elements of the party-state apparatus may be seen to be undermining cultural heritage protection—through, for example, the promotion of mass tourism—other agencies are actively involved in heritage protection. The most obvious example is the State Administration of Cultural Heritage (Guojia Wenwuju, 国家文物局) and its counterparts at provincial, municipal, and prefectural levels. Non-government organizations dedicated to cultural heritage education and protection are an example of a form of non-state activism (although it should be noted that in China there are many NGOs directly funded and administered by the government, which the literature refers to as "government nongovernment organizations"). Finally, individuals and groups, often in the form of a grassroots community (Nitzky 2013), are another important instance of cultural heritage activism in contemporary China, which, along with NGOs, make up the buds of an emerging heritage-orientated civil society.

Building on the work of James M. Jasper, I will refer to these various state and non-state actors as "players." Broadly defined, players are "those who engage in strategic action with some goal in mind" (Jasper 2015: 10). The space in which these players operate is an "arena," which Jasper describes as "a bundle of rules and resources that allow or encourage certain kinds of interactions to proceed, with something at stake" (14). An arena consists of formal and informal aspects. Formal aspects include, for example, the body of relevant heritage laws. Informal aspects might refer to the unwritten rules of social interaction, such as, in the Chinese case, the notion of *guanxi* (关系), which refers to the important role of mobilizing personal relationships (Yang 1994). Rules in this instance are flexible, can be changed, or can even be ignored. This is especially so in the case study in regional China that will be examined here where the Chinese saying "Heaven is high and the emperor far away" (*Tian gao, Huangdi yuan*, 天高皇帝远) is apposite when describing how locals get around heritage restrictions.

The location of this chapter's case study is the historic village of Xizhou (喜洲) in Dali Bai Autonomous Prefecture, approximately twenty kilometers from the famous old town of Dali (大理) and not far from the shores of Erhai Lake to the east and the Cangshan mountains to the west (see Figure 3.1). Dali Prefecture is part of Yunnan Province (云南省). Yunnan, which literally means "south of the clouds," is located in China's southwest and shares domestic borders with Sichuan, Guizhou, Guangxi, and Tibet and international borders with Myanmar, Laos, and Vietnam. Dali is thus firmly located in China's extensive "borderlands." It is one of the most topographically

Figure 3.1. Map of the People's Republic of China. Adapted by Gary Sigley from the original map by Koryakov Yuri, via Wikimedia Commons (CC BY-SA 3.0).

and culturally diverse regions on the planet. The chapter further focuses on one particular "player," the Linden family. Brian and Jeanee Linden are an American couple who operate a boutique hotel and cultural programming center—the Linden Centre—in Xizhou. Brian Linden, who will be the main focus here, reminds us that in the field of cultural heritage activism, we should not assume the activist is always a local national subject or that "activism" necessarily expresses itself as a form of open resistance to the state. As the notion of player suggests, heritage activism is about building alliances, articulating a mission, marshaling resources, and constantly negotiating.

In building the Linden Centre, the Lindens have had to engage in these activities within the local cultural heritage scene constituted as a coming together of other institutions and players. Brian Linden himself can be situated as a unique player within China, that is, as the "exemplary foreigner." By exemplary foreigner, I refer both to the important role of the "exemplar" or "model" (*mofan*, 模范) in Chinese culture (Bakken 2000) and to the status of the "foreigner" in the PRC as an outsider who performs a certain role that cannot be played by the national subject. Brian Linden, as a charismatic, skilled, and passionate player takes on the act of performance, crossing adroitly between Western and Chinese culture well aware of the different cultural nuances including in speech and body language, that reminds one strongly of Erving Goffman's (1956) pioneering research on the role of performance in everyday life. In the Maoist period, the exemplary foreigner had little scope in adjusting the performance. As Anne-Marie Brady (2003a) notes, the foreigner was "made to serve China," and much of the power was clearly in the hands of the party-state and in particular the system of "foreign affairs." In the post-1978 reform era, there is much greater scope for foreign players to act out their performance according to their own desires and missions.

Nonetheless, to do so effectively still demands that the foreign player is well aware of the boundaries and formal and informal rules. In this regard, the Lindens have proved particularly flexible and are a good example of the exemplary foreigner/s in the contemporary context when it comes to grassroots cultural heritage activism. What the Lindens are doing can hardly be described as a "social movement," which Alain Touraine (2002: 90) describes as "organized conflicts or as conflicts between organized actors over the social use of common cultural values." On the contrary, the players within the cultural heritage field in Dali tend to avoid open conflict. As will be explained, this is not because the power of the party-state is overwhelming but rather because the autonomy of grassroots communities allows them space to make their own decisions about cultural heritage, whether for good or ill. In the face of government priorities that overwhelmingly prioritize economic development and a desire to avoid stirring up ethnic discontent (thus, for example, not upholding the strict cultural heritage regulations that pertain to what villagers can do with their property), it is not surprising that cultural heritage preservation finds itself in a disadvantaged position. It is into this space, in the absence of a broad based social movement, that the Linden Centre marks out its position and attempts to define a positive alternative to cultural heritage preservation.

The rest of the chapter is divided into four sections. First, I outline in more detail the trends, paradoxes, and contradictions in what I refer to as China's "cultural heritage revolution." Next, I turn our attention to the emerging field, or arena, of cultural heritage activism in the PRC. Then I provide the necessary background and introduction to the historic village of Xizhou and the Linden Centre. Finally, I focus exclusively on Brian Linden as an exemplary foreign player in the Xizhou cultural heritage arena.

China's Cultural Heritage Revolution

The PRC is undergoing a cultural heritage revolution. By "revolution," I mean a radical repudiation of the previous approach to cultural heritage and its replacement with a new approach, one that is informed by quite different assumptions (although of course not without some level of continuity). The official party-state approach to cultural heritage in the PRC can be divided into three major periods since 1949. The Maoist period (1949–1978) was characterized by an orthodox Marxist approach to cultural heritage. During this period, cultural heritage was primarily viewed through the grid of class analysis. Tangible and intangible culture was divided into that which was the product of "good classes"—the workers and peasants—and that which was the product of "bad classes"—feudal and bourgeois ruling classes (including that of "foreign imperialists"). This critique was backed up by concrete measures aimed at destroying the physical vestiges of material culture—or converting them into modern and secular functions such as schools, factories, and offices—and prohibiting the continuing practice and dissemination of intangible culture. In its place, the party-state claimed a new "socialist culture" was being created (this also involved "sanitizing" some forms of traditional culture and readapting them for the party-state's mission). The number of players was also strictly limited and controlled. The agency of individuals and communities at the grassroots was significantly curtailed, although acts of resistance did take place through, for example, the hiding of cultural artifacts and the secret transmission of some cultural practices.[2]

The ushering in of the policies of "reform and openness" (*gaige kaifang*, 改革开放) constitutes the beginning of the second period. This transitionary period (1978–1992) witnesses a reversal in the official position on traditional culture. Physical attacks on material culture ceased, and the prohibitions against many forms of intangible cultural practices were lifted. The party-state institutions credited with cultural heritage preservation became much more active and increased contact with external agencies (thereby facilitating the absorption of a more standardized and global cultural heritage discourse such as the ratification of the Convention Concerning the Protection of the World Cultural and Natural Heritage in 1985).

During the 1980s, as the party-state began to reassess the position of "traditional culture" (*chuantong wenhua*, 传统文化) and even openly declared it to have a positive function in social development (alongside what have now ironically become known as the "socialist traditions" (*shehuizhuyi chuantong*, 社会主义传统) or "red traditions" (*hongse chuantong*, 红色传统)), cultural affairs bureaus were severely underfunded and encouraged to find innovative ways to generate revenue. This sometimes resulted in cultural heritage buildings being turned into pool halls or rented out for other forms of entertainment purposes. These practices were later prohibited, but it did not stop the cultural heritage sector seeking for more stable and lucrative forms of revenue, an ongoing issue that has been somewhat alleviated by considerable increases in state funding in recent years and the development of mass tourism. In particular, intangible cultural heritage at the grassroots began to experience a revival during this transitionary period, especially in regard to religious practices. Much of this grassroots revival was part of a general revival of cultural identity taking place across China in the wake of the Maoist period, both among China's fifty-five officially recognized ethnic minorities and the Han Chinese, the latter itself an incredibly diverse group with many regional cultural variations (Sautman 1997).

The third period, which carries us into the present, begins in 1992 with the official declaration by then President and Party Secretary General Jiang Zemin at the 14th National Congress that henceforth the goal of the party is to construct a "socialist market economy." This is the first time "market economy" is given official sanction as part of national policy. It coincides with the call for local governments across China to engage with "market forces" to promote economic growth. This also included the development of a "cultural market" (*wenhua shichang*, 文化市场). In what has been called the "cultural turn" (Nitzky 2013; Oakes 2006a) local governments were henceforth actively encouraged to find "cultural resources" that could be mobilized to promote economic growth, especially for the then rapidly growing domestic tourism economy. Hence, the aforementioned revival of "folk religion," "popular festivals," and other "traditions" associated with "cultural heritage" now gain a new value as resources to be exploited within the planning and developmental mentality of local, provincial, and national government.

During this third period, we see the emergence of many new players. Of particular importance is the emergence of the business sector and partnerships between business and government in the field of cultural heritage. As the domestic tourism economy grows, local governments partner with business developers—some of whom we might consider "cultural entrepreneurs"—to create "scenic zones" (*jingqu*, 景区). The scenic zone model of tourism development is the preferred model of mass tourism in the PRC (Nyiri 2006). A scenic zone can consist of natural or cultural attractions, or a combination of both. They are regulated and spatially demarcated zones that require entrance fees. These consumption spaces are specifically developed to cater for very large numbers of tourists, most of whom are experiencing the scenic zone through organized group tours.

This scenic zone model has significant consequences for both material and nonmaterial cultural heritage. The most important impact is the commodification of cultural heritage within a model that is clearly geared toward large-scale tourism and profit maximization. Even UNESCO World Heritage status—which has been granted to several sites across China—is no guarantee of preservation. On the contrary, local governments see World Heritage inscription as a means of increasing market share and developing their particular "brand." This hails the arrival of a bureaucratized and commercialized "heritage industry." The Yunnanese heritage town of Lijiang, inscribed as World Heritage in 1997, is a well-studied case (McKhann 2001; Su and Teo 2009).

This model has also been applied to the commercial development of "old towns." In this scheme of things, the local governments of historic towns and villages form contracts with business developers to convert the site into a scenic zone. In some cases, the entire local community is moved out of the village or town. Entrance fees are applied, and the site is converted into an "experience" for tourists. There is a strong sense of affinity between the commercialization and commodification of old towns and more general developments in Chinese consumer culture and middle-class/new rich aspirational lifestyles. In recent years, the mass tourism scenic zone model has been supplemented by the development of more independent forms of tourism. Of particular interest here is the arrival on the scene of a new player in the form of China's nouveau riche, colloquially known as the "hillbilly rich" (*tuhao*, 土豪). With vast amounts of disposable income, the new rich are active in asserting their "tastes" and "cultural capital," a point I will return to when I examine the case study more closely.

At the same time, the processes of industrialization and urbanization that began in the 1980s have greatly accelerated. While traditional culture is no longer attacked, and indeed is increasingly used a means of essentializing a form of state-sponsored "Chineseness," the wrecking balls of urbanization and industrialization have laid waste to much material heritage landscape, especially of China's rich vernacular architecture as old residential quarters are bulldozed. It would be fair to say there has been more destruction of tangible heritage in the reform era as a result of these processes, combined with a severe lack of enforcement of heritage provisions, than there was during the entire Maoist era.[3] As a result, Chinese cities have taken on a uniform, and some would say drab, appearance. Local authorities seek to revitalize what heritage areas are remaining through redevelopment, as mentioned earlier, in the form of commercial pedestrian malls. The commercial redevelopment of the historic Qianmen area in Beijing is a good example (Layton 2007).

Thus, in the shift over the past thirty years from the Maoist period to the present, the PRC has experienced a cultural heritage revolution. The previous orthodox Marxist approach is now itself a "thing of the past." Cultural heritage has become an artifact for both the party-state and commercial forces. It is an object used by the party-state, where it sees fit, to educate the citizenry in a contemporary form of cultural nationalism. Alongside these trends are grassroots movements, which often seek some patronage or support from both the government and private sector, seeking to revitalize their own cultural heritage identity.

Cultural Heritage Activism in Contemporary China

As noted earlier, the party-state was the dominant player when it came to the appropriation of cultural heritage during the Maoist period. In this scheme of things, the other players, such as intellectuals working within the cultural heritage field and the local communities from which the cultural objects originally derived, had very little or no agency. However, as China entered the post-1978 reform era, the arena within which this dynamic operates underwent radical change. While the party-state retains a vast resource capacity, it retreats from the politicization of daily life, thereby giving individuals and local communities greater scope in shaping and distributing their own cultural objects and revitalizing their own cultural and religious traditions. The role of intellectuals and other "cultural workers" (writers, artists, filmmakers, etc.) is also less severely regulated, thereby creating a broader and more diverse approach to both the critique and production of cultural objects. Of pivotal importance in all this is the emergence of the cultural market, especially since the heralding of the socialist market economy in 1992. Thus, the cultural heritage scene in the PRC now has two "masters": the party-state on the one hand and the market on the other.[4] Into this scene have emerged several new forms of cultural heritage activism. In addition to the formal institutions of the party-state, such as the State Administration of Cultural Heritage and its counterparts at local, provincial, municipal, and national levels, we can now discern three other forms of players: the corporate sector (or cultural entrepreneurs), grassroots communities and individuals, and nongovernment organizations.

Cultural Entrepreneurs

In a culture where the party-state has been the dominant financial and resource backer for the cultural field for over half a century, it is not surprising that corporate support for intangible heritage in China is almost nonexistent (interview with the deputy director of the Grand National Theatre, May 2015). However, there is much greater scope for corporate support, and indeed outright management, of material cultural heritage. Here I refer to the role of cultural entrepreneurs. Cultural entrepreneurs are a motley crew. They primarily consist of registered businesses. They can also refer to "freelancing" intellectuals operating as consultants. More often than not, they work in contractual partnership with local governments, particularly local cultural heritage bureaus and/or tourism bureaus. This alliance between the market and the party-state is largely responsible for the construction and proliferation of the scenic zone model. Intellectuals working as consultants play an important role in the application and approval process by providing the imprimatur of expertise and legitimation. Tourism, of course, is the major business. This model is well established across China, and I have examined it previously with regard to the development of the Ancient Tea Horse Road (Sigley 2013a, 2015). It is also dominant in the development of culturally orientated theme parks and exploitation of old towns. While it is difficult to generalize, this model is commercially driven and promotes the commodification of material and nonmaterial culture. At the same time, the resultant products also work toward reinforcing the party-state's cultural nationalist narrative. This is not surprising given the active role of government in this alliance, but I would also argue the ideological and pedagogic position that is presented is also regarded as "common sense" by those developers, intellectuals, and other parties involved. It fits well with Gramscian notions of how cultural hegemony is reproduced (Gramsci 1971).

Local Communities and Individuals

The official rhetoric of cultural heritage protection and development of cultural heritage resources explicitly calls upon community participation

(Nitzky 2013). This is in part an extension of the development of notions of community participation in development projects that began in the 1990s and part of the absorption of global heritage discourse that takes community participation as important. The Principles for the Conservation of Heritage Sites in China (commonly called the China Principles) states this very clearly. However, as Hilary du Cros and Yok-Shiu Lee (2007: 140) argue, the China Principles, unlike other international codes and charters, has "avoided ... stakeholder involvement in conservation planning":

> Undertaking conservation work in the national interest and for rational economic reasons appear foremost in the document. Gaining consensus from non-experts as part of the planning process is not, however. In fact, local communities are often relocated, en masse, as part of urban renewal or conservation projects without giving much thought to how this might have weakened and dissolved the connectivity of the communities and their living culture. (124)

Hence, community participation in tourism planning, especially in ethnic minority regions (despite the 1984 Law of Regional Ethnic Autonomy (amended in 2001), which proclaims minorities have the right of autonomy including practicing and developing their own cultures and religions and using their own languages) is limited (Jigang and Jiuxia 2007; Wang et al. 2010). In places where the management/administration is functional/able to resolve problems and distribute tourism resources/benefits fairly, the lack of participation does not seem to be an issue (Li 2005); indeed, lack of participation is the norm in China. In cases where there has been meaningful community participation, the overall result has been better for all concerned (Ying and Zhou 2007).

The local community, thus while not always an active player in the planning, development, and management of such cultural heritage tourism projects, is nonetheless involved insofar that they are often subcontracted by the scenic zone company to provide support services and activities in the form of, for example, horse rides, catering facilities, song and dance performances, tour guides, and sanitation services. When compared to the Maoist period, there is not much scope for agency in this model either (although, once again, it is dangerous to generalize). However, at certain moments, the community can be mobilized against such development when it infringes on aspects of their heritage they feel strongly about.[5]

In other instances, local communities may be actively involved in reconstituting the history of their own village or clan. This has become quite common all across China but especially in the villages of the rapidly industrializing and urbanizing Yangtze and Pearl river deltas. After the destruction of the Maoist period, many villages worked to recover their heritage by either rebuilding lost material heritage and/or reconstructing lineage genealogies. There is also often a significant gendered dimension to this, as it is more likely, given that the family line is traced through male descent, that men will be actively involved in ancestral heritage.[6] In some instances, local cultural relic/heritage bureaus may have already designated certain buildings for preservation (the homes of historical and revolutionary figures is a case in point). This can lead to conflict and contestation with local communities over the display, use, and interpretation of this heritage (Svensson 2006).

Into this grassroots heritage mix we should also consider examples beyond the scenic zone model that are attempting to identify and preserve China's rich intangible culture. In this regard, Anne McLaren's (2011) study of the epic songs of the Yangtze River Delta is a salient example. The Yangtze River Delta has a very rich and diverse cultural heritage. This heritage has been gradually lost over the course of the past century through urbanization, industrialization, migration, and, of course, the trials and tribulations of political and ideological campaigns. The once village-orientated agricultural lifestyle that supported certain intangible cultural practices has been more or less displaced. The epic songs sung by locals in local dialects were thought to have disappeared and in some cases were not even known to exist. It was not until the 1980s, with the aforementioned revival of scholarship on grassroots cultural heritage, that they were "discovered" to still reside among the memory of many elderly individuals. Suffice to say, overall, the impact of the scenic zone model and the forces of commercialization and commodification have the upper hand.[7]

Nongovernment Organizations

The last form of "new player" to be examined here is the cultural heritage orientated nongovernment organization. The number of NGOs operating in China across a broad spectrum of social, cultural, educational, and environmental areas has increased dramatically in recent years. The party-state has not been very comfortable with the rise of the NGO, especially in the wake of the "color revolutions" and its fear of a "westernized civil society" (Sigley 2013a). The government has thus devised measures to control NGO activities and ensure that explicit political work is prohibited.[8] One method has been for government departments to create and endorse their own NGOs, which are tautologically known in the literature as government nongovernment organizations (GONGOs). All NGOs are required to register with the Ministry of Civil Affairs.[9] NGOs thus tend to operate in a gray area. Many avoid trouble with the authorities by focusing on supporting government programs and policies. It is certainly not wise for an NGO to take on a more adversarial role as is common for NGOs in Western societies.

Research on cultural-heritage-orientated NGOs in China is almost nonexistent. Part of the reason may be because the number of such NGOs is itself rather miniscule compared to the much larger number of environmental, education, gender, or more general culturally orientated NGOs. One of the best examples in recent years is the Beijing Cultural Heritage Protection Center (CHP). The CHP is registered under the Beijing Municipal Administration of Cultural Heritage (the director of the CHP is reputedly also an official in this supervisory body). This seems to have been, at least initially, a productive partnership. The CHP's mission is to "to assist local communities to preserve tangible and intangible local culture through training and capacity building." The mission statement concludes by stating:

> Large portions of China's rich cultural heritage are at risk due to low awareness and poor enforcement of heritage protection laws, as well as short-sighted policies that sacrifice cultural rights and values to short-term economic gain. Chinese government laws and policies in the field of cultural heritage protection are generally well-conceived, but are not well understood and are often poorly implemented. CHP has been established to address and tackle these issues. (CHP 2019)

Although these objectives could easily be conceived as adversarial, even the CHP's own website says its activities must "not hassle the government." One can clearly discern possible conflicts between government supported commercial development and CHP supported cultural heritage protection.

In this regard, the CHP claims two major victories in the battle against the demolition of heritage buildings and neighborhoods in Beijing. First, the CHP successfully lobbied for the protection of the former residence of Liang Sicheng (a famous modern architect / urban planner and the son of conservative scholar/activist Liang Qichao) against proposed demolition. Second, the CHP was instrumental in advocating for the cancellation of the proposed Drum and Bell Tower neighborhood redevelopment. Both of these were achieved in 2010. However, both of the commercial development projects that threatened these material sites were reinstated a short time later. I have been informed by anonymous sources that the CHP was instructed to disengage from contact with foreign NGOs and donors.[10] Since 2014, the former CHP website, in both English and Chinese, has ceased to operate. I am informed the website is still active but that it no longer seeks a public profile and has significantly scaled back its operations. This clearly indicates that commercial forces are much stronger than those of the grassroots cultural heritage movement in contemporary China. Cultural-heritage-orientated NGOs thus play only a limited role in this environment. NGOs that do not successfully navigate this terrain will face many obstacles and even possible deregistration. I will return to this notion of "navigation" when I examine how the Lindens have been able to work within the formal and informal rules of cultural heritage in Xizhou.

Studies of social movements in the PRC are generally framed in terms of a "party-state versus society" binary. However, not all activism is about resistance or open conflict (see chapter 1). In proceeding to the case study section of this chapter, we shall see the ability to navigate and negotiate within a particular arena in ways that create alliances is a much more effective strategy than outright conflict. This does not mean there is no place for meaningful critique, but it does suggest players need to make strategic choices about how they can best promote a progressive position while not destabilizing or upsetting the status quo.

Dali, Xizhou, and the Linden Centre

Dali City is a prefectural city and administrative center of Dali Bai Autonomous Prefecture in the southwest province of Yunnan.[11] Dali is situated on the fertile basin between Erhai Lake and the Cangshan mountains. The average altitude of two thousand meters and the latitude of 26.88983 provide Dali with a mild climate year-round. The basin is dominated by two large population centers: the new administrative town of Xiaguan and the historic old town of Dali. The rest of the basin consists of numerous villages, large and small. The Indigenous people of the Erhai basin are the Bai (白族), a people with a Sinicized culture but still with many unique cultural traditions (including, of course, a distinctive language). The region is also home to many other ethnic groups including Hui (Chinese Muslims), Yi, and Han. Dali sits at the crossroads of several important trading routes, most notably the Southern Silk Road and Ancient Tea Horse Road. It was the capital of two important kingdoms: the Nanzhao (737–937) and the Dali Kingdom (937–1253). After the Mongol conquest leading to the establishment of the Yuan Dynasty (1271–1368), the political and cultural center shifted to Kunming (Yang 2008), but Dali remained an important corridor for the movement of people, commodities, and ideas.

Like much of eastern China, Dali is experiencing rapid change. Dali, with its relatively mild climate, picturesque scenery, attractive architecture, and colorful culture, has in recent years become a popular tourist destination. In addition to the general processes of development (growing population, building of transport infrastructure, urbanization of towns and villages, etc.), the rapid development of tourism has had a huge impact on Dali (Notar 2006). Dali now includes several popular scenic zones, ranging from those of a cultural-historical nature to those based on famous films and novels.[12] In 2014, Dali received approximately four million tourists. More recently,

Dali has become a favored lifestyle migration destination for people seeking to escape the pollution, congestion, and pressures of urban life in China's eastern seaboard (Sigley 2016). In short, along with the loss of material and nonmaterial culture typically associated with the forces of "modernization," the Bai culture has experienced waves of commercialization and commodification as a direct result of the rapid development of mass tourism.

While some remain rather pessimistic about the ability of Bai culture to respond to these challenges, a family of American citizens—the Lindens—has taken up the challenge by developing an innovative boutique hotel and cultural heritage tourism business in the large historic village of Xizhou, situated on the northern end of the Erhai basin. Xizhou is a short distance, about twenty kilometers, from Dali old town and is well known for being the home of many successful merchant families, especially those who plied the caravan trade within China's southwest and beyond to Myanmar, Nepal, and India (Wang and Zhou 2008). With commercial success, the merchants built many beautiful courtyard mansions, temples, and other buildings. Most of the remaining structures date from the late Qing and Republican periods. The Lindens completed renovations on one of these family mansions in 2008. Since then, it has been operating as a sixteen-room boutique hotel. In 2011, they completed renovations on an Art Deco–influenced building now functioning as an education and cultural programs center. The third site opened in 2015 and consists of a culinary school and an art and textile studio. Collectively, these sites and activities are the Linden Centre (Xi Lin Yuan, 喜林苑), representing a total investment of $1,600,000 and many years of hard work, planning, and negotiation.

According to its official website,[13] the Linden Centre focuses "on cultural sustainability and heritage preservation," explaining that, "we believe that China has suffered too much damage to its tangible and intangible culture ... The Linden Centres [sic] offer China a more sustainable and enlightened option." The website proceeds to declare the Linden Centre is dedicated to:

> Preserving and sharing the cultural heritage of Asia's timeless villages;
> Creating and inspiring experiential learning opportunities;
> Developing partnerships to build innovative, cultural programs;
> Providing an elegant and unprecedented heritage hotel for our guests.

The gamut of the Linden Centre is thus quite broad, much more than just a functioning hotel. In this regard, the Lindens have taken direct inspiration from organizations such as the Aspen Institute. Hence, in addition to providing a rich cultural immersion experience for guests and visitors, the Linden Centre seeks to establish itself as a locus for a broad range of cultural and educational activities. Much of this focuses on presenting the rich cultural heritage of Dali to the rest of China and the world, but also in bringing other cultural experiences and practices to Dali to foster a sense of mutual respect and understanding. The center hosts international scholars from a wide variety of backgrounds in the humanities and social sciences, along with artists, musicians, and writers. It holds frequent cultural events, workshops, and exchanges in music, photography, and painting. Students from China and abroad also visit the center on a regular basis and take advantage of its location and facilities (which includes a resource room with three thousand items). One of the hallmarks of the Linden Centre is its interactions with the local community. Community interaction is facilitated through daily "market tours," "antique hunting," other guided tours, and interactions with local musicians and schools. In its short span of years, the Linden Centre has become highly respected and welcomed in the Xizhou community. Brian Linden is a well-known figure and jokingly referred to by the locals as the Mayor of Xizhou.

The boutique hotel designed by the Lindens also flies in the face of the aesthetic demands of the burgeoning Chinese luxury hotel market. The rooms, for example, do not have television sets, which goes against most Chinese expectations. As Brian Linden notes, many Chinese guests judge the quality of their room by the size of the television, the origin of the furniture (did it come from Italy?), and the overall sense of grandeur (interview, September 2015). The Lindens' approach can be seen as a form of aesthetic challenge to the tastes of the new rich, yet it also fits well with a traditional aesthetic Chinese approach, captured in Chan (Zen) Buddhism, which sees virtue in the rustic and simplistic. The model adopted by the Lindens has been successful. The Linden Centre has won many tourism, sustainable tourism, and business awards, including the US Secretary of State's Award for Corporate Excellence and the TripAdvisor Travelers' Choice Award for China's Top Small Hotels. The Lindens have faced some major challenges in securing the long-term viability of the project. First is the status of "ownership." In China, no matter whether in rural or urban settings, nobody owns freehold title to the land. In rural areas, the land is owned collectively by the local village or township. In urban areas, it is owned by the relevant government department concerned with land. Instead, individuals, families, and companies take out long-term leases of up to ninety-nine years. In effect, this amounts to a form of de facto ownership. However, the situation for foreigners is even more complex, especially in rural contexts such as Xizhou. The Lindens own the brand "The Linden Centre" and are in a cooperative arrangement with the local Xizhou government when it comes to the buildings and property. Brian is quoted as saying, "We never were building equity in the buildings, because we don't own them ... Our equity in the future is really just our brand. And that's tied so much to Jeanee's and my story" (Ives 2013).

The Exemplary Foreigner: The Outsider and Cultural Heritage Preservation in Xizhou

The success of the Linden Centre no doubt rests on the skills and hard work of the Linden family. Brian's passion, determination, and commitment shine through; he is a "mountain changer" with a mission (for more on mountain changers, see Sigley 2015). It is possible to situate the Lindens in a family tree of foreigners in China. Understanding how foreigners operate within this environment—while of course acknowledging the differing social and political conditions that separate them over time—will better enable us to make sense of Brian's particular form of cultural heritage activism. Brian fits within a long-standing history of foreigners who have become deeply enamored with China, its cultures, and its peoples. These foreigners, men and women from a diverse range of national and ethnic backgrounds, have committed themselves to deep immersion in Chinese language, culture, and society. Many these people have been active in recording, studying, promoting, and preserving China's rich cultural heritage. Joseph Needham, an English scientist, developed a career-long interest in the history of Chinese science (Winchester 2009). Joseph Rock, an Austrian-American botanist, explorer, and ethnographer, revealed to the world the unique culture of the Naxi people (in Lijiang, Yunnan, not far from Dali) (Yoshinaga et al. 2011). William Lindesay has been active in promoting the preservation of the Great Wall (www.wildwall.com). Ed Jocelyn, through his tea road exploration and tourism business, has likewise raised awareness of Yunnan's network of ancient trading routes (www.redrocktrek.com).

Cultural heritage activism is often understood as an expression of cultural nationalism in which the assumed subject is the concerned citizen, that is, the nationalist subject. However, in this instance, a foreigner is performing the role of cultural heritage activists. The role, and performance, of the foreign cultural heritage player is quite different to that of the nationalist subject. In the case of the PRC, foreigners, as noncitizens, have clear advantages and disadvantages. On the positive side of ledger, a foreigner can get away with saying and doing things that nationalist subjects cannot. Foreigners are seen as more honest and trustworthy, a result perhaps of the cynicism and distrust engendered by the Chinese political system over the decades. While there are clear limitations to what anyone can say within public discourse in the PRC, a foreigner, nonetheless, is generally given more leeway. Foreigners also have a certain level of exotic appeal, especially if they speak good Mandarin. They can use this to attract more attention to their cause, as Chinese people are genuinely interested to read and hear what a foreigner has to say. Brian uses this attribute particularly well.

On the negative side of the ledger, foreigners in the PRC can have great difficulty in being fully accepted. First, the PRC does not recognize dual citizenship or have an effective "green card" system for long-term residents. Instead, foreign residents need to engage in an ongoing process of securing visa status. This can be quite onerous. Many long-term foreign residents feel this process devalues the contributions they are making to Chinese society. Foreigners who have worked and lived in China during the reform period have also expressed discontent with the way the system and society in general treats them as a form of "sojourner." In this sense, there is dissatisfaction that no matter how long or how committed a foreigner is to China, they will never be "fully accepted." In some extreme cases, the enamored foreign subject "falls out of love" with China (see Kitto 2013). For people such as Brian who have a long-term commitment to China, this is an issue always in mind and perhaps something that could contribute to adjusting one's conduct so as to not generate open conflict or adverse criticism.

There are also some xenophobic tendencies among some Chinese who, in Brian's words, "feel that only they 'own' tradition, and that only they can effectively package their culture." In pitching the Linden Centre as a form of auxiliary "Chinese soft power," Brian argues the foreigner has distinct advantages when it comes to packaging and presenting Chinese culture to a global audience: "I would argue that their inability to place Chinese culture in a world context and objectively understand its perceived strengths and weaknesses always leads to a hackneyed presentation/packaging of their culture" (email correspondence, November 2015). Despite these restrictions, the scope for foreigners to be actively involved in cultural heritage activism in the PRC has dramatically broadened. Foreigners during the Maoist period served the clear role of legitimizing the newly founded PRC in the eyes of the world.[14] In the reform era, the foreign resident now has much greater scope in determining what one will say and do. It is important, however, for the exemplary foreigner to ensure the positives outweigh the negatives and, to be successful, the foreigner both knows how to perform and is adept in creating their "China story."

Brian Linden speaks openly of the important role his story has in the success of the Linden Centre. The story is one of a foreigner who not only came to China and fell in love with its rich culture, history, and people but also is grateful of the opportunity that China gave to him to advance his career and rise in social and economic status. Brian describes the sense of passion and respect for Chinese culture that he projects to a Chinese audience as pivotal in getting the project up and going:

> The government was taking a bit of risk with us. We didn't have a lot of money—by which I mean there wasn't any chance of corruption or financial gain for cer-

tain officials—there was no precedence for what we were proposing to do—even to this day in China there aren't any other national heritage buildings like this one operating in private hands. This was an experiment. We were far enough away from Beijing to avoid direct intervention. I don't think they would have given this to a Chinese person, at least in those days, for fear that the outcome would have been deemed too commercial and culturally inappropriate. When Beijing did finally get down here to have a look at what we were doing the hard work was already done and they were very supportive. (Interview, September 2015)

Brian had a less-than-affluent upbringing and had to work in part-time jobs throughout high school and to pay for his college studies. Fortunately, he did very well academically and ended up in China in the 1984, first at the Beijing Language Institute (now the Beijing Language and Culture University) and later working for CBS News in Beijing. He became fascinated with all things Chinese and from that point forward began his career in Chinese language, culture, and education. This is thus the story of someone from humble origins whose path to success just happened to lead him to China. For that, Brian is very grateful and through his efforts wishes to pay respects to Chinese culture and people by giving something back. That "something" just happens to be a passionate effort to preserve the Bai culture of Xizhou and develop the Linden Centre. Brian says his "China story" is one of the key elements that attracts not only Chinese media attention but also Chinese guests to the Linden Centre. In this sense, Brian and his family are not only the managers and cultural entrepreneurs but also part of the attraction itself.

Brian's story fits well with Chinese notions of overcoming adversity and especially of the role of education in transforming the self (a long tradition in China going back to Confucius and beyond). Chinese stories of personal transformation often center on education, a process that invariably involves a teacher. In the course of the twentieth century, in adopting modern concepts, students began to describe this process as one of "enlightenment" (*qimeng*, 启蒙) and the teachers that were pivotal in the process as "enlightenment teachers" (*qimeng laoshi*, 启蒙老师). Brian's story of "before and after China" fits well with this "enlightenment narrative":

> Before China, I was cleaning carpets to get through community college. I'd never even heard of Stanford let alone dreamed [I'd] get a scholarship to pursue a PhD there. For that reason, I approach China differently. I don't see China as a place to make a profit. These projects are like my teachers, like the professor who changes your life. (Interview, September 2015)

In following the strictures of Confucian teaching, Brian eschews the profit motive in describing his actions. Brian's commitment to China therefore presents as pure and unadulterated by pecuniary interest, the latter being a major feature of the emerging Chinese consumer society and at once a source of admiration for those who aspire to greater wealth and a target for critique, as many associated this with greed and hedonism to the detriment of social advancement. This in turn puts Brian in a privileged position, not without its appeal to the role of the "Confucian gentleman" (*junzi*, 君子), to critique what even the Chinese media lament as the cultural poor taste of the "hillbilly rich." As Brian himself noted in a comment on TripAdvisor, "Hotels claim that they are heritage projects, but most are doing nothing more than gutting 50–100 year old [sic] structures and injecting the same 'face' luxuries that China's nouveau rich require (bathtub televisions, bathrooms with glass windows looking out into the bedroom!)."

Outlined here is a kind of Sinicized "American Dream." That is, it demonstrates the aspirational ethos that with hard work, education, and opportunity, an individual can rise up the social ladder and become a "success." The "Sinicized" part of this equation simply refers to the fact that this American Dream unfolded largely in China. But even more than that, Brian invests the very notion of his identity in China, or, as he says, "China created who I am." However, Brian is clear that, however you want to call it, it is not a Chinese Dream, at least not the "Chinese Dream" (*Zhongguo meng*, 中国梦) referred to by the Chinese Communist Party in recent years (Barmé 2013). That Chinese Dream is only for Chinese people. It is projected at Chinese national subjects to the exclusion of foreign residents. When asked to reflect on the Chinese Dream, Brian responded:

> I tell them very clearly that China's Dream should embrace the world. I tell them that the China Dream is a very narrow, chauvinistic, and selfish dream. The way the China Dream is depicted, it is only a dream for Chinese people; outsiders aren't included. The American Dream is open to anyone and has been a major motivation for migrants as well as born and bred Americans. I've invested everything I have, employ over seventy people, could live here all my life, but I still have to apply for a visa every year, and I will never be treated as "a local." What is my China Dream? China has to grow and it has to grow and embrace the outside world and make room for those who also have respect for Chinese culture and China's cultural heritage. (Interview, September 2015)

There is a veiled ambivalence here. On the one hand, there is a gratefulness for China's influence in shaping personal identity, yet discontent on the other that the process does not allow entry into the racialized club of "being Chinese." At the same time, we must not forget that foreign subjects such as Brian also occupy a privileged position vis-à-vis Chinese nationals that allowed his China story to unfold.[15] For better or for worse, Brian is clearly marked as a "foreigner." Despite the difficulties and even insults, Brian can take solace in the fact that he is not just a foreigner. Brian Linden is a contemporary manifestation of the exemplary foreigner.

Brian Linden's Dali Critique

Brian is also driven by a strong sense of civic responsibility. This may be attributed to his American cultural inheritance. This topic also came up in our discussions on the core problems facing cultural heritage preservation in the villages of Dali. Before proceeding to discuss this in detail, I would like to first outline Brian's critique of tourism, development, and cultural heritage preservation in Dali. The Lindens' choice of Dali for their cultural heritage project has worked out well. As Brian notes, "Dali really attracted us because of its openness, its acceptance of outsiders, Dali has a kind of seductive charm" (interview, September 2015). In recent years, millions of tourists and thousands of lifestyle migrants have also been attracted to Dali.

Brian makes clear that by "seductive charm," he implies Dali's Indigenous culture and natural beauty are his personal attraction. While certainly many tourists and mountain changers are also attracted to these qualities, Brian broadens out "seductive charm" to include desires of a more base nature, that is, a form of "cultural sex appeal" that attracts outsiders, whether Chinese or foreign, to consume Dali in disrespectful and shallow ways:

> Dali is a slut.[16] Dali has a lot of sex appeal; everybody wants to come to Dali and live out their own erotic fantasies, but in a couple of years they will be looking for the next object of desire. So the trick is to get beyond the shallow sense of seduction and go deeper, build some personality, create some insight. Dali shouldn't just prostitute itself to anyone who comes here; it needs to be a lot more discerning. (Interview, September 2015)

This is the core of Brian's critique of the mass tourism, lifestyle migration, and development of Dali. In a speech given in Chinese to local Dali government officials, Brian said:

> Travel in China has now become so sanitized and luxury-driven that it has lost much of its allure ... Most foreign travellers are turned off by these superficial and soulless destinations. However, because the nascent domestic Chinese travel market is so large and predominantly driven by comfort and familiarity, the future of Chinese travel will be filled with more of these commercial re-creations.

Brian's answer to this predicament is the Linden Centre. In the same speech, he continued:

> My greatest disappointment (and the reason why we established the Linden Centre) is the loss in China of any sense of place, any *genius loci*. This loss, which strikes at the interaction of people with their living spaces, exacerbates 70 years of languid social ties. Physical characteristics embodied in old architecture and material culture can help communities overcome some of these weaknesses, encouraging a sense of solidarity, providing them with a tangible reminder of a common past. However, the homogenization of China's cities, including the indiscriminate incorporation of Western structures into China's cityscapes, is intensifying the destruction of the already-weakened foundations of China's cultural traditions. (Linden 2014)

Brian is thus highly cognizant of the close relations between traditional vernacular spaces and community identity. If you take away the former, you will invariably transform and lose the latter. The same goes for removing the community from their residential spaces, as has been done in many of China's old towns. Once the community is removed, the village or town becomes "soulless" and "museumified." Brian also takes aim at the new rich both as hotel patrons and developers, as indicated in a comment on TripAdvisor:

> We regularly see said companies turning to glitzy, non-indigenous hotels built out of glass and steel and responsible for the destruction of the communities within which they are located ... These places, while beautiful, reflect nothing more than a desire to target a nouveau riche Chinese customer whose only requirement is a glass view of Lake Erhai and a barrier from the "lazy" and "dirty" locals.

While declaring, "We are proud to be a part of the renaissance of China's culture," Brian urges the Chinese authorities, developers, and people to consider carefully how to understand and project Chinese culture to the world as China rises.

The "losing battle" Brian refers to is being waged across Dali, in Dali old town, and in the numerous villages on the Erhai basin. With the tourism and building boom, local and outside developers are demolishing old buildings and erecting modern concrete and glass structures in their place. The 2002 Law Protecting Cultural Relics is the principal legal framework for identifying and protecting China's cultural relics (the law applies only to tangible cultural heritage). However, as Lisa Rogers (2004) notes in her study of the law, various factors, including the sheer geographic size of China, lack of understanding of legal processes and responsibilities, a cavalier attitude toward material cultural heritage, and so on, mean that in reality the law is seldom put into effect. When asked why he thinks this is the case, Brian raised the complex imperative of the government's "social stability" (*weiwen* 维稳) program (Sigley 2013b):

The government is always going to err on the side of stability in the villages. There are detailed heritage laws. Nothing should be touched in Xizhou but buildings are being destroyed all the time. Originally we had 110 protected structures and now it is down to about eighty . . . So the developers go to a village and tell them "let me lease this for fifteen years, I'll build a new modern building and in fifteen years you will have a new home." The development is so fast and large that it's happening everywhere. The government knows if they try to enforce heritage rules the villages will be up against them. This is the irony. In the West we think of the Chinese government as all powerful and draconian. The reality is that in these villages the people have an incredible amount of freedom. They don't care what the government says.

It is at this point that the crucial cultural differences between American and Chinese forms of "governmentality" come to the fore.

Liberal forms of governmentality, while not without despotic tendencies, tend to encourage citizen-subjects to take an active part in their own government. This can be manifested in the active role community groups, NGOs, and individuals take in the grassroots, including in cultural heritage preservation. In China, by contrast, the party-state has encouraged a passive role for those being governed. It actively discourages genuine community participation, especially in recent years, when it fears the consequences of social instability. While there are always exceptions, as noted in the foregoing discussion of community participation in tourism development, Chinese rural communities are dominated by an "administrative mentality." As Brian puts it:

> In America I like this practice we have; you might call it a social contract between society and the government. Local communities have a lot of civic pride and genuine concern—and most importantly participation—in their community. In China I don't see that civic pride manifest in same way. The villagers only care about themselves and what they can do as a household to get ahead. (Interview, September 2015)

There is an interesting contradiction here. On the one hand, the government hesitates to intervene in the villages to impose the heritage and zoning laws for fear of upsetting the villagers (it also must be said that it is also not high on the government's priorities). As part of the social stability maintenance program, it figures that to intervene may be more trouble than it's worth. On the other hand, the problem is further exacerbated by the lack of genuine participation in their own government by the villagers. They are simply bystanders to what is happening (while once again noting that at times villagers can be mobilized to protect community heritage in the form of temples and ancestral halls).

Conclusion

As the conditions prevalent in Dali and Xizhou indicate, there is no place for a broad cultural heritage social movement in China that does not conform to the general determinants outlined by the party-state. With little scope for meaningful NGO activity in the cultural heritage arena, it often falls to specific individuals to become champions of cultural heritage preservation and revitalization. Brian Linden and the Linden Centre provide a useful case study in this regard. Brian occupies a relatively unique position as an exemplary foreigner in the local cultural heritage arena. While drawing on state-sanctioned tradition of exemplary foreigners, Brian is able to straddle the cultural divide between China and the West and in so doing create a cultural heritage enterprise that stands as a counterexample to China's current fascination with mass tourism. Whether entities like the Linden Centre are able to influence change within their arena in the long term remains to be seen. Nonetheless, it is important to note that in contemporary China there are many such people and institutions, Chinese and foreign alike, that inhabit the spaces made available by the reform process. To this date, little attention has been given to such "cultural heritage players," and the case study provided here offers but a first step in examining the broader implications of ongoing reform and development in China as it relates to various different forms—contested and uncontested—of participation in cultural heritage preservation.

Gary Sigley is Professor in the School of Land and Tourism at Luoyang Normal University. His research interests are broadly based within the social sciences and cultural studies with a particular focus on tourism and heritage in the context of a rapidly changing China. A research project investigating cultural heritage and regional identity in southwest China along the Ancient Tea Horse Road is near completion.

NOTES

1. This approach to understanding the relations between state, society, and cultural heritage is not exclusive to the context of China but is indicative of a broader approach across cultural contexts (see Graham et al. 2000).
2. Sometimes certain local cultural practices merged with the dominant Maoist ideology in innovative ways. I once interviewed a Jingpo (景颇族) shaman in Dehong (德宏) (on the Yunnanese border with Myanmar) who explained he continued performing his rituals and chants during the Maoist period by substituting the traditional content with extracts from the famous "little red book," *Quotations from Chairman Mao Tse-tung*.

3. An official survey of cultural relics and sites conducted by the State Administration of Cultural Heritage in 2014 discovered at least thirty thousand items on the 1982 survey list have disappeared (Branigan 2009).
4. This has been a difficult transition for many culturally orientated institutions. The Chinese bureaucracy distinguishes between two forms of "enterprise": *qiye danwei* 企业单位, which are commercially orientated, and *shiye danwei* (事业单位), which are nonprofit socially orientated. The latter relied almost exclusively on state sponsorship. While some more nationally recognized cultural forms receive strong financial support from the government, such as Peking opera, other forms of local opera, for example, have had to rely more on ticket sales to shore up revenue.
5. I am aware of one instance, for example, that took place in the historic town of Shuhe in Lijiang where locals successfully demonstrated against the removal of ancestral graves to make way for a tourist development. In the same region, a local *dongba* (东巴)—the Naxi people's equivalent of a native "shaman"—decided not to work within the formally established tourist attraction—a kind of *dongba* theme park. Instead, he opted to work with small groups of visitors in his village courtyard house, where he argued he could provide a more fulfilling and authentic experience (from fieldwork conducted in 2013).
6. It should be also noted that even in this gendered area of the clan, genealogy change is taking place. I am aware of cases where genealogies now include reference to the outstanding achievements of female descendants.
7. Mayfair Yang (2004) provides another good example in her study of conflict over the use of space or religious or secular activities in the Wenzhou region (Zhejiang Province). Her study reminds us that even into the 1990s local government was still attempting to limit and contain the construction of local temples within the folk religion tradition. Local villagers deployed various tactics to sidestep the intentions of the secularizing state.
8. The Chinese government passed a Foreign NGO Management Law in 2016.
9. NGOs, of the non-GONGO variety, have also been required to affiliate with relevant government departments, a process that many describe as particularly arduous and counterproductive given that the government department is often the very entity the NGO is seeking to monitor thereby limiting the NGOs scope and creating clear conflicts of interest.
10. The campaign against development in the Drum and Bell Tower neighborhood enlisted many local foreign residents.
11. "Dali" can refer to the "old town" of Dali, the prefectural city, and the prefecture itself. Hereafter, "Dali" refers to the prefectural city. "Dali old town" and "Dali prefecture" will be used to denote the other geographic uses of "Dali."
12. Dali old town is not "gated," that is, there is no on-site collection of entrance fees. Individuals gain free entry. However, as of 1 September 2015, the government is levying an "entrance fee" on all persons within organized tour groups and a one per cent fee from all registered business (CNTA 2015).
13. http://www.linden-centre.com/. Retrieved in May 2016. The Linden Center website has since been updated.
14. Rewi Alley, a socialist hailing from New Zealand who spent much of his life in the PRC, is a good example (Brady 2003b).
15. I would like to thank Tod Jones for reinforcing this point.

16. Describing Dali as a "slut" is shocking for several reasons, most notably that it involves a negative sexualization and feminization of the cultural subject that seemingly only the virtuous foreigner can protect. This is in line with a long tradition of Orientalist discourse pitching the white male protagonist as the worthy protector of the colonial (female) subject. My understanding is that this comment was made to an audience of local Dali officials and was mobilized precisely for its shock effect. In my observations and interactions with the Lindens, I did not detect any widespread sexism, but nonetheless the positions of "savior" and "saved" are noteworthy. Thanks to the reviewers for helping clarify this point.

REFERENCES

Bakken, Børge. 2000. *The Exemplary Society: Human Improvement, Social Control, and the Dangers of Modernity*. New York: Clarendon Press.
Barmé, Geremie R. 2013. "Chinese Dreams (Zhongguo meng 中国梦)." *China Story Yearbook 2013: Civilising China*, ed. Geremie R. Barmé and Jeremy Goldkorn, 4–13. Canberra: Australian National University.
Brady, Anne-Marie. 2003a. *Making the Foreign Serve China: Managing Foreigners in the People's Republic*. London: Rowman & Littlefield.
———. 2003b. *Friend of China: The Myth of Rewi Alley*. London: RoutledgeCurzon.
Branigan, Tania. 2009. "China Loses Thousands of Historic Sites." *The Guardian*, 14 December.
CHP (Beijing Cultural Heritage Protection Center). "Our Mission." Accessed 19 June. http://en.bjchp.org/?page_id=15.
CNTA (China National Tourism Administration). 2015. "Tourists to Pay Maintenance Free for Ancient City of Dalit." 14 September.
du Cros, Hilary and Yok-Shiu F. Lee, eds. 2007. *Cultural Heritage Management in China Preserving the Cities of the Pearl River Delta*. London: Routledge.
Economist. 2015. "Uncivil Society." 22 August. https://www.economist.com/china/2015/08/22/uncivil-society.
Goffman, Erving. 1956. *The Presentation of Self in Everyday Life*. Edinburgh: University of Edinburgh Press.
Graham, Brian, Gregory J. Ashworth, and John E. Tunbridge. 2000. *A Geography of Heritage: Power, Culture and Economy*. London: Taylor & Francis.
Gramsci, Antonio. 1971. *Selections from the Prison Notebooks of Antonio Gramsci*. London: Lawrence & Wishart.
Ives, Mike. 2013. "From Outsiders to Innkeepers in China's Sleepy Countryside." *New York Times*, 14 August.
Jasper, James M. 2014. "Introduction: Playing the Game." In *Players and Arenas: The Interactive Dynamics of Protest*, ed. James M. Jasper & J. W. Duyvendak, 9–32. Amsterdam: Amsterdam University Press.
Jigang, Bao, and Sun Jiuxia. 2007. "Differences in Community Participation in Tourism Development between China and the West." *Chinese Sociology and Anthropology* 39 (3): 9–27. https://doi.org/10.2753/CSA0009-4625390301.
Kitto, Mark. 2012. "You'll Never Be Chinese." *Prospect*, 8 August. http://www.prospectmagazine.co.uk/features/mark-kitto-youll-never-be-chinese-leaving-china.

Layton, Kelly. 2007. "Qianmen, Gateway to a Beijing Heritage." *China Heritage Quarterly* 12. http://www.chinaheritagequarterly.org/articles.php?searchterm=012_qianmen.inc&issue=012.
Li, WenJun. 2005. "Community Decision Making: Participation in Development." *Annals of Tourism Research* 33 (1): 132–143. https://doi.org/10.1016/j.annals.2005.07.003.
Linden, Brian. 2014. "China's Culture in an Era of Mass Tourism." Speech given at Linden Center, September. http://www.linden-centre.com/2014/09/chinascultureinaneraofmasstourismbrian.
McKhann, Charles F. 2001. "The Good, the Bad, and the Ugly: Observations and Reflections on Tourism Development in Lijiang, China." In *Anthropology, Tourism, and Chinese Society*, ed. Chee-Beng Tan, Sidney Cheung, and Hui Yang, 147–166. Bangkok: White Lotus Press.
McLaren, Anne E. 2011. "Eco-sites, Song Traditions and Cultural Heritage in the Lower Yangzi Delta." *Asian Studies Review* 35 (4): 457–475. https://doi.org/10.1080/10357823.2011.628276.
Mozaffari, Ali. 2015. "The Heritage 'NGO': A Case Study on the Role of Grass Roots Heritage Societies in Iran and Their Perception of Cultural Heritage." *International Journal of Heritage Studies* 21 (9): 1–19. https://doi.org/10.1080/13527258.2015.1028961.
Nitzky, William. 2013. "Community Empowerment at the Periphery? Participatory Approaches to Heritage Protection in Guizhou, China." In *Cultural Heritage Politics in China*, ed. Tami Blumenfield and Helaine Silverman, 205–232. New York: Springer.
Notar, Beth E. 2006. *Displacing Desire: Travel and Popular Culture in China*. Honolulu: University of Hawaii Press.
Nyiri, Pal. 2006. *Scenic Spots: Chinese Tourism, the State, and Cultural Authority*. Seattle: Washington University Press.
Oakes, Tim. 2006a. "Cultural Strategies of Development: Implications for Village Governance in China." *Pacific Review* 19 (1): 13–37. https://doi.org/10.1080/09512740500417616.
Rogers, Lisa. 2004. "'The Heavens are High and the Emperor Is Far Away': Cultural Heritage Law and Management in China." *Historic Environment* 17 (3): 38–43.
Sautman, Barry. 1997. "Myths of Descent, Racial Nationalism and Ethnic Minorities in the People's Republic of China." In *The Construction of Racial Identities in China and Japan: Historical and Contemporary Perspectives*, ed. Frank Dikötter, 75–95. Honolulu: University of Hawaii Press.
Sigley, Gary. 2013a. "The Ancient Tea Horse Road and the Politics of Cultural Heritage in Southwest China: Regional Identity in the Context of a Rising China." In *Cultural Heritage Politics in China*, ed. Tami Blumenfield and Helaine Silverman, 235–246. New York: Springer.
———. 2013b. "From Revolution to Government, From Contradictions to Harmony: Urban Community Policing in Post-Deng China." In *Policing Cities: Urban Securitization and Regulation in a 21st Century World*, ed. Randy K. Lippert and Kevin Walby, 29–42 London: Routledge.
———. 2015. "From 'Backwater' to 'Bridgehead': Culture, Modernity and the Reimagining of Yunnan." In *China's Frontier Regions: Ethnicity, Economic Integration, and Foreign Relations*, ed. Michael E. Clarke and Doug Smith, 171–203. London: I.B. Taurus.

———. 2016. "The Mountain Changers: Lifestyle Migration in Southwest China." *Asian Highlands Perspectives* 40 (1): 233–296.
Su, Xiaobo, and Peggy Teo. 2009. *The Politics of Heritage Tourism in China: A View from Lijiang*. London: Routledge.
Svensson, Marina. 2006. "'In the Ancestors' Shadow: Cultural Heritage Contestations in Chinese Villages." Working paper in Contemporary Asian Studies no. 17. Sweden: Lund University.
Touraine, Alain. 2002. "In Importance of Social Movements." *Social Movement Studies: Journal of Social, Cultural and Political Protest* 1 (1): 89–95. https://doi.org/10.1080/14742830120118918.
Tunbridge, John E., and Gregory J. Ashworth. 1996. *Dissonant Heritage: The Management of the Past as a Resource in Conflict*. Chichester: J. Wiley.
Wang, Mingda, and Xilu Zhou. 2008. 马帮文化 [Horse caravan culture]. Kunming: Yunnan People's Publishing House.
Wang, Hui, Zhaoping Yang, Li Chen, Jingjing Yang, and Rui Li. 2010. "Minority Community Participation in Tourism: A Case of Kanas Tuva Villages in Xinjiang, China." *Tourism Management* 31 (6): 759–764. https://doi.org/10.1016/j.tourman.2009.08.002.
Winchester, Simon. 2009. *The Man Who Loved China: The Fantastic Story of the Eccentric Scientist Who Unlocked the Mysteries of the Middle Kingdom*. London: Harper Perennial.
Yang, Bin. 2008. *Between Winds and Cloud: The Making of Yunnan*. New York: Columbia University Press.
Yang, Mayfair Mei-Hui. 1994. *Gifts, Favors, and Banquets: The Art of Social Relationships in China*. New York: Cornell University Press.
———. 2004. "Spatial Struggles: Postcolonial Complex, State Disenchantment, and Popular Reappropriation of Space in Rural Southeast China." *Journal of Asian Studies* 63 (3): 719–755. https://doi.org/10.1017/S002191180400169X.
Ying, Tianyu, and Yongguang Zhou. 2007. "Community, Governments and External Capitals in China's Rural Cultural Tourism: A Comparative Study of Two Adjacent Villages." *Tourism Management* 28 (1): 96–107. https://doi.org/10.1016/j.tourman.2005.12.025.
Yoshinaga, Alvin, He Hangyu, Paul Weissich, Paul Harris, and Margaret Byrne Swain. 2011. "Classifying Joseph Rock: Metamorphic, Conglomerate, and Sedimentary." In *Explorers and Scientists in China's Borderlands, 1880–1950*, ed. Denise M. Glover, Stevan Harrell, Charles F. McKhann, and Margaret Byrne Swain, 116–118. Seattle: University of Washington Press.

 CHAPTER 4

Heritage Activism in Singapore
Terence Chong

Heritage activism is the struggle for recognition. Old buildings, ancient burial sites, historic towns—these are proxies in the bigger struggle for acknowledgment of a group's existence. To advocate for heritage, or to make meaning of the past, is to tell stories about ourselves in order to mark our civilizational lineage and anchor our place in the world. In short, at the core of heritage are notions of self-worth, community, dignity, and identity. Heritage activism is thus a political activity because of the claims it makes, the voices it articulates, and the pasts it unravels. Like all forms of social activity, heritage activism requires alliances and networks as much as it encounters resistance and confrontation. Heritage activism is also a simultaneously inclusive and exclusive activity. On the one hand, it adopts and absorbs lessons from other heritage sites and experts while, on the other, is unique because of the particular site it champions and its history. If heritage activism is a political activity, then it is also socially constructed and shaped by local histories, politics, and economics. In capitalist and politically pluralist societies, heritage activism may be subtle or confrontational, often enlisting the help of mainstream media, while in other, more authoritarian societies, heritage advocacy needs to negotiate with a strong state and its agencies. Heritage activism, like all forms of civil society activity, learns to exploit and utilize existing institutions and structures for its interests.

Conversely, the state has particular imaginations of heritage. Heritage is imagined to be a vital yet unproblematic tool for nation-building. Community heritage is expected to be understood and accepted by diverse cross-sections of society and, in the process, produce a unifying national identity. State-sponsored heritage is thus imagined as a site where national culture can be expressed in order to anchor citizens in a global age. Like heritage advocates, the state is also in the meaning-making business. The state seeks to imbue key narratives, ideologies, and values into heritage sites to elevate the material to a state of timelessness and sacredness in the face of fluid modernity. This condition of timelessness and sacredness is crucial to creating a certain type of authentic experience. However, such imaginations of heritage may also be presumed to be inclusive and unproblematic without the messy cultural politics that arise from tensions between an ethnic majority and minorities. For this very reason, these heritage imaginations often are banal celebrations of nostalgia and historical reminiscing for popular consumption. It is the duty of activism to criticize these projects for their nostalgia and reminiscing, for they often obscure the multiple nuanced stories and meanings that are embodied in heritage sites. In much the same way state-imagined heritage homogenizes narratives and reduces complexities, heritage activism seeks to expose such imaginations for what they are—the political sterilization of the past.

This chapter looks at heritage activism in Singapore. It begins with a broad overview of the state's relationship with heritage development, arguing that heritage was largely neglected by the Singapore postcolonial government during the early years of independence. During an extended period of economic growth and nation-building in the 1970s and 1980s, the state selectively used heritage conservation to showcase the cultures of the country's main ethnic groups in order to underline its multicultural ethos. Nevertheless, by the 1980s, a middle class had developed and, along with it, new sensibilities toward heritage. The next section looks at the different modalities of heritage activism in Singapore and argues the strong state has resulted in a variety of ways heritage activism is performed in Singapore. Within conventional modes, from civil society advocacy to backroom activism where personal influence and relations prevail, heritage activism has adjusted and adapted to contemporary Singaporean politics.

Heritage and the State in Singapore

Heritage activism differs between locations. In Chennai, India, heritage activism has been observed to be primarily an elitist activity and isolated from the concerns of the broader community (Arabindoo 2010). Such forms of activism are generally exclusive in nature, requiring personal or professional connections in order to produce results. For others, there is little difference between heritage activists and political activists because of political decentralization, which has, in turn, spurred greater democratic involvement of ordinary citizens (Blackwood 2008). Such modes of activism tend to be more broad-based with greater grassroots participation. Heritage advocates may also be part of international networks. Here, local cultural groups, through transnational linkages, are able to bring global attention to specific sites, thus heightening awareness and applying pressure on local governments. Naturally, heritage activists may be seen as the "unrealistic enemy" by developers and the state, who characterize activists as not being able to see the "bottom line" and as "enemies of progress" (McMordie and Pannekoek 2004: 7). This false dichotomy between conservation and progress erroneously frames heritage as something that is at odds with modernity. It ignores the ways modernity is able to retain the local and the indigenous for constant reinvention and reinterpretation of the past.

In Singapore, heritage was treated with benign neglect by the postcolonial People's Action Party (PAP) government during the early years of industrialization. Upon independence in 1965, the immediate national concerns were economic growth, mass public housing, and tackling unemployment because the PAP understood these issues, and not heritage, would ensure reelection. Compounding this neglect was the survivalist mentality of the ruling elite borne from the city-state's lack of natural resources and its separation from Malaysia, thus spelling the end for dreams of a hinterland and a common market. This survivalist mentality served to heighten the national sense of vulnerability and insecurity, or what scholars have called "ideology of survival" (Chan 1971). To perpetuate this ideology, the ruling elite constantly replayed the "historical trauma" (Yao 2007) of separation, thus nurturing a "garrison mentality" (Brown 1994) or the political "staging of crises" (Birch 1993), to remind Singaporeans of their precarious position as an island state and the economic and political vulnerabilities that accompany it. This notion of vulnerability has been hardwired into the nation's sense of sovereignty, such that the latter cannot be discussed without reviving the former.

This survivalist mentality demanded the imagination of a Singapore cast firmly in the future, where heritage and history were consigned to textbooks. Singapore was imagined by the ruling elite as a global city first and a nation second; the elite believed that only as the former could the latter exist. Naturally, legal tools passed down from the British colonial government, like the Land Acquisitions Act, made clearing private orchids and small rural villages for urban development politically expedient. Many of the previous inhabitants were moved to new public flats around the island. At a time when the leadership was intent on forging a multicultural society, the elites' view that heritage awareness was but a few small steps from cultural superiority and ethnic differentiation was politically significant. The PAP government was acutely aware of the power of heritage. It understood its embodiment of cultural sovereignty and communal identity, and was constantly vigilant over the ways ethnic groups articulated their heritage. Any grassroots championing—for instance, of Chinese or Malay heritage—would be met with suspicion because the ruling elite believed it could provoke a response from other ethnic groups. The multiethnic complexion of the immigrant population required "selective amnesia" in order to create the nation as a tabula rasa, thus allowing the PAP government to exorcize the "ancestral ghosts" of different ethnic groups for universally accessible myths such as multiculturalism and meritocracy (see Hong and Jianli 2008). Under these conditions, the conservation-progress dichotomy was presented as a hard but necessary choice of progress. Summing up the government's stance on heritage is the pithy retort from Kim San Lim (1985), a pioneer politician who, when faced with public protest over grave exhumations in Tiong Bahru during the 1960s, asserted: "Do you want me to look after our dead grandparents, or do you want to look after your grandchildren?"

Likewise, the development of heritage activism in Singapore has been profoundly influenced by the particularities of the broader state–civil society relationship. Singapore's experience as a one-party state has influenced the political opportunities for, and imagination of, activism. The early taming of unions and their eventual consolidation under a state-friendly congress in the 1960s and 1970s, as well as the closure of several media outlets, placed limits on dissent. These limits, it is argued, have also impacted the way activism and civil society have been shaped in Singapore. Several key pieces of legislation, for example, such as amendments to the 1964 Industrial Relations Act and the 1982 Trade Union Bill, have served to limit the negotiating rights of the local workforce in order to meet the demands of global capital. The absence of competitive politics, together with the managerial efficiency of the PAP and its punctual delivery of public goods, allowed the PAP to move considerations of civil society and advocacy to the margins of public consciousness. As such, during the 1960s and 1970s, heritage activism was scarce for a variety of reasons: low public awareness of the importance of heritage; an unsympathetic government more concerned with industrial development; stringent laws and regulations that limited advocacy; and a weak civil society.

Heritage, however, was not completely marginalized by the government. Rather, it was, like arts and culture, relegated to the bottom of national priorities but trotted out for tourists and nation-building purposes. For instance, the state adroitly used heritage to advance its ideology of "multiracialism." It was not uncommon to see dancers from the three main "races"—Chinese, Malay, and Indian—clad in their respective ethnic costumes (*qipao* for Chinese, *sarong kebaya* for Malay, and *sari* for Indian). Accompanying these performances were highly recognizable cultural accouterments such as Chinese *erhu*, the Malay *kompang*, and the Indian *sitar* to represent distinct "races." In the same way, such cultural dances were performed in schools and National Day Parades, and so too was heritage occasionally used to create and enhance tourist attractions.

By the early 1980s, the country had grown in material affluence. Coming into the game much later than most postcolonial countries, Singapore began to turn to its local ethnic cultures as a draw for tourists. The Tourism Task Force was set up in 1984, and the Committee on Heritage was established four years later, in 1988, and tasked with creating more awareness of multicultural history for nation-building purposes. Entrenching patterns of ethnic-centric locations that began with the British colonial administration, the Urban Redevelopment Authority (URA) began gazetting buildings in so-called ethnic enclaves like Chinatown, Kampong Glam, Serangoon Road, and the Civil District in the late 1980s. In addition to creating ethnic enclaves for tourists, the gazetting of these areas was meant to underline for Singaporeans the immigrant heritage of the Chinese (Chinatown) and the Indians (Serangoon Road), the Indigenous Malays (Kampong Glam) and the country's colonial legacy (Civic District). Such forms of state-sponsored heritage dovetailed with its administrative categorization of Singaporean society into Chinese, Malay, Indian, and "Others." This use of heritage allowed the state to underline its narrative of a multicultural society and to appease tourists. Nevertheless, by the 1980s, in response to changing demographics, heritage underwent subtle shifts in perception. The emergence of a discernible middle class and intelligentsia heralded the advocacy of local heritage beyond colonial legacies, coinciding with the establishment of the Singapore Heritage Society (SHS) in 1986. The 1980s was when heritage discourse entered into the language and concerns of the chattering class. This gave rise to the perception that heritage was an elitist activity, a perception that still holds among civil servants today.

Nevertheless, a succession of prime ministers, from Lee Kuan Yew to Goh Chok Tong to Lee Hsien Loong, has seen a gradual relaxing of regulations restricting activism and civil society in a variety of areas. Goh Chok Tong's succession of Lee Kuan Yew as prime minister in November 1990 was popularly hailed as the beginning of a more inclusive corporatist approach in Singapore. Inclusive corporatism, David Brown (1994: 69) explains, "is where the organic community is built on a more genuinely consensual partnership between state and society." With inclusive corporatism, a more democratic, but not necessarily liberal, process occurs "in which the network of corporatist institutions for controlled, mobilized participation is broadened to incorporate wider segments of society, to the point where it begins to provide the dominant basis for politics" (72). Lee Hsien Loong's succession as prime minister in August 2004 and his rhetoric of an "open and inclusive society" built on Goh's "kinder and gentler society" slogan (Chan and Liang 2014), but it stopped short of substantially empowering interest groups.

A key influence on the way the state imagined heritage was the desire to be a global city. This, in turn, saw further commodification of heritage for tourist consumption. The policy to turn the city-state into a "Global City for the Arts" was part of the broader attempt to reinvent the country as a financial, medical, and education hub that would attract highly skilled professionals. Heritage was thus packaged accordingly for the tourist's gaze. This was nowhere more obvious than the Chinatown debacle in 1998. The proposal by the then Singapore Tourist Promotion Board (STPB) to transform Chinatown into a thematic landscape, complete with stereotypical representations of Chinese culture, was criticized by civil society, the SHS among them, for catering to the taste and expectations of international, typically Western, tourists instead of respecting local sensibilities and priorities. Indeed, Haw Par Villa, a tranquil public garden famous for dioramas of Chinese mythology, after passing into the hands of STPB in 1988, found itself renamed Haw Par Villa Dragon World and turned into an American-style theme park replete with laser shows, acrobats, and boat rides. Its exorbitant entry fee and inauthenticity subsequently turned locals away, thus forcing STPB to make entry free again in 1998. In the aftermath of these two experiments with heritage and tourism, authorities have grown more circumspect and have been sensitized to the pitfalls of packaging heritage only for tourist consumption. Local audiences cannot be alienated if such heritage attractions are to be sustainable, which means retaining authenticity and relevance for citizens.

Yet, while still far from a liberal democracy, there has been more space granted to alternative views, such as the establishment of Speaker's Corner in Hong Lim Park, while the growth of social media and online news have made political proscription harder, if not impossible. Understanding that the younger generation of a better-educated and well-traveled polity cannot be managed like their parents, the PAP government has learned to publicly express its desire to be more consultative when it comes to policy decisions. However, consultation does not mean the public has become the coauthor of policy. Instead, it essentially means gathering public feedback before policy announcements in order to better anticipate public reactions.

Modalities of Heritage Activism

Heritage activism in Singapore must continuously adjust to two contradictory realities. On the one hand, the PAP state continues to hold a monopoly over resources and power, while, on the other, the undeniable widening of civil society space has resulted in greater leeway for non-state actors to engage with heritage. The result is that heritage activism now has developed multiple modalities to achieve its goals. These modalities, or the utilization of the specific means and resources at the disposal of individuals or groups, are expressed by different heritage groups that sometimes compete with each other for recognition and funding. The modalities of activism are not mutually exclusive with advocates able to engage with the state or other actors through different modalities, at times simultaneously.

Intellectual Activism: The SHS and the Shaping of Public Opinion

The most conventional form of heritage activism is through civil society organizations like the SHS. As mentioned, the SHS was established in 1986 at a time when a Singaporean middle class was taking shape. Rising incomes, higher levels of education, and greater leisure time combined to fuel an interest in local history and heritage. The English-speaking middle class began to explore questions of national identity and culture. This is nowhere more evident than in theater. Local plays began to reflect the preoccupations of the predominantly English-speaking middle class. For example, Kuo Pao Kun's first English language play, *The Coffin is Too Big for the Hole* (1984), critiqued the uneven power relationship between citizens and government, Eleanor Wong's *Jackson on a Jaunt* (1989) explored the sexual liberation of a consumer middle class, and the challenges of multiracialism and multiculturalism were articulated in Haresh Sharma's *Mixed Blessings* (1993). The use of Singlish was also explored as an Indigenous vehicle for articulating local narratives and in keeping with issues of multiple identities and lifestyle choices accentuated by material affluence and a cosmopolitan education.

The SHS was part of this English-educated middle-class formation. Its founding president was William Lim, a renowned architect, and the SHS has been led by lawyers and academics since. As a convergence point for local intelligentsia to discuss and rally behind heritage, the SHS was initially met with suspicion by the government. The government had two general reservations with regard to SHS. First, the state believed the elitist concerns of highly educated Singaporeans were driving the NGO, and the SHS was thus not representative of the concerns of ordinary citizens. Second, it was framed by civil servants as anti-progress and antidevelopment, preferring to privilege the country's past over its future. Because of such perceptions, the SHS was tolerated rather than embraced. However, there were exceptions like Tommy Koh, then chairman of the National Arts Council, and George Yeo, then Minister for Information and the Arts, who were more willing than most to engage with the NGO. Nevertheless, the society's public stance on two major national controversies cemented its public role in heritage conservation.

The first was the demolition of the Old National Library Building on Stamford Road. Built by the then Public Works Department, the National Library opened in late 1960 by Singaporean President Yusof Ishak. Generations of Singaporeans were familiar with the iconic red-bricked building, where they had cultivated their love for reading. In late 1998, the public was alerted to the possibility of the library's demolition when building plans for the upcoming Singapore Management University (SMU) were revealed. The SMU's city campus would be sited on Bras Basah Road and would occupy the location where the library stood. There was an unprecedented display of public dissent in the months that followed. Numerous letters were published in the mainstream press supporting the library's preservation, while features on disappearing heritage sites and buildings only underlined the sense of impending loss. To mitigate this discontent, the SMU held a public symposium in March 1999 at the St. Joseph Institution (now the Singapore Art Museum) across the road from the library. The symposium saw long, impassioned pleas to save the library from members of the public lasting more than four hours. The SHS was a prominent player in this public dissent, offering itself as a thought leader by crystallizing arguments for heritage for the public through forums and opinion pieces. This outcry took the government by surprise. Unfamiliar with calls to preserve old buildings from the public, the URA responded with insensitivity by claiming the National Library "was not of great architectural merit and should not be conserved" (Nirmala 1999). Six years later, in 2005, the National Library was torn down to make way for the Fort Canning Tunnel.

While heritage activists failed to save the National Library, the incident allowed activists, intellectuals, and heritage experts to mobilize themselves for the first time to engage with a state agency. The public gathering of these individuals served to energize the civil society landscape and gave rise to a more defined sense of civic consciousness among younger Singaporeans. On the state's part, the event marked the beginning of the ongoing lesson in engaging publicly with civil society. No longer was it possible to announce urban decisions that were detrimental to historic buildings or sites without the expectation of public response, thus forcing younger generations of civil servants to sensitize themselves to the interests of heritage community. Meanwhile, the National Library saga became remembered as a byword for the triumph of pragmatism over social memory.

The second controversy erupted in 1998. On 26 September, the Singapore Tourism Board (STB) announced a $97.5 million plan to "revitalize" Chinatown (*Straits Times* 1998). To attract more tourists, the STB had intended to impose different color-coded districts in the area, build an elemental garden (earth, water, fire, etc.), and create a village-temple complex. A month later, an exhibition of Chinatown's enhancement plans was opened, triggering public outcry. Letters to the mainstream press, particularly the Chinese-language papers, accused the tourism agency of being insensitive to the living heritage of Chinatown. Instead of developing the uniqueness of Chinatown, the STB had chosen cultural homogenization and kitsch with its thematic plans. The SHS, again, played a public role in crystallizing the opinions of the public with its letter to the Chinese press. The SHS warned against developing the site as a theme park only for tourists while ignoring the local residents there as this would result in an artificial Chinatown. The STB denied that its revitalization plans would degrade Chinatown's heritage and held a public forum in Kreta Ayer Community Club on 1 February 1999 to address public concerns. The exchange between the STB and members of the public was heated and candid, lasting two hours longer than its scheduled duration. Later, the STB's head, Kenneth Liang, acknowledged the strong public resistance to some designs in the enhancement proposal but also said the public would grow fond of them over time (Kwok et al. 2000). Eventually, realizing it needed to be seen to make overtures to public concerns, the STB announced it had found common ground with the SHS on the issue, while the SHS informed its members that the STB had assured it of being committed to an ongoing consultation process.

The Chinatown case was remarkable as a self-orientalizing exercise. Rather than revitalizing the historic site according to the needs of residents and demonstrating sensitivity to its immigrant history, the STB was more concerned with the tourist's gaze. Heritage became a purposefully manufactured commodity to satisfy stereotypes and caricatures of Chinese identity and culture. This Disneyfication of Chinatown was designed to make a historically complex site more easily accessible to tourists. In place of historical narratives of immigrant poverty and squalor, vice and alienation became neatly colored zones with self-contained themes. The episode demonstrated with painful clarity how far ahead heritage activists of the time were, vis-à-vis urban planners and tourist officials, in terms of cultural sensitivity and the politics of representation. The lesson was that while local civil servants continued to be faultlessly efficient and dependable, the widening of the middle class and intelligentsia since the 1980s meant they no longer held a monopoly over cultural knowledge, sophistication, and taste.

These two controversies underlined three broad points. First, at a similar time, the National Library and Chinatown debates made it clear that heritage and history were increasingly important to ordinary Singaporeans. They mark a watershed in the nation's relationship with its past, signifying a period where material affluence had spilled over into a deeper appreciation for shared memories and social practices. Second, the public role the SHS played made it impossible for the government and civil servants to ignore its opinions and activities. No longer at the margins, the SHS had moved to the center of heritage debates by shaping and crystallizing public opinion through opinion pieces or letters to the mainstream press, articulations in public forums, and interviews. Third, and most pertinent, the modality of the SHS's activism was conditioned by its political opportunities. Nonconfrontational, eschewing public demonstrations, and continually seeking to engage the state, the SHS capitalizes on its strengths such as academics, heritage, and conservation experts in order to raise heritage awareness in the country.

The most recent heritage controversy was over the plans to develop Bukit Brown Cemetery for residential use in 2011. Bukit Brown, nestled in the middle of the island, was a 160-hectare site that dated back to the mid-nineteenth century. It was turned into a municipal cemetery in 1922, and was a burial place for the Chinese community until it closed in 1973. The URA later announced an eight-lane road built across Bukit Brown would be completed in 2016. Subsequent research revealed the Bukit Brown Cemetery and the three surrounding Chinese clan cemeteries collectively formed the single largest Chinese cemetery complex outside China with possibly more than two hundred thousand graves.

To raise public awareness of Bukit Brown, the SHS and other civil society groups began to co-opt the cemetery into the national narrative. Instead of allowing the government to present the cemetery as a space for development, civil society groups highlighted the graves of immigrant pioneers who had contributed to the building of modern-day Singapore. These groups mimicked the annual National Day Parade (NDP) by staging their own ritual on 9 August entitled Nation's Deceased Pioneers. The Bukit Brown NDP ceremony comprised the singing of the national anthem, the waving of national flags, pledge recital, tours of the cemetery, and goody bags containing symbolic items like medicated oil, matchboxes, and colored incense paper (see Chong 2015). Prominent personalities like Tan Lark Sye, Chew Boon Lay, Gan Eng Seng, and Lim Chong Pang, who had been imprisoned there, are no longer disparate pioneers from a forgotten past but reinterpreted as agents of progress and benefactors of a nascent community that would become a nation. In doing so, these civil society groups have learned to use national narratives and national identity to the advantage of heritage conservation. In addition to championing heritage for the sake of heritage, Bukit Brown cemetery is framed as a crucial and tangible repository of a young nation's past. As a Chinese cemetery, the space is recognized not only as an important feature of ethnic identity but also as a multicultural space that hosts elements of other ethnic groups such as Sikh guards and Peranakan tiles, and thus fitted the broader multicultural narrative of the country.

In addition to nationalizing heritage spaces, civil society groups in Singapore have learned to win global recognition for local causes. In October 2013,

Bukit Brown was included in the 2014 World Monuments Watch list, which contained sixty-seven international heritage sites that were vulnerable to destruction. Local civil society groups had submitted a dossier on Bukit Brown to the New York–based World Monuments Fund in order to be on the watch list. This immediately lent the cemetery an international profile (see Chong and Ai Lin 2014). This mode of activism underlines the importance of going global. As a global city dependent on international networks and flows, Singapore has had to calibrate local practices to international norms. Whether in the areas of banking and finance, law, shipping, or trade, local regulations and practices have had to be synthesized with international ones. By lodging Bukit Brown in the international watch list, the cemetery came to be judged by international heritage norms. This, in turn, allowed local activists to make a stronger case for its preservation and to argue for local heritage practices and norms to be calibrated to international ones.

Cause-Specific Activism

One of the disadvantages facing NGOs like the SHS is the wide array of heritage issues it must contend with at any single time. Whether it's the development of Pulau Ubin, the touristification of Chinatown, or the building of a highway through Bukit Brown Cemetery, broad-based NGOs like the SHS are expected to have an informed position on very different sites. Unsurprisingly, the SHS is unable to respond or address every issue with the same degree of coherence because its members and executive committee are volunteers. This is where cause-specific groups have the advantage. Members of the public may come together and organize themselves over a specific issue. In the area of environmental advocacy, for example, the Waterways Watch Society is committed singularly to keeping local rivers and canals clean. In the area of animal welfare advocacy, cause-specific groups like the Cat Welfare Society are able to focus limited resources and labor on particular issues.

On the heritage landscape, single-cause groups include a.t.Bukit Brown (All Things Bukit Brown) and SOS Bukit Brown, both of which were established by ordinary Singaporeans to promote awareness of Bukit Brown cemetery. Groups like the SHS provided the initial flurry of heritage activism. The society's position paper offered an intellectual pathway for activists to understand the significance of the site and to engage with government officials (see Chong 2012). Not long after, a.t.Bukit Brown was formed when a group of strangers interested in the fate and heritage of Bukit Brown became acquainted through social media platforms such as Facebook. A.t.Bukit Brown offers both public and private tours around the cemetery and has even helped members of the public to locate the tombs of their ancestors. In

2014, a.t.Bukit Brown was recognized as the Advocacy Organisation of the Year by the Singapore Advocacy Awards, a civil society initiative to acknowledge impactful NGOs and individuals. A smaller group, SOS Bukit Brown, also offers tours and carries out advocacy work.

The civil society groups around Bukit Brown also offer up an interesting observation. The groups most closely associated with the site are the SHS, a.t.Bukit Brown, and SOS Bukit Brown. Collectively, they share the same concerns but function rather differently. As the biggest and most established of the NGOs, the SHS engages with government agencies more frequently on a variety of heritage issues. A working relationship with civil servants is possible because the SHS's executive committee holds a moderate position on heritage and conservation. This means agreeing to disagree with the government on issues when an acceptable compromise cannot be reached while keeping the channels for discussion open for the sake of other heritage matters. It entails accepting engineering and technical limitations when it comes to conservation, being open to urban development and infrastructural improvements to the landscape, and agreeing to compromise once all conservation options have been exhausted. Meanwhile, a.t.Bukit Brown, as a cause-specific group, has emerged as the leading authority on the cemetery. The heavy involvement of its members in conducting tours, recovering gravestones for members of the public, constant exploration, and giving public talks has seen a wealth of domain knowledge accumulated by the group's members. As such, a.t.Bukit Brown serves as on-the-ground expertise on the cemetery, its history, and the many stories from among the gravestones. The repository of knowledge offered by the group continues to be vital to contemporary research. SOS Bukit Brown sees itself as a more advocacy-oriented group. It is constantly seeking to highlight the vulnerability of the site and the need to reconsider development plans. Collectively these three different groups work in complementary ways.

Myqueenstown is another single-cause activist group on the local heritage landscape. It was formed in 2009 by ordinary citizens to raise awareness of the heritage significance of Queenstown, one of the oldest satellite towns in the country. The group carries out documentation of old buildings, provides heritage tours, and partners government agencies to showcase and protect parts of the town. The advantage that cause-specific activism has over broad-based activism is not only a stronger focus on issues but also more straightforward relationships with government agencies. For example, the SHS cannot afford to allow its activism over a particular heritage site alienate government agencies because it must work with the same agencies over a variety of issues. As such, the SHS must compromise, negotiate, and, when unsuccessful in achieving its objects, move on to other heritage sites. Cause-specific activism, on the other hand, does not have this burden to shoulder and can thus be more assertive without worrying about other heritage sites or issues in its dealings with government agencies.

Backroom Activism

Heritage activism in Singapore can also be divided into public activism and backroom activism. The former practices conventional forms of dissent such as public petitions, protests, grassroots mobilization, self-organization, public dialogues and forums, and so on. Backroom activism, on the other hand, is unseen activism removed from the public gaze. This is where heritage advocates work behind-the-scenes to influence, cajole, and warn government officials and state representatives over heritage decisions. Backroom activism allows both heritage advocates and civil servants to speak candidly and without fear of being misrepresented in the media or public. Politically sensitive matters, technical limitations, and the reversal of government decisions can be discussed in such scenarios. There are several ways backroom activism takes place.

One institutionalized platform for backroom activism is co-option. The co-option of technical experts is one of the key features of a corporatist state. The state's elitist selection process sees highly credentialed civil servants in the top ranks of the bureaucracy. Heritage-related portfolios, which include custodial bodies like the National Heritage Board under the Ministry of Culture, Community and Youth, are administered by civil servants who may or may not have an interest in the arts. To compensate for the absence of technical knowledge or expertise, technical experts, heritage academics, or practitioners are co-opted through invitations to sit on committees or resource panels for their domain expertise. This self-reflexive bureaucracy is conscious of its own limitations, prompting the co-option of experts and practitioners into its fold when preparing for major heritage decisions. The presence of heritage experts on government committees and resource panels allows the state to mitigate activism while benefiting from their expertise. In exchange, such experts enjoy positions that allow them to wield some influence over policy or regulatory decisions.

Another more personal mode of backroom activism is through the standing of a respected heritage advocate. Here, a well-known and trusted heritage expert who has personal access to high-ranking civil servants may advise the latter over impending heritage decisions. Alternatively, such civil servants may consult heritage experts privately for their views before proceeding with public announcements. One such example was the breakfast meeting between the then SHS President Kevin Tan and the CEOs of URA and the Land Transport Authority (LTA) in August 2011. The meeting was for the two CEOs to inform Tan in advance of the government's decision to build a highway that would cut across Bukit Brown Cemetery to reduce traffic congestion on Lornie Road. With the decision as *fait accompli*, Tan was able to advise the two government agencies to mitigate public outcry by commissioning a documentation of the graves that would have to be exhumed for the highway. Such forms of backroom activism can be effective when there is mutual trust and respect between heritage advocates and civil servants.

Conclusion

In October 2015, a small group of heritage advocates were invited to a closed-door meeting held by the LTA. The new Circle Line of the MRT (Mass Rapid Transit, or subway) was being planned, and one of the new stations would require the temporary dismantling of the historic Tanjong Pagar railway station. At the meeting, the LTA carefully explained the engineering demands of installing railway tracks and the layout options available for building the new MRT station. The heritage advocates present were persuaded by the rationale and supported the decision. This meeting, however, may not have taken place at all. The initial decision was to proceed with the dismantling without the meeting until one of the architects involved suggested the authorities meet with these heritage advocates because they "don't want a repeat of Bukit Brown." The reference was to the strident public dissatisfaction that followed the construction of the road through the Chinese cemetery. It also alluded to the perceived lack of public consultation prior. It is clear that heritage activism in Singapore is not as confrontational or vociferous as occurs elsewhere. Nonetheless, it has had a momentum of its own. From being the sole preserve of middle class intelligentsia that the state once brushed aside as an elitist pastime, it has evolved into a broader spectrum of civil society efforts that takes into account contemporary politics and obstacles.

One of the main reasons for increased heritage activism in Singapore has been the cultural awakening of younger Singaporeans. Better educated, widely traveled, and more concerned with matters beyond issues of basic economic security, younger Singaporeans have been crucial to the different forms of heritage activism that have grown. It has become more difficult to frame heritage as "antidevelopment" or "antiprogress" because of the impulse for a stronger national identity and culture. Globalization and immigration into the city-state have pushed national identity to the forefront of many public debates raising questions such as "What does it mean to be Singaporean?" and "What is Singapore culture?" Heritage activism has been able to position itself a constructive voice as citizens attempt to answer such questions.

Terence Chong is Deputy Director of the ISEAS–Yusof Ishak Institute (Singapore). He has a PhD in Sociology from the University of Warwick, and his research interests include Christianity in Southeast Asia, heritage, cultural policies and politics in Singapore, and the sociology of religion and deviance. He has published in academic journals such as the *Journal of Contemporary Asia*, *Critical Asian Studies*, the *Journal of Southeast Asian Studies*, *Modern Asian Studies*, and *Asian Studies Review*. He is the author of *The Theatre and the State in Singapore: Orthodoxy and Resistance* (2010), coauthor of *Different Under God: A Survey of Church-Going Protestants in Singapore* (2013), and editor of *The AWARE Saga: Civil Society and Public Morality in Singapore* (2010). He is a member of the Heritage Advisory Panel at the National Heritage Board and of the Arts Advisory Panel at the National Arts Council, and he served as Vice President of the Singapore Heritage Society from 2013 to 2015.

REFERENCES

Arabindoo, Pushpa. 2010. "Isolated by Elitism: The Pitfalls of Recent Heritage Conservation Attempts in Chennai." In *New Architecture and Urbanism: Development of Indian Traditions*, ed. Deependra Prashad and Saswati Chetia, 155–160. Newcastle upon Tyne: Cambridge Scholars Publishing.

Birch, David. 1993. "Staging Crisis: Media and Citizenship." In *Singapore Changes Guard: Social, Political and Economic Directions in the 1990s*, ed. Garry Rodan, 72–83. Melbourne: Longman.

Blackwood, Robert J. 2008. *The State, the Activists and the Islanders: Language Policy on Corsica*. New York: Springer.

Brown, David. 1994. *The State and Ethnic Politics in Southeast Asia*. London: Routledge.

Chan, Heng Chee. 1971. *Singapore: The Politics of Survival, 1965–1967*. Singapore: Oxford University Press.

Chan, Robin, and Lim Yan Liang. 2014. "National Day Rally Speech: 10 Years of Bold Moves . . . and Babies." *Straits Times*, 16 August.

Chong, Terence. 2012. "Position Paper on Bukit Brown." Singapore Heritage Society, January. http://www.singaporeheritage.org/wp-content/uploads/2011/11/SHS_BB_Position_Paper.pdf.

Chong, Terence. 2015. "Bukit Brown Municipal Cemetery: Contesting Imaginations of the Good Life in Singapore." In *Worlding Multiculturalisms: The Politics of Inter-Asian Dwelling*, ed. Daniel P. S. Goh, 161–181. New York: Routledge.

Chong, Terence, and Chu Ai Lin. 2014. "The Multiple Spaces of Bukit Brown." In *Public Space in Urban Asia*, ed. William S. W. Lim, 26–55. Singapore: World Scientific Publishing.

Hong, Lysa, and Huang Jianli. 2008. *The Scripting of a National History: Singapore and Its Pasts*. Singapore: NUS Press.

Kwok, Kian-Woon, C. J. Wee Wan-ling, and Karen Chia. 2000. *Rethinking Chinatown and Heritage Conservation in Singapore*. Singapore: Singapore Heritage Society.

Lim, Kim San. 1985. Oral History Interview. Accession no. 000526121. Singapore: Oral History Centre.
McMordie, Michael, and Frits Pannekoek. 2004. "Introduction." In *Heritage Covenants and Preservation: The Calgary Civic Trust*, ed. Michael McMordie and Frits Pannekoek, 1–15. Calgary: University of Calgary Press.
Nirmala, Murugaian. 1999. "National Library to Go." *Straits Times*, 14 March.
Straits Times. 1998. "$97.5m Plan to Revitalize Chinatown." 26 September.
Yao, Souchou. 2007. *Singapore: The State and the Culture of Excess*. London: Routledge.

CHAPTER 5

Riverscape as Biocultural Heritage
A Local Indigenous Social Movement Contests a National Park in Nepal

Sudeep Jana Thing

Introduction

At the northern tip of the lower Karnali River Delta, adjacent to the Bardia National Park, the Sonaha people constructed a makeshift shelter on a river island. The location, locally known as Nakchikla, is a popular site for the Sonahas to take refuge away from their village settlement while fishing and panning for gold dust in the River Karnali. The river island, surrounded by the river, was not accessible without a canoe. It provided a safe refuge from human intruders and wildlife. The makeshift shelter was built on the edge of a huge log that had drifted onto the sand, and used thin plastic sheets and blankets. Two Sonaha couples had been taking refuge there for the past two weeks. Several other Sonaha men from different villages in the delta were sheltering nearby. The Sonaha men in pairs often went fishing at night upstream of the island. Canoes were beached close to the shelter. Women prepared daily meals and panned for gold on the riverbanks nearby. The men spent the afternoon catching up on sleep, and weaving broken fishing nets under the shed on a sand bank. A flock of cormorants fished nearby, and vultures watched from the branches of a *simal* (red cotton tree). Forests conserved by local communities surrounded the river island, providing a corridor for megafauna (including Asian elephants and greater one horned rhinoceros) moving in and out of the Park. Occasionally river dolphins, gharials, and otters could be spotted in the river.

These observations from my fieldwork in March 2012 convey a sense of special interactions, connections, and relationships of the Sonaha Indigenous minority group with the natural environment in the river delta, in the mid-western Nepalese lowland (see Figure 5.1). This chapter examines and analyses the Sonahas social movement as they contest exclusionary state conservation interventions and policies. After the creation of the Bardiya National Park (hereafter the Park), the largest lowland protected areas in Nepal, around the delta in the early 1970s for wildlife conservation, the Sonahas have been alienated from their ancestral riverine territory and were eventually pushed to settlements in the buffer zones (on the periphery of the Park) or outside it. I argue the Sonahas' history, interactions, and relationships with the riverscape and its natural environment, worldviews, associated river-based traditional livelihoods, collective identities, and claims all underpin, reconstruct, and reproduce the Sonaha biocultural heritage that is marginalized by the dominant conservation regime and discourse of the Nepalese state. The biocultural heritage is claimed and takes shape through the Sonaha social movement.

Examining the little understood social movement of the Sonahas, I will show it offers a critical counter-discourse to the dominant conservation regime and natural heritage conservation. At the same time, I contend the international discourse and paradigm of biocultural heritage has until now been overlooked by the state, the Sonaha movement, and supporting civil society organizations. I argue the concept and spatial approach of biocultural heritage—as adopted in the local context through the Sonaha social movement—is useful for the analysis of the contestations between Sonaha and Park management in support of just solutions by advancing a rights-based approach to conservation. This chapter is empirically grounded in the ethnographic fieldwork conducted in Nepal between 2011 and 2013. I undertook fieldwork[1] in several Sonaha villages in the delta that are located in the close proximity to the Karnali River or its branch Geruwa River that forms the western boundary of the Park (see Figures 5.1 and 5.2).

Locations of Sonaha villages in the delta are not only significant to their livelihoods but also have important ramifications in their movement and Sonaha social movement dynamics, as explored in this chapter. These villages include settlements of predominantly Hinduized Sonaha such as Rajipur, Sarkhol, and Khutiyana at Patabhar village development committee (VDC),[2] and Saijana at Manau VDC, which is another major Sonaha village with a mix of Christianized and Hinduized Sonahas, located closest to the Park boundary. Both these VDCs are located in the Park buffer zone. There are other Sonaha villages such as Murghauwa and Chanaura at Daulatpur VDC, located outside the Park buffer zone (Figures 5.1 and 5.2), that have predominantly Christianized populations. As of 2012, out of the total Sonaha population in the country (1,249), there were 810 Sonaha people residing in the delta. The delta has a total population of 94,424 with the largest

Riverscape as Biocultural Heritage • 125

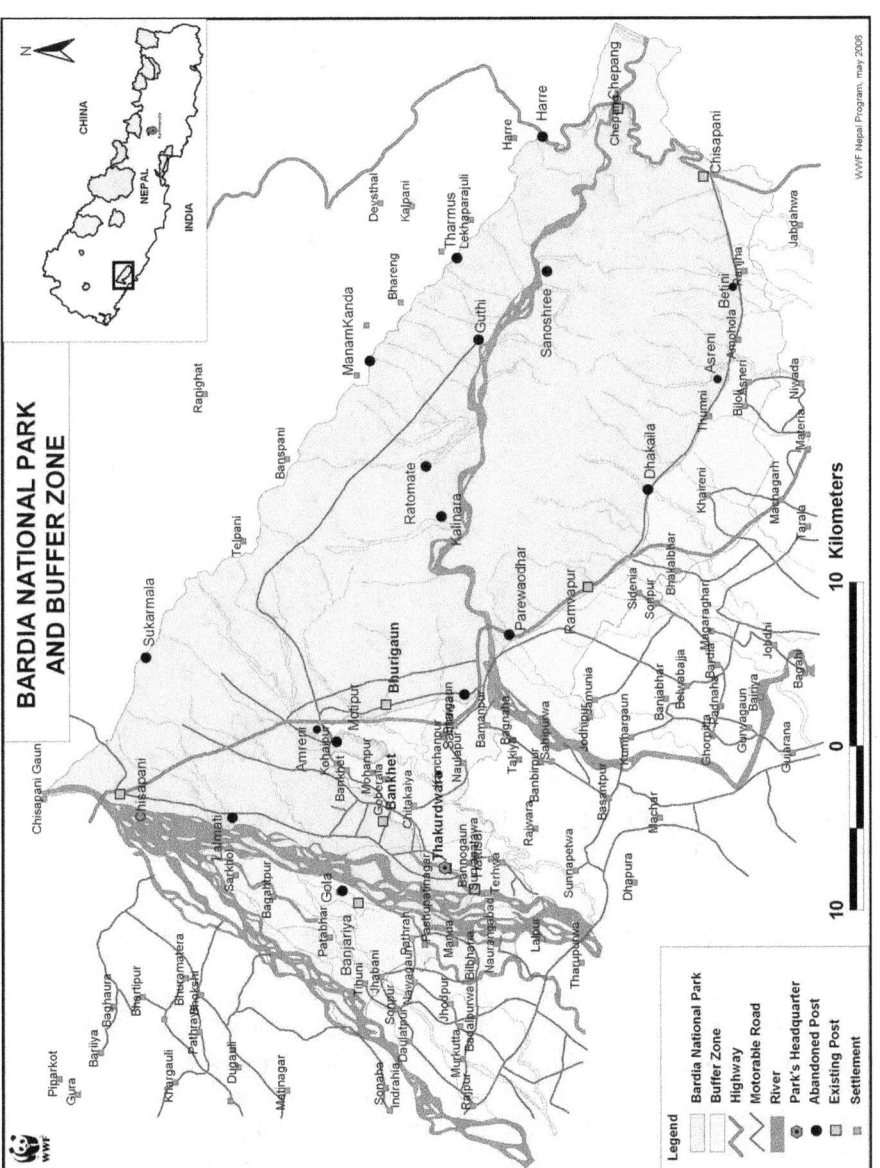

Figure 5.1. Lower Karnali River Delta to the west of Bardia National Park. Manau VDC is labeled as Manau, courtesy of WWF Nepal (© Sudeep Jana Thing).

126 • Sudeep Jana Thing

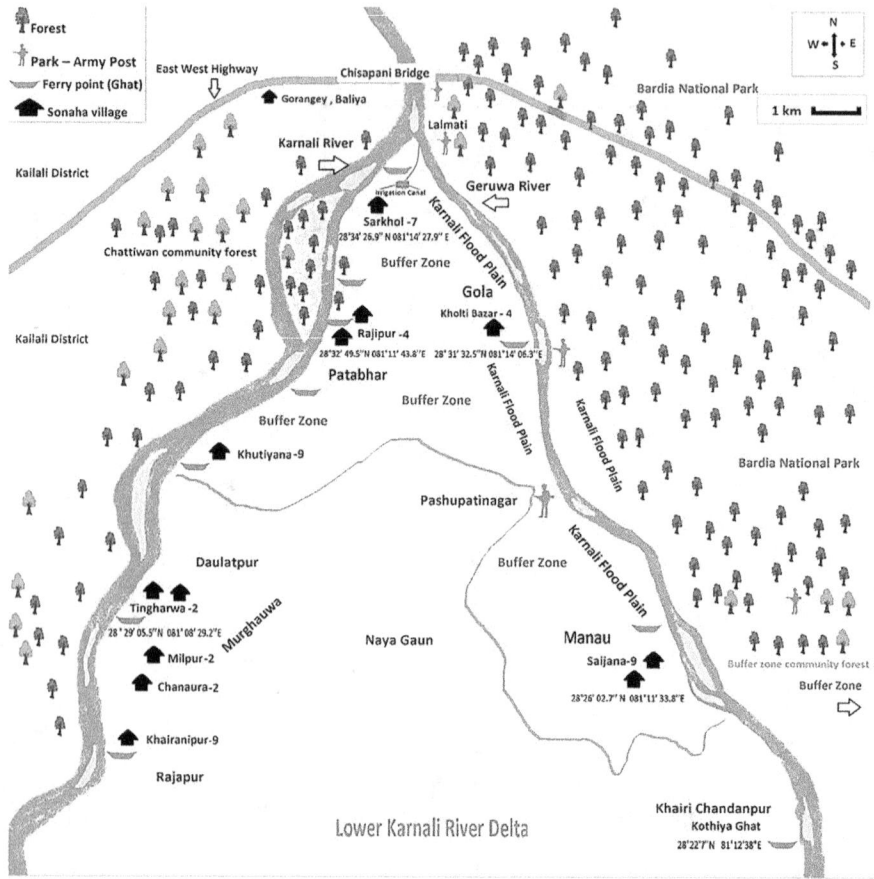

Figure 5.2. Sketch map of the river delta locating the Sonaha settlements (© Sudeep Jana Thing).

group being the Tharu, the largest Indigenous people of the lowland plains of Nepal, across eleven VDCs.

This chapter begins by exploring the emerging concept and movement of biocultural heritage internationally. It then discusses the relevance of the field of political ecology that informs my analysis. The second section introduces the Sonahas' ancestral territory and reconceptualizes the riverscape as the Sonaha biocultural heritage. The third section highlights the contestations between the Sonahas and the state conservation interventions in the national park with particular attention to the clash of two opposing worldviews, natural heritage for nature conservation, and the Sonaha heritage with respect to the riverscape. In this pretext, the chapter then digs deeper into the trajectories of the Sonaha social movement that underpins meanings and politics of the Sonaha biocultural heritage. Finally, I will make a case for biocultural heritage as an alternative pathway that can be pursued by Indigenous social movements, as well as the Nepalese state in the context of the contested riverscape conservation.

Concept of Biocultural Heritage and Political Ecology

The International Institute for Environment and Development (IIED), an advocate for biocultural heritage, defines it as "a complex system of interdependent parts centred on the relationship between Indigenous Peoples and their natural environment [including] biological resources, from the genetic to the landscape level; and long standing traditions, practices and knowledge for adaptation to environmental change and sustainable use of biodiversity" (see IIED 2019). The concept also refers to landscapes that Indigenous peoples create and inhabit, and their holistic worldview. Janice Cumberbatch and Catrina Hinds (2013) conceptualize it as the complex interrelationships between native people and the natural environment. In this section, I provide a brief history of the development of biocultural heritage concept, outline its relationship with political ecology, and explore why it is a useful concept for Indigenous social movements like the Sonaha.

Recent research has broadened the concept of biocultural heritage beyond the domain of Indigenous peoples as a conceptual framework for approaches to sustainable development. Biocultural heritage entails linkages between innovation, practices, and knowledges of Indigenous peoples and local communities, and those communities' complex linkages to the territory, economy, cultural, and spiritual values, customary laws, and biodiversity (Davidson-Hunt et al. 2012; Swiderska 2006). Biocultural heritage is also conceived as both tangible and intangible with respect to "eco-cultural landscape," referring to intimate relationships between people and nature, and it is respectively urged to be prioritized in the field of conservation (Rotherham 2015). The concept of a collective biocultural heritage evolved from the work of an international Indigenous rights social movement driven by NGOs such as Asociación ANDES, Call of the Earth / Laimando de la Tierra, and IIED in the mid-2000s (Davidson-Hunt et al. 2012). The workshop organized by IIED and ANDES in Cusco, Peru, in 2005 first defined collective biocultural heritage (see IIED 2005). The work of ANDES and Andean Quechua communities in Potato Park in Peru on Indigenous biocultural heritage also popularized the concept (Davidson-Hunt et al. 2012).[3]

In the domain of conservation organizations, the biocultural heritage approach is attributed to the work of members of the Commission on Environment, Economic and Social Policy of the International Union for Conservation of Nature to document biocultural diversity. It also has roots in the emerging framework and initiatives of biocultural diversity conservation internationally (Davidson-Hunt et al. 2012; Maffi and Woodley 2010). It has now found expressions in the emerging discourses and practices of biocultural approach to conservation (Gavin et al. 2015), new conservation paradigm (Stevens 2014), and global movements of biocultural diversity conserved by Indigenous peoples and local communities (see ICCA Consortium 2019). The field of political ecology offers opportunities to understand and contribute to the dynamics and politics of biocultural heritage. T. Garrett Graddy (2013) engages political ecology with biocultural heritage by exploring agro-biodiversity in Indigenous biocultural heritage in the Peruvian Andes. Likewise, Thomas Leatherman (2005) used biocultural relationships within a political-ecological approach by considering issues of power and inequality within the human-environment interface and then addressing these relationships at global-local intersections. The framework of political ecology has focused on issues of unequal power relations among social groups and actors, marginalization, conflicts and contestations over natural resources, and politics of environmental conservation (e.g., Bryant and Bailey 1997; Robbins 2012).

The framework of political ecology is particularly relevant to understand the social movement of marginalized Indigenous peoples such as the Sonahas in the light of the national park management and associated politics of conservation (Jana 2013, 2014). Social movements are "sustained, intentional efforts to foster or retard broad legal and social changes, primarily outside the normal institutional channels endorsed by authorities" (Jasper 2014a: 5). Although social movements constitute an important theme in political ecological inquiry as demonstrated by Arturo Escobar (1998), Wendy Wolford and Sara Keene (2015) contend the engagement of political ecology with social movements has been inadequate.

It is worth noting the concepts of indigeneity, Indigenous environmental knowledge, and conservation are contested and debated (Dove 2006). Scholars have provided a critical examination of Indigenous peoples' social movements with respect to a biodiversity conservation (e.g., Escobar 1998), and the politics and construction of environmental identities (e.g., Ulloa 2005). While the conflicting relations between modern conservation and Indigenous peoples have been recognized (Dowie 2009), exclusionary conservation has been criticized for violating Indigenous peoples' rights (e.g., Colchester 2004). There are ample experiences of grassroots social movement of marginalized Indigenous peoples against the national park policy of the state (e.g., Jana 2007). However, trends of convergence between "global environmentalism" and "global indigenism" also suggest meaningful collaborations between Indigenous peoples and conservationists (Brockington et al. 2008: 130). Likewise, David Carruthers (1996) examines a nexus between contemporary environmentalism and Indigenous resistance in Mexico, the alliances between environmental and Indigenous social movement organizations to safeguard traditional ecological knowledge. This chapter attempts to advance political ecology's engagement with social movement of Indigenous peoples through considerations of Indigenous biocultural heritage in the pretext of the contested natural heritage.

The Riverscape as Sonaha Biocultural Heritage and Its Marginalization

The Sonahas consider the riverine areas of the delta (see Figure 5.2) their ancestral riverine territory because of their long-standing history of occupation, interactions, and special relationship with the river, the riparian areas, and the forests. Oral histories of the Sonaha elders trace their presence in the delta as far back as the eighteenth-century preunification period of Nepal. The Sonaha elders recall stories of their ancestors being engaged in the battles against Muslims during *Lawabi Din* (days of Nawabs, ruling elites and Muslim landlords from the adjoining region of Oudh (Awadh), farther south in India) when the region of Bardiya was under the control of British India (1816–1861). Sonaha ancestors led a semimobile way of life in the rivers, fishing and panning for gold, ferrying, and hunting and gathering in the forests while pursuing a subsistence lifestyle. They occupied lands only temporarily in the delta by clearing forest to sow seeds. The Sonaha ancestors' historical preference of semimobile lives along the rivers rather than agrarian settled lives in the delta is attributed by the present generations as a key factor behind landlessness and small landholdings of most Sonahas today.

The Sonahas have had a history of both conflicting and cooperative relationships with the dominant majority of the Tharu people in the delta. Sonahas elders exchanged their fish catch and ferrying service with the agricultural products and alcohols produced by Tharu, and they participate in each other's festivities. Sonahas also work as agricultural laborers on Tharu farms. There are also memories of Sonaha exploitation by big Tharu landlords in the delta. Historically, Sonaha acclaim their status as Jal Thakuri (Thakuri describes them as a higher caste group, of the water/rivers), and elders considered their ethnicity superior to the Tharu. However, the economically and politically powerful Tharu majority wield more social power in daily lives and community affairs.[4]

The relationship between Sonaha, their livelihood practices, cultural identity, and the riverscape is complex and cannot be separated. Temporary shelters on the river islands where Sonaha men and women take refuge during their fishing and gold panning trips are called either *dyara* or *dera*. Customary *dera* existed on both sides of the rivers in the delta (see Figure 5.1). While Sonaha men fish with gill nets—in the past using cast nets and spears—from wooden canoes, women pan gold dust in the riverbanks manually with wooden equipment and fish from the banks. Their immense knowledge of the river and riverine ecology are critical to their adaptation and livelihoods. The Sonaha way of life and livelihoods in the delta are increasingly diversified (now including labor migration and wage labor). Fishing and gold panning practices continue to be important to their livelihoods, as well as central to their sociocultural lives.

Many Sonahas still continue a way of life that follows customary *dera*, staying on the river as long as one month. Sonaha river-based livelihoods and their interactions with the river are also shaped by their appreciation of the dynamic nature and shifting flows of the river. River flow and water volume are closely associated to the availabilities of fish and gold, which in turn also influence Sonahas' mobility in the rivers, which ignores the confines of the Park buffer zone. Sonahas' holistic view of the riverscape and their historical interactions are incompatible to the scientific view of the Park authorities and conservationists about the buffer zone areas separated from the core zone of the Park by the natural boundaries of the river (see Figure 5.1). The current policy and management of the Park and its buffer zone does not address the dynamic and complex socio-ecological processes of Sonaha mobility in the delta.[5]

Until the early 1990s, the Sonahas practiced a customary system of regulating and managing sacred gold panning areas along the riverbank called *kafthans*. The eldest and most respected members of the Sonaha clan would allocate such locations equally to the fellow Sonahas who wanted to pan gold after performing rituals. Although the practice, documented elsewhere at length (Jana 2013, 2014), is nonexistent today, Sonaha elders and adults still have strong memories of those practices. The Sonahas refer to such sacred customary locations as *gaun*. Memories of *kafthans* across the river delta are a record of Sonahas' historical ties to the riverscape.

Considering the worldviews, lived experiences, and livelihood practices of the Sonahas, one can reconceptualize this riverscape as a biocultural space (Jana 2013) or biocultural heritage of the Sonahas. Drawing inspiration from the work of Henri Lefebvre (1991)—which provides a radical and dynamic conception of space as produced, multidimensional, and symbolic—the riverscape for the Sonahas, in a holistic sense, is at once perceived (physical-material), conceived (mentally constructed), and lived space (symbolic). It entails a complex nature-culture hybrid constitutive of the Sonahas' epistemology, ontology, and cosmology. Sonahas' long-standing history, unique interactions, ties with the riverscape, embedded river-based livelihoods, and cultural identities all underpin and reproduce Sonaha biocultural heritage. The contestations between the Sonahas and the Park management can also be attributed to the different and competing meanings and values associated to the riverscape. The Sonaha collective resistance to the Park regime can also be understood as the politics and assertion of Sonaha biocultural heritage against contemporary Nepalese state practices of natural heritage conservation.

Unpacking the Sonaha Social Movement

The passive and silent resistance (Scott 1985) of the Sonahas to the Park regime continues today (Jana 2014), mainly in terms of occasional trespassing of the Park boundary for fishing and panning for gold. This section focuses on the trajectories of the Sonaha social movement's collective and organized resistance between 2006 and 2014, which was led by the national association of the Sonahas and supported by several rights based nongovernmental organizations in Nepal. Although their explicit engagement with the international discourse of biocultural heritage was absent, collective struggles of the Sonahas for rights provide an avenue to understand the articulation of the Sonaha biocultural heritage, as well as its associated politics and complexities.

The Sonaha men had made attempts in the past to organize themselves as a Fish Farming Group and later as a Unified Sonaha Struggle Committee, but these organizations failed to materialize. After 1990, Nepal experienced an expanded democratic space for civil society organizations and organizing of marginalized social groups, allowing the entry of the NGOs into the delta. These NGOs raised consciousness about rights among the Sonahas. The Sonahas still recall how the NGO Environment Conservation Society (ECOS), based in the district of Bardiya, in the 1990s facilitated microcredit and saving groups for Sonaha women. These activities triggered local discussion of rights violations as a result of Park policies. The NGO also supported Sonahas to put an end to unjust private fishing contracts, and extraction of undue fees from the Sonahas charged by a local institution that manages riparian forests as a community forests. Although ECOS publicized the Park administration's violation of fishing rights, it suspended its activities with the Sonahas during the state of emergency during the fighting between Maoist groups and the government that began in 2001. Thus, ECOS's initial attempts to trigger a fishing rights campaign for Sonahas petered out in the early 2000s.

In 2006, the political situation in Nepal changed drastically after the nonviolent people's movement against the direct rule by monarchy. This was followed by a comprehensive peace agreement between the government and the Maoist rebels. Amid the favorable political climate and a democratic transition, rights-based NGOs and local activists from political parties affiliated with NGOs began to engage with the Sonahas in the delta. In October 2006, Sonahas from different parts of the delta gathered in the village of Rajipur, located in the Park buffer zone (see Figure 5.2), for their first-ever *sammeylan* (conference). The *sammeylan* was a moment of cultural festivity and collective deliberation pressing issues regarding Sonaha rights. The predominant Tharu ethnic groups and hill migrants politically and economically dominate historically marginalized Sonahas. The *sammeylan* was an empowering moment. The Sonaha mass assembly endorsed the Rajipur Declaration witnessed by invited local journalists, NGO representatives, and politicians from the Bardiya district. The declaration articulated their collective demands that the Nepalese state "guarantee unhindered access to rivers within and beside the national parks; . . . ensure the traditional rights of the Sonahas over forests and rivers . . . [and] identify the Sonahas as Indigenous peoples and take the necessary steps to protect their language and culture" (Jana 2008: 23).

This first mass gathering was a key moment to energize and connect the Sonahas in the delta. It gave birth to the Nepal Sonaha Adhikar Sangh (Nepal Sonaha Rights Association), which was later legally registered as the Nepal Sonaha Sangh (NSS) in 2007. The NSS was the first national organization of the Sonahas to advocate for their welfare and rights, and became a key player and the primary backbone of the Sonaha movement (see Figure 5.3). The NSS and its activists eventually gained support to their movement from several players in different arenas (Jasper 2014b), including peoples' organizations and institutions in the Park buffer zone, the NGOs, and local political party activists affiliated with NGOs.

The movement strengthened as the NSS leaders aligned with activists of another emerging network of locals residing in the Park buffer zone who resented rules of the Park restricting local access to resources, harassments by the Park guards, and lack of compensation for damage to person and property from wildlife. This was a time when grassroots mobilization and actions in other parts of the country were forging a national alliance called the National Park Victims Struggle Committee. The committee, which was later transformed into the Samrachit Chetra Jana Adhikar Magasangh (Protected Areas People's Rights Federation—SCJAM), an ad hoc national forum of local populations resisting protected area policies in the country,[6] was a key ally of the NSS.

In addition to the leaders of the SCJAM in Bardiya, Sonaha leaders' engagements with activists of four NGOs have been crucial (see Table 5.1). First, a Bardiya-based human rights and developmental NGO called the

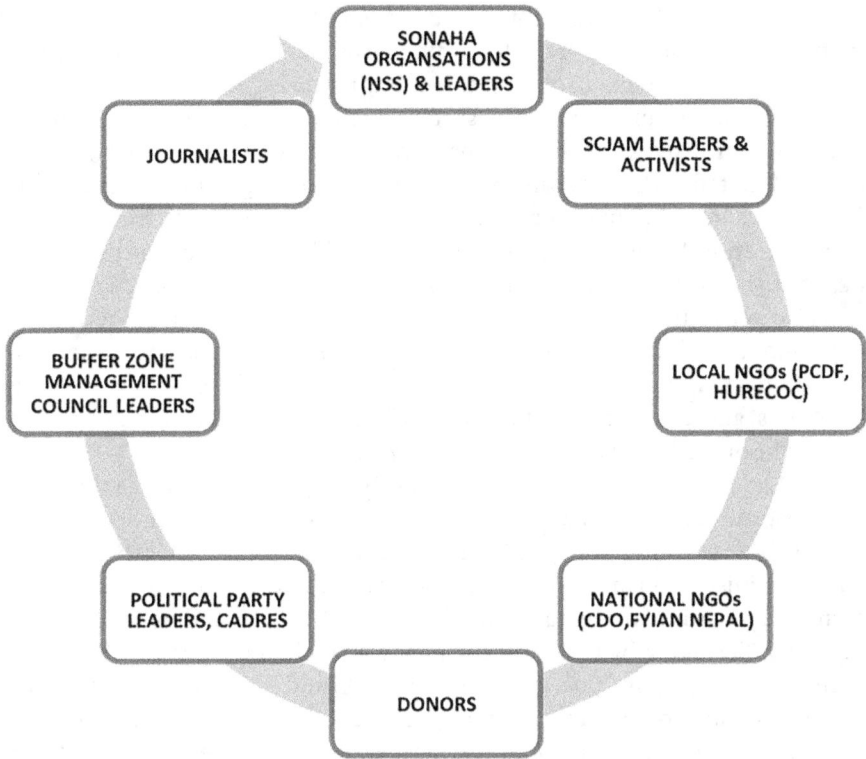

Figure 5.3. Key players and supporters of the Sonaha social movement (© Sudeep Jana Thing).

People-Centered Development Forum (PCDF) has been working with the Sonahas since 2006. Second, the Human Rights and Environment Concern Centre (HURECOC), another local NGO of human rights lawyers, has been working with the Sonahas since 2011. Third, the Community Development Organization (CDO), a national rights-based NGO that grew out of engagement with a grassroots movement of Indigenous fishing minorities in Chitwan National Park, began advocating for the rights of local populations affected by protected area interventions and policies in Nepal in the mid-1990s (Jana 2007; Tanaka 2011). The CDO, the key NGO that was facilitating campaigns led by the SCJAM (Jana 2008), has prioritized the actions of Sonahas in its project funding[7] for the SCJAM since 2006. Fourth, the Food-First Information and Action Network (FIAN) Nepal, another national human rights NGO working on food rights issues, began working with the Sonahas in 2011.

These NGOs played crucial roles in increasing the capacities of Sonahas and supporting their collective actions for Sonaha rights (See Figure 5.2).

These actions included small funding support to the NSS to organize and mobilize the Sonahas in the delta, training the Sonahas about human rights and strategies of social campaigns, facilitating dialogues with the Park administration, and providing exposure to the Sonahas to the media, politicians, and bureaucrats at the national level. The role of a local Tharu student leader affiliated with a left-wing political party, working as an employee of the PCDF, was instrumental in advocating Sonaha fishing rights with the Park administration between 2006 and 2008. The NSS main agenda then was to negotiate rights to fishing and panning of gold dusts in the rivers. The PCDF was also active in mobilizing other local population and SCJAM activists in the region. During this period, the NSS leaders and activists together with SCJAM participated in series of actions such as mass rallies, demonstrations, dialogues, and delegation to the Park warden (see Table 5.1) directed toward the plight of the locals in the Park buffer zone.

On 12 January 2007, the SCJAM-Bardiya organized a mass rally and a demonstration near the Park headquarters, where hundreds of Sonaha took part. This mass protest led to an agreement between the SCJAM-Bardiya, the Park administration and the Buffer Zone Management Council[8] (BZMC) to address demands of the agitating park victims. Their demands toward reforming the policy and governance of the Park also included the issue of Sonahas' access to the rivers. In 2007, activists of the NSS and the SCJAM-Bardiya padlocked the office of the ranger/guard post in the delta to protest the failure of the Park administration to comply with their demands. The same year, during the joint delegation of the SCJAM-Bardiya and the BZMC to Kathmandu—the capital city—the participating NSS activists also highlighted plight of their community before the high-level government officials and the parliamentarians. National print media covered the news of Sonaha.

The NSS began negotiations with the Park administration for fishing concessions. The Park administration put forth several restrictive conditions and provisions to regulate fishing and address conservation issues in the rivers. Some of these include: a ban on night fishing, fishing restrictions in the river branches flowing inside the Park and during fish spawning seasons, and allowing only Sonahas residing in the Park buffer zone to apply for permits. The provision on the eligibility of the Sonahas based on current residence within the buffer zone generated a dilemma in the movement, as it would exclude the Sonahas residing outside the Park buffer zone (such as in Daulatpur VDC). Whether to compromise and accept fishing concessions for the Sonahas in the buffer zone despite its restrictive provisions or to completely forgo this crucial opportunity to secure the permits and continue demanding concessions for all posed a key challenge to the NSS leaders.

Amid the internal disputes, NSS leaders from villages within and outside the Park buffer zone forged a general consensus to acquire the fishing per-

Table 5.1. Key Events in the Sonaha social movement

Dates	Actions/events
1998	Mass assembly at Rajipur village, Bardiya
2–4 October 2006	First Sonaha Peoples Conference at Rajipur, Bardiya
12 January 2007	Mass rally and demonstration at the Park headquarters
15 February 2007	Dialogue between the Sonahas, the leaders of local Park victims, the Buffer Zone Management Council (BZMC), and the Park officials
29–30 March 2007	Formation of the national coalition of protected area victims (SCJAM)
June 2007	Application lodged for the enlistment and recognition of Sonaha ethnic identity by the government
27 June 2007	Padlocking of the office of the Banjariya Range Post
30 September 2007	Torching of a copy of the national law of protected areas by locals in the buffer zone
6–7 November 2007	Collective delegation of the Sonahas, the Park victims, and the BZMC members to the forest bureaucracy
2 February 2008	Fishing permits granted to the Sonahas by the Park
18 February 2011	Mass cycle rally, demonstration, and dialogue with the Park authorities
30–31 March 2011	Second Sonaha Peoples Conference at Rajipur, Bardiya
23 June 2011	Sonahas delegation and appeal to the forest minister and the national park department in Kathmandu
26–27 April 2013	Sonahas participated in the national gathering of endangered Indigenous groups in the nearby district of Kailali
July 2013	Sonaha delegation sent to Kathmandu
1 April 2014	Sonaha leaders dialogue with constituent assembly members and government authorities
12 October 2014	Sonaha filed a public interest litigation in the Supreme Court

Note: Updated and adapted from Jana (2008).

mits while continuing to struggle for the fishing rights of the Sonahas residing outside the Park buffer zone. In the aftermath of these actions, on 2 February 2008, the Sonahas from the delta—excluding those residing in Daulatpur VDC—acquired nine-month fishing permits for the first time. Nonetheless, the Sonahas in general were jubilant after acquiring the fishing permits. The NSS leaders and activists considered this their movement's victory despite the discontent of the Sonahas from Daulatpur. This was an initial yet crucial step in the process of reclaiming their biocultural heritage.

However, the victory was short lived. Since April 2008, the Park administration has discontinued further renewal and issuance of licenses following an incident where two Sonaha youth from the village of Saijana (Manau VDC) were arrested for illegally selling a rhino horn taken from a dead rhino at the Park boundary. The permit-issuing warden of the Park said:

> While issuing the licenses we had told the Sonahas that they had to report to the Park administration about illegal activities in the area. But the permit [license] holders ferried hunters [indicating poachers]. They contravened an agreement with the administration ... the licenses were suspended when one Sonaha was found to have been involved in rhino poaching. (Interview, 25 May 2011)

Although this was the first incident in their history, it was a major setback for the entire Sonaha community. Between 2008 and 2010, the Sonaha movement ebbed. The NSS leaders attribute this to three main reasons. First, the main channel of the river held its course, so most of the Sonaha began fishing in the Karnali River outside the Park jurisdiction. The absence of fishing permits did not constrain the Sonaha from fishing. The founding president of the NSS said:

> Now the river is big on our side [the Karnali], there is no need for fishing licenses, so the people [his fellow Sonahas] do not see their value now. But when the river goes back to the Geruwa, and when they can't fish freely there, then they will realize the importance of our *andolan* [movement]. (Interview, 28 April 2011)

Second, the tenure of the NGO projects supporting their movement ended. Third, internal discord and politics among the NSS leaders from different villages in the delta seriously affected the functioning of the NSS.

The Movement Revived

> If the Park does not give us licenses when we are begging, we will have to acquire them even if we have to seize them [by pressure]. If we all approach the Park, maybe one brother will die but another brother will still be alive. (Interview, 21 March 2011)

This quote from a Sonaha women leader regarding the marginalization of Sonaha by the Park management demonstrates how her strong emotions and feelings are central to the Sonaha social movement (Jasper 1998). Some Sonaha leaders continue to maintain tactical relations with government project officials and the Park administration. The Sonahas from the village of Saijana acquired four hours of fishing licenses and a onetime weeklong permit to pan gold in the Geruwa River from the Park administration in 2011. The Park officials issued permits on an ad hoc and temporary basis rather than making a policy decision. However, the leaders in this village reported they returned them back to the Park headquarters since it was impractical. This, however, raised suspicion among the leaders of Sonaha at Rajipur who contended negotiation of such feeble permits without wider discussion among the Sonaha villages in the delta would only weaken their movement.

From mid-2010, HURECOC, another local NGO, met the Sonahas, as the national NGO, CDO, began work in Bardiya with funding from the UK Department for International Development. Support of these NGOs triggered further actions of the NSS and the SCJAM-Bardiya (see Table 5.1). In their major action, the NSS organized to claim their rights over the riverscape through a mass rally at the Park headquarters on 28 February 2011. The protest was primarily planned by the leaders of NSS from the village of Rajipur and backed by the SCJAM-Bardiya and supporting NGOs. The Sonahas from different villages of the delta (both inside and outside the buffer zone) took part in the protest. "Sonaha should be allowed to fish. We need our fishing licenses" and "fishing and gold washing are our traditional occupations" were among the slogans vigorously chanted. During the dialogue with the Park warden that followed the demonstration, the NSS leaders demanded their fishing licenses be resumed. The Park warden on the contrary expressed concerns about the impact of Sonaha fishing practices on the conservation of aquatic species.

Meanwhile, a leader from the village of Murghauwa (Daulatpur VDC), then the president of the NSS, raised the issue of their exclusion from the fishing permits that were issued in 2008. He argued the Sonahas from Murghauwa also once lived closer to the Park but moved away because of the Park restrictions. He demanded alternative livelihood options for Sonahas. The Park warden hinted that because they reside outside the Park jurisdiction, they are ineligible. Sonaha leaders contest such logic and argue that despite their current residence outside the Park buffer zone, they interact with the rivers and have a stake in the permits. This also reemphasizes mismatch between the state view of the Park and buffer zone management and the Sonahas view of the riverscape as a biocultural heritage. Likewise, whether to reclaim customary livelihoods (for example, access to the rivers in the Park) or demand alternative livelihoods has also been an issue of contentions among the Sonaha leaders. The dialogue ended inconclusively, and no workable solutions were negotiated. Discord between the leaders from different Sonaha villages was evident.

Intra-Sonaha Dynamics and Tensions in the NSS

Frictions between the Sonaha leaders and activists were a significant challenge to the Sonaha social movement. Internal tensions were largely rooted in the exclusion of the Sonahas from Daulatpur VDC from acquiring fishing permits in 2008. The discriminatory policy of the Park administration has been a contentious issue triggering intra Sonaha dynamics and tensions. The tension heightened further in the crisis of the NSS leadership. The Sonahas from Rajipur strongly challenged the outgoing president of the NSS (a Christian Sonaha from Murghauwa), accusing him of incompetently leading their movement. In 2012, there was a heated discussion among the Sonahas in deciding the venue of the second Sonaha *sammeylan* and on affairs of the NSS convention to elect new leaders. The Sonaha leaders from Rajipur with much closer ties with the supporting NGOs, in the face of opposition from leaders and activists from Daulatpur who were aspiring to organize the events in their village, organized the *sammeylan* and the NSS convention at Rajipur on March 2012. While there were representatives of Sonahas from other smaller settlements in the delta, the Sonahas from Saijana (Manau) and Murghauwa (Daulatpur) boycotted the event.

Forming a new NSS leadership without significant representation of Sonahas from these two major Sonaha villages led to the formation of another competing Sonaha organization called the Sonaha Bikash Samaj. Likewise, religious faith has also been a major factor of discords among the leaders—primarily between leaders of Rajipur village (Hinduized Sonahas) and Murghauwa village (predominantly Christianized Sonahas). The clash and factions among the leaders of these three major Sonaha villages in the delta (Rajipur, Saijana, and Murghauwa) is a significant setback to the Sonaha movement. Intra-Sonaha dynamics thus have weakened the collective claims for rights and access to the rivers, and claims for recognition Sonaha biocultural heritage. The new NSS leadership with NGO support immediately organized a delegation to the Ministry of Forests and the Department of National Parks and Wildlife Conservation in the capital city of Kathmandu in June 2012. The NSS leaders also employed a strategy to highlight the Sonaha cause and struggles by inviting journalists and media personnel to their villages, or giving interviews on the FM radio and organizing press conferences. These and other sporadic attempts of the Sonahas thereafter have failed to negotiate any concrete solutions with the Park administration.

Politics and Struggle for Ethnic Identity

> Our fight is not only with the Park warden; it is with the government [Nepalese state] too for recognition of our ethnicity. We have to put pressure on the government. (Interview, 21 April 2011)

This narrative of a Sonaha leader suggests the movement for fishing and gold panning rights in the Park rivers increasingly became infused with the collective ethnic consciousness, and the politics of ethnic identity as a Janajati, or an ethnic group that has been legally recognized as an Indigenous nationality of Nepal. The 2006 Rajipur Declaration of the NSS that, among others, articulated Sonaha collective demands about ancestral occupation in their riverine territory had also appealed the Nepalese state to "identify Sonahas as *adivasi Janajati* including both Hindu and Christianized" and to take necessary steps "to protect their language and culture" (Jana 2008: 23).

The Sonahas are currently not included among the fifty-nine officially recognized Indigenous nationalities of Nepal, as per the National Foundation for the Development of Indigenous Nationalities (NFDIN) Act 2002.[9] In the wake of their movement in 2007, the NSS leaders had lodged an application at the office of the NFDIN in Kathmandu, seeking legal recognition of their ethnic identity. The application stressed the recognition of Sonahas' ethnicity and their legal listing as a distinct Janajati. The supporting document to the application, entitled "Sonaha: Ethnic Introduction," says the Sonahas' claim to be Loponmukh Jati (an endangered ethnic group). It also asserts their ethnic identity, cultural practices, and ancestral occupations as being distinct. The Sonaha leaders and activists have increasingly realized the importance of such legal recognition in their ongoing struggle, as it would be critical to bargain and negotiate their rights with the Nepalese state.

The Sonahas' assertion of ethnic identity, as well as the struggle for Indigenous rights, should be situated within the sociopolitical transformations, ethnic conflicts and heightened discourses, mobilization, and movements around ethnic identities in Nepal since the 1990s (Hangen and Lawoti 2013; Whelpton et al. 2008). In 2009, in response to the pressure generated from Janajati movements, the Nepali government formed a high-level task force to revise the existing schedule and classification of Janajati groups. This task force, after field-based research, submitted its report to the government with a recommendation for a revised schedule to include twenty-nine more groups including the Sonahas (Gurung 2010).

Since 2011, FIAN Nepal has been providing occasional support for the sporadic efforts of the Sonaha leaders from the NSS and Sonaha Bikash Samaj to advocate and lobby for the legal recognition of the Sonahas. The NSS leaders participated in the collective alliances of "endangered Janajati" groups in the country to highlight their demands. In their other strategy to legitimize their ethnicity identity and presence in the delta, the Sonahas acquired recommendation letters from the local government that recognize their distinct identity and habitation in the delta. In response to a writ petition filed by the Sonaha leaders in 2014 with a legal aid from an

NGO, Juri-Nepal, the Supreme Court in 2015 ordered the government to enlist Sonahas as an "endangered Indigenous group." At the time of writing in 2018, the Nepalese government had not revised the listing of Indigenous peoples in Nepal. The Sonaha struggle for legal status of their ethnic identity is continuing.

For many Sonahas, *purkheuli pesa* (ancestral occupation) constitutes part of their collective identity, history, and biocultural heritage that are considered integral to both Sonaha culture and ongoing struggles. Most of the Sonaha leaders during my conversation expressed strong attachment to their ancestral occupations. A leader of the NSS from Rajipur emphasized the importance of ancestors: "Our *purkhauli pesa* is the foundation of our ethnic identity. If we are demanding with the government to be listed as *Janajati* then this very ancestral occupation is important; we should not give them up without viable alternatives." Likewise, the founding president of the NSS from Rajipur affirmed: "Fishing and gold panning are our ancestral occupations. These are what identify us as Sonahas and these are also our culture" (interview, 25 March 2011). The perspective of a former NSS president, a Christianized Sonaha from Daulatpur and a leader of Sonaha Bikash Samaj, contrasts with the views and sentiments of the NSS leaders above. He said: "It is because of these occupations [fishing and gold panning] that we have not been able to uplift our lives, we are still backward." He went on to argue the Sonahas should move beyond their ancestral occupations (interview, 26 February 2012). However, this leader also asserted government recognition of their ethnicity is essential to be entitled to claim state incentives and privileges accorded to marginalized Janajati groups in Nepal. This alludes to the fact that meanings ascribed to the Sonaha biocultural heritage is not uniform.

The formation and politics of collective identity are central features of social movements (Castells 2009; Polletta and Jasper 2001). The assertion and struggles for recognition of ethnic identity as a Janajati have been central to the Sonaha movement. This can be attributed to five key reasons. First, there has been increased consciousness about their minority status, and concerns about their endangered status among the Sonahas. The Sonahas perceive legal recognition of their ethnic status is vital to prevent assimilation into other communities. Second, the Sonahas often express their discontent when their ethnic identity is confounded with other ethnic groups such as the Tharu people. The Sonahas feel awareness about their distinct ethnic identity in the country is limited. Thus, it has become integral to their honor and dignity. Third, the Sonahas perceive recognition of ethnic identity would empower their community and elevate their sociocultural status in the delta dominated by majority of Tharu and hill migrants. Fourth, assertion of Sonaha identity as a Janajati with a long history of occupation and ties with the river delta, and unique ancestral occupations have been vital for the Sonahas to claim their rights to customary occupation with the Park administration and the state. Fifth, Sonaha leaders have seen opportunities of developmental projects of the government and NGO often enjoyed by other marginalized Janajatis of Nepal.

Conclusions and Policy Implications

The Sonaha social movement was triggered by the crisis of customary livelihoods resulting from restrictive policies of the Bardiya National Park. The NSS transformed the silent resistance of the Sonahas into an organized movement that was backed by multiple players including rights NGOs, leaders, and activists who agitated against the regulation of the buffer zone by the Park management. Over time, the movement became increasingly exposed to and shaped by the discourse of Indigenous rights in the context of national parks by employing diverse strategies in multiple arenas such as NSS gatherings, NGO projects, mass rallies, and negotiations at the Park administration, as well as lobbying with the politicians and bureaucrats at the capital, and a legal action. The supporting civil society organizations' adoption of national discourse of Janajati rights, as well as global discourses on human rights of Indigenous peoples and, in particular, discussions about Indigenous people's rights in the international conservation forums, was influential in framing the agenda of the Sonaha movement. The Sonahas themselves have increasingly reconstructed their customary occupations and claims of access to rivers as Indigenous rights; the Park caused livelihood crises and displacements from the ancestral territory, which are violations of their human rights. The discourse of Janajati rights with respect to the riverscape is embodied in the Sonaha movement and reproduced by it. This discourse confronts and challenges the dominant conservation discourse and practice of the Nepalese state in Nepal that excludes the Sonahas, and entails politics of Sonaha biocultural heritage.

The Sonaha movement has also been increasingly shaped by consciousness and reassertions of collective ethnic identity as their distinct ethnicity is yet to receive a legal recognition form the state. The Sonaha struggles to pursue their livelihoods have now merged with their ongoing struggles for legal recognition of their ethnic identity. The Sonaha social movement thus articulates a complex interface and interweaving of Janajati rights, ethnic consciousness, and preexisting collective identity. The movement is an arena and a site of collective resistance to state conservation regime, reassertion of their history and relationships with the ancestral territory, reproduction of counter discourse of Janajati rights, and politics of ethnic identity and biocultural heritage. This movement enacts cultural politics (Alvarez et al. 1998), on the one hand implicitly contesting the dominant meanings and values of the riverscape associated with conservation and natural heritage, and on the other hand reconstructing the complex Sonaha view and meanings of the lived river space, their interactions, and embedded identities that underpin Sonaha biocultural heritage.

The movement has ebbed lately because of the reasons discussed in the preceding two sections. For economically disadvantaged and sociopolitically marginalized minority groups like the Sonahas, waging and sustaining a persistent collective movement against the conservationist state is challenging without civil society support. One of the lacunae of the movement and its allying NGOs is the emphasis only on rights violations. The movement strategies have been largely directed toward contesting the Park policies and management, and demanding rights to customary occupations to secure threatened livelihoods. While the Sonaha biocultural heritage was marginalized by the conservationist state, its politics and meaningful deliberations have yet to find prominence as critical alternatives.

Sonaha struggle has yet to forge links with the global discourse, networks, and initiatives of biocultural heritage. However, an increased appreciation of the Sonaha biocultural heritage and understanding of its political ecology as articulated in the social movement could be informed by the broader paradigm and global discussions on biocultural heritage. There is an opportunity to forge meaningful partnerships and collaborations between local populations, state conservation authorities, civil society, and private actors; to envision and operationalize locally adapted plans to manage and govern the riverscape for effective conservation; and to respect and strengthen the heritage of groups like the Sonaha. It thus offers just an alternative that reconciles rights, livelihoods, and heritage with the conservation priorities and natural heritage of national parks.

Sudeep Jana Thing is an early career researcher affiliated with planning and geography in the School of Design and Build Environment at Curtin University, where he earned his PhD in Social Sciences in 2014. He is currently involved in teaching geography courses as a sessional academic. He is involved in forest tenure research with the research organization ForestAction Nepal. His doctoral dissertation examines the contestations between a marginalized Sonaha Indigenous minority group and a national park management in Nepal and resultant spatial politics and is a contribution to the political ecology of conservation. He continues his research on the changing lives and livelihoods of Sonaha people in the Karnali River Delta, midwestern lowlands regions of Nepal. Before his academic career, he was involved with several civil society organizations in Nepal as a researcher in the field of sociopolitical and equity dimensions of conservation, natural resource governance and conflicts, community-based conservation, sustainable rural livelihoods, and grassroots social movements. He has contributed several peer-reviewed articles, chapters, and research outputs. He is an associate member of the ICCA Consortium, a global civil society organization that supports areas and territories conserved by Indigenous peoples and local communities. He is a member of the World Commission on Protected Areas and the Institute of Australian Geographers.

NOTES

1. The fieldwork included interviews with key activists and leaders of civil society organizations, NGOs actively supporting the Sonaha movement, and officials of the Park administration.
2. VDC is the lowest-level political and administrative unit of governance in Nepal.
3. For the evolution of the concept and discourse of biocultural heritage, see Davidson-Hunt et al. (2012).
4. For further details about the complex Sonaha-Tharu relations in the delta, see Jana (2014).
5. For instance, many Sonahas outside the Park buffer zone (in particular, villages in Daulatpur VDC) who historically interacted with the Geruwa River (closer to the Park) now fish on the upper tip of the delta, in the buffer zone but outside the jurisdiction of the Park.
6. For the detailed actions of SCJAM between 2006 and 2010, see Jana (2008).
7. The project was funded by Human Rights and Good Governance Unit of the Danish International Development Agency.
8. Legally recognized institution of the local population that comanages and administers development and conservation activities in villages with the buffer zone along with protected area administration.
9. The act founded an exclusive and semiautonomous institution also known as the NFDIN for the welfare and development of Janajati in Nepal. The law in its schedule lists fifty-nine Janajati. They are categorized as endangered, highly marginalized, marginalized, disadvantaged, and advanced, located over several geographical locations such as the mountains, hills, inner Terai, and Terai lowlands (Gurung 2010).

REFERENCES

Alvarez, Sonia E., Evelina Dagnino, and Arturo Escobar. 1998. "Introduction: The Cultural and Political in Latin American Social Movements." In *Culture of Politics, Politics of Culture: Re-visioning Latin American Social Movements*, ed. Sonia E. Alvarez, Evelina Dagnino, and Arturo Escobar 1–29. Boulder, CO: Westview Press.

Brockington, Dan, Rosaleen Duffy, and Jim Igoe. 2008. *Nature Unbound: Conservation Capitalism and the Future of Protected Areas*. London: Earthscan.

Bryant, Raymond L., and S. Bailey. 1997. *Third World Political Ecology*. London: Routledge.
Carruthers, David V. 1996. "Indigenous Ecology and the Politics of Linkage in Mexican Social Movements." *Third World Quarterly* 17 (5): 1007–1028. https://doi.org/10.1080/01436599615236.
Castells, Manuel. 2009. *The Power of Identity*. 2nd ed. Malden, MA: Wiley-Blackwell.
Colchester, Marcus. 2004. "Conservation Policy and Indigenous Peoples." *Environmental Science & Policy* 7 (3): 145–153. http://dx.doi.org/10.1016/j.envsci.2004.02.004.
Cumberbatch, Janice A., and Catrina J. Hinds. 2013. "Barbadian Bio-cultural Heritage: An Analysis of the Flying Fish." *International Journal of Intangible Heritage* 8: 118–34.
Davidson-Hunt, Iain J., Katherine L. Turner, Aroha Te Pareake Mead, Juanita Cabrera-Lopez, Richard Bolton, C. Julián Idrobo, Inna Miretski, et al. 2012. "Biocultural Design: A New Conceptual Framework for Sustainable Development in Rural Indigenous and Local Communities." *S.A.P.I.E.N.S.* 5 (2): 33–45. http://sapiens.revues.org/1382.
Dove, Michael R. 2006. "Indigenous People and Environmental Politics." *Annual Review of Anthropology* 35: 191–208. https://doi.org/10.1146/annurev.anthro.35.081705.123235.
Dowie, Mark. 2009. *The Hundred-Year Conflict between Global Conservation and Native Peoples*. Cambridge, MA: MIT Press.
Escobar, Arturo. 1998. "Whose Knowledge, Whose Nature? Biodiversity, Conservation, and the Political Ecology of Social Movements." *Journal of Political Ecology* 5 (1): 53–82. https://doi.org/10.2458/v5i1.21397.
Gavin, Michael C., Joe McCarter, Aroha Mead, Fikret Berkes, John Richard Stepp, Debora Peterson, and Ruifei Tang. 2015. "Defining Biocultural Approaches to Conservation." *Trends in Ecology & Evolution* 30 (3): 140–145. http://dx.doi.org/10.1016/j.tree.2014.12.005.
Graddy, T. Garrett. 2013. "Regarding Biocultural Heritage: In Situ Political Ecology of Agricultural Biodiversity in the Peruvian Andes." *Agriculture and Human Values* 30 (4): 587–604. https://doi.org/10.1007/s10460-013-9428-8.
Gurung, Om. 2010. "Nepal Ma Adivasi *Janajati* Andolan Ko Itihash." [History of Indigenous nationalities in Nepal]. *Journal of Indigenous Nationalities* 3: 13–28.
Hangen, Susan, and Mahendra Lawoti. 2013. "Introduction: Nationalism and Ethnic Conflict in Nepal." In *Nationalism and Ethnic Conflict in Nepal: Identities and Mobilisation after 1990*, ed. M. Lawoti and S. Hangen, 5–34. London: Routledge.
ICCA Consortium. 2019. "What we do." Accessed 1 July. https://www.iccaconsortium.org/.
IIED (International Institute for Environment and Development) 2005. "Protecting Community Rights over Traditional Knowledge: Implications of Customary Laws and Practices." Research Planning Workshop, Cusco, Peru, 20–25 May. https://pubs.iied.org/pdfs/G01090.pdf.
———. "About Biocultural Heritage." Accessed 19 June. http://biocultural.iied.org/about-biocultural-heritage.
Jana, Sudeep. 2007. *Working towards Environmental Justice: An Indigenous Fishing Minority's Movement in Chitwan National Park, Nepal*. Lalitpur, Nepal: International Centre for Integrated Mountain Development.

———. 2008. *"Protecting People in Protected Areas": Recapitulating Rights Campaign in Lowland Protected Areas of Nepal.* Kathmandu: Community Development Organization.

———. 2013. "A National Park, River-Dependent Sonahas and a Biocultural Space in Peril." In *The Right to Responsibility: Resisting and Engaging Development, Conservation, and the Law in Asia,* ed. Holly Jonas, Harry Jonas, and Suneetha M. Subramanian, 99–119. Malaysia: Institute of Advanced Studies, Natural Justice and United Nations University.

———2014. "The Polemics and Discourse of Conservation in Nepal: A Case Study of Sonaha Indigenous Minorities and Bardia National Park." PhD dissertation, Western Australia: Curtin University.

Jasper, James M. 1998. "The Emotions of Protest: Affective and Reactive Emotions in and around Social Movements." *Sociological Forum* 13 (3): 397–424. https://doi.org/10.1023/A:1022175308081.

———. 2014a. *Protest: A Cultural Introduction to Social Movements.* Chichester: John Wiley & Sons.

———. 2014b. "Playing the Game." In *Players and Arenas: The Interactive Dynamics of Protest,* ed. James M. Jasper and Jan Willem Duyvendak, 9–34. Amsterdam: Amsterdam University Press.

Leatherman, Thomas. 2005. "A Space of Vulnerability in Poverty and Health: Political-Ecology and Biocultural Analysis." *Ethos* 33 (1): 46–70. https://doi.org/10.1525/eth.2005.33.1.046.

Lefebvre, Henri. 1991. *The Production of Space.* Trans. Donald Nicholson-Smith. Oxford: Blackwell.

Maffi, Luisa, and Ellen Woodley. 2010. *Biocultural Diversity Conservation: A Global Source Book.* London: Earthscan.

Polletta, Francesa, and James M. Jasper. 2001. "Collective Identity and Social Movements." *Annual Review of Sociology* 27: 283–305. https://doi.org/10.1146/annurev.soc.27.1.283.

Robbins, Paul. 2012. *Political Ecology: A Critical Introduction.* Chichester: John Wiley & Sons.

Rotherham, Ian D. 2015. "Bio-cultural Heritage and Biodiversity: Emerging Paradigms in Conservation and Planning." *Biodiversity and Conservation* 24 (13): 3405–3429. https://doi.org/10.1007/s10531-015-1006-5.

Scott, James C. 1985. *Weapons of the Weak: Everyday Forms of Peasant Resistance.* New Haven, CT: Yale University Press.

Stevens, Stan. 2014. "A New Protected Area Paradigm." In *Indigenous Peoples, National Parks, and Protected Areas: A New Paradigm Linking Conservation, Culture, and Rights,* ed. Stan Stevens, 47–83. Tucson: University of Arizona Press.

Swiderska, Krystyna. 2006. "Protecting Traditional Knowledge: A Framework based on Customary Laws and Bio-cultural Heritage Sustainable Agriculture, Biodiversity and Livelihoods Programme." Paper presented at the International Conference on Endogenous Development and Bio-cultural Diversity, Geneva, 3–5 October.

Tanaka, Masako. 2011. "The Changing Roles of NGOs in Nepal: Promoting Emerging Rights-Holder Organizations for Inclusive Aid." *VOLUNTAS: International Journal of Voluntary and Nonprofit Organizations* 22 (3): 494–517. https://doi.org/10.1007/s11266-010-9173-1.

Ulloa, Astrid. 2005. *The Ecological Native: Indigenous Peoples' Movements and Eco-governmentality in Colombia*. New York: Routledge.
Whelpton, Joanna, David N. Gellner, and Joanna Pfaff-Czarnecka. 2008. "New Nepal, New Ethnicities: Changes Since the Mid 1990s." In *Nationalism and Ethnicity in Nepal*, 2nd ed., ed. David N. Gellner, Joanna Pfaff-Cznarnecka, and John Whelpton, xvii–xlvii. Kathmandu: Vajra Publications.
Wolford, Wendy, and Sara Keene. 2015. "Social Movement." In *The Routledge Handbook of Political Ecology*, ed. James McCarthy, Gavin Bridge, and Tom A. Perreault, 626–637. London: Routledge.

 CHAPTER 6

Heritage for Whom?
Caste and Contestation among Sri Lanka's Dumbara Rata Weavers
Aimée Douglas

> Although the patrimony serves to unify each nation, the inequalities in its formation and appropriation require that it also be studied as a space of material and symbolic struggle between classes, ethnic groups, and other groups. (Canclini 1995: 136)

> Too much is asked of heritage. In the same breath, we commend national patrimony, regional and ethnic legacies and a global heritage shared and sheltered in common. We forget that these aims are usually incompatible. (Lowenthal 1998: 227)

In Sri Lanka, as elsewhere, policy debates framed in terms of the protection of heritage and traditional knowledge have necessarily entailed a consideration of "how far the preservation of this knowledge must be limited to [its] traditional bearers" (Silva 2015: 248). This question is one of central concern to legal scholars presently trying to "[strike] a balance between cultural preservation and access to knowledge" and is typically posed with reference to the disenfranchisement of local communities by corporate interests seeking to gain from indigenous technical knowledge, musical and artistic productions, and genetic material (Andanda 2012). At a moment when "liberal state-based regimes of protection of patrimony" seem to have given ground to "marketized relationships that position cultural heritage as a resource" (Coombe and Weiss 2015: 43), the question is not only relevant for "big business." It is also battled out within those communities whose presumed harmony remains central to the imaginations of consumers, government officials, and others whose activities support the "development of craft" in

South Asia.[1] Drawing on ethnographic research carried out among weavers engaged in an industry popularly regarded as exemplary of Sri Lanka's cultural heritage, I focus here on one such battle. In a place where the figure of the "crafts entrepreneur" has emerged alongside (and to some extent displaced that of) the "traditional craftsmen" in state-sponsored narratives, this contestation is a powerful evocation of the struggle to which Néstor García Canclini refers in the epigraph. As I aim to demonstrate here, it instantiates a globally observed tension between, on the one hand, the neoliberal promises of economic freedom and individuation and, on the other, the salience of local categories of identification (and the inequalities they might entail) that emerge out of and give form to social life everywhere.

In the central Sri Lankan village of Redigama,[2] a postwar and largely tourism-driven surge in demand for the unique textiles produced in the village has helped drive a dispute over entitlement to the regionally distinctive weaving industry for which it is known, or *Dumbara Rata* (Dumbara designs). An anthropological examination of this dispute offers insight into the kinds of locally meaningful forms and interests that animate that nebulous terrain called heritage politics. In Redigama, the industry's historically recognized heirs and the relative newcomers employed in the former's workshops over the past forty years articulate competing notions of the knowledge and skills entailed in Dumbara Rata weaving in order to justify their respective claims to the industry. In doing so, they enact a tension very much like that identified by David Lowenthal in the epigraph between local or communalist legacies and collectively shared and stewarded "global heritage." While those who have long controlled the industry ground their claims in ideas of identity, inherited ability, and descent-based proprietorship, those who challenge this control articulate recognizably neoliberal notions of entitlement based on shared knowledge, economic freedom, and individual, self-taught skill. In an instance of the revelatory heritage politics taken up in this chapter, I find that caste, a category of identification publicly disavowed as anachronistic in a modern, democratic Sri Lanka, both conditions and is re-energized by the manner in which those on each side of this dispute qualify the nature of their relationship to Dumbara Rata weaving and the knowledge it requires.

Dumbara Rata Textile Production in Redigama

As is the case with many of what are today regarded as Sri Lanka's "traditional handicrafts," the production of Dumbara Rata textiles has long been recognized as an occupation performed by individuals at one of the lowest rungs of a Sinhala caste hierarchy, in this instance the Berava. While official census reports in Sri Lanka do not account for caste, unofficial estimates indicate that of the approximately four hundred Sinhala Buddhist living in Redigama, a roughly one-thousand-acre swath of land in Sri Lanka's Central Province, a small minority identify as Berava, while the vast majority identify as "highest caste," or Govigama (cultivator caste).[3] Ananda Coomaraswamy's (1908) early twentieth-century *Medieval Sinhalese Art* and oral history accounts from Redigama's current residents suggest that from at least the late nineteenth century until around the 1970s, the Berava of Redigama produced minimally decorated cotton material for local consumption while performing duties as ceremonial drummers and, like others in the area, engaging in paddy and chena cultivation—in seeming accordance with a popular and to some extent scholarly conviction that caste among the Sinhalese has waned to a point of irrelevance. However, since the 1970s, not only the Berava have been weaving Dumbara Rata textiles. Since that time, the extended kin network of individuals who separately own and manage several Dumbara Rata weaving workshops in Redigama have employed their relatively impoverished but high-caste neighbors in filling orders for decorative cotton wall hangings, cushions covers, table mats, and other items destined for high-end crafts emporia and handloom galleries in the island's more affluent urban centers. This industry arrangement has largely set the stage for the present contestation over Dumbara Rata.

To explain how Redigama's high-caste residents came to weave in the workshops of their low-caste neighbors, over the course of the twentieth century, and in particular following the country's political independence in 1948, governmental and nongovernmental initiatives to develop the rural economy have converged with interests—many of them expressly nationalistic—to promote the country's "arts and crafts." By the 1970s, the combination of a growing market for Dumbara Rata textiles following the sudden influx of foreign tourists to the island and Redigama's location in one the most economically vulnerable areas of the Mahaweli River basin positioned the village as one site of such convergence (Dowling 2000). The Sri Lankan government began funding training programs in and around Redigama in which self-described "highest-caste" men and women learned to weave under the instruction of their Berava neighbors. From 1972 until 1980, for instance, the Department of Small Industries funded a weaving training center in which every two years a group of ten students from the area learned to weave Dumbara Rata textiles from, at least initially, one of the then oldest members of the extended family that has historically dominated the industry. An early feud between two siblings belonging to this family over an order from a major buyer had helped solidify an arrangement by which members of the family managed separate workshops, catering to and vying for the business of different government and private dealers in Kandy and

Colombo. When private and government-owned shops in these two cities began increasing their orders for Dumbara Rata items in the early 1980s, newly trained, high-caste weavers were readily absorbed by the low-caste, family-owned workshops now struggling to keep up with demand.

According to all my interlocutors in Redigama, there has always been a certain competition among the village's Berava weavers, hereafter also referred to as "the family." Such business-oriented rivalry is reported to have become especially pronounced following the end of the country's nearly thirty-year war in 2009 when, according to some family members, a rebounding tourism industry and overall strengthening of the country's economy resulted in a tenfold increase in demand for Dumbara Rata textiles. When I first visited the village, narratives of such competition—including one about a man breaking into his cousin's workshop and, in a drunken, jealous rage, slashing the threads on her loom—were in wide circulation among the Berava. When I returned one year later in 2013, however, such narratives were almost entirely eclipsed by tales featuring a new antagonist: non-related workshop employees and others demanding the right to weave Dumbara Rata textiles independently of the family.

The general impetus for this shift from intra-family rivalry to tension between Berava family members and their high caste, non-relative neighbors is undoubtedly located in the postwar surge in demand for Dumbara Rata textiles and the perceived opportunity for economic gain. The more proximate cause, however, is the move by Redigama's high-caste weavers to actively pursue their interest in using the knowledge and skills they have acquired in training programs and as employees of their Berava neighbors to weave and conduct business independently or at least beyond the workshops of the latter. At the time of my visit in 2013, they found encouragement for these ambitions in at least some of the government-appointed poverty alleviation officers assigned to the area. It was in this context that their Berava neighbors reasserted their own claims over the industry in terms that, as we will see, would be discounted by the government officers as evidence of "narrow-minded" thinking.

Contention over Dumbara Rata Heritage

While the conversations I had with many in Redigama centered on the contestation over Dumbara Rata weaving, my own direct observations of the dispute were limited to the rare occasions on which the tension erupted publicly. One such occasion was in November of 2013, when Redigama's Samurdhi Program officer convened an annual meeting to elect the program's local governing board members for the coming year. The Samurdhi Program, a government microfinance scheme introduced in 1995 with the goal of eradicating rural poverty, has been reinvigorated as a result of its recent incorporation into Divi Neguma, a large-scale development initiative launched in 2011 to establish "one million household economic units" (MED 2013: 1). Alongside home gardening, fisheries, and animal husbandry, Divi Neguma's microfinance and infrastructure development programs have been oriented toward cottage industries, including the domestic production of handloom textiles.

On this particular day, I accompanied about thirty men and women, all qualifying as low-income earners and therefore eligible for Samurdhi funds, who had assembled to learn more about the programs that would be available to them in the coming year.[4] Gathered in the shade in front of the home in which the Samurdhi officer meets with residents during his weekly visits to Redigama, they inquired about support for home gardens, the use of Samurdhi funds to defray the costs of hospital visits, and how to galvanize participation in the village's defunct children's society. Twenty minutes into the meeting, a side conversation among a group of women abruptly escalated into a verbal scuffle between meeting attendees and Rukshan, a man belonging to the extended family of Berava weavers who own and manage the village's Dumbara Rata weaving workshops.

A suddenly nervous-looking Rukshan addressed the group of women sitting across from him: "If you all take loans to weave these textiles, then you all should demonstrate that you are doing them." A woman shot back, "Rukshan, people are not weaving alone! They are weaving for your family. You *know* that!" "Yes," agreed another, "we can take loans, Rukshan, but then we should have the right to weave alone. How can we pay back the loans when we are weaving for someone else?" After a moment, Rukshan declared with an air of uneasy confidence, "Everyone in the country knows that Dumbara Rata is *only* done in Redigama and that it is our *own* family who is doing it. Everyone in the world knows that."

To this, an outspoken woman in the audience replied, "But Rukshan, now there are a lot of people who *can actually do* Dumbara Rata. So, someone should go and say that there is no point in giving [government] funds because only one family is doing it! Why bother making proposals to develop the small industries?" Shouting in agreement, a middle-aged man agreed, "Now, *anyone* in the village can weave!" An elderly woman noted that a Dumbara Rata wall hanging at a bank in town had in fact been woven by a young man unrelated to the family. Rukshan rejected the suggestion and asked, "How could *he* have done that?" At this, a man in attendance gestured toward another sitting beside him and asked, "Now, if this man knows carpentry, does that mean that someone who works under him can't go and open up his own place to do carpentry?"

The argument that followed focused on whether Rukshan's family could rightfully prevent others from using Samurdhi loans to start their own weaving businesses and whether it was fair for the family members to take credit for textiles woven by their workshop employees. A rare public eruption of the tension to which the latter's attempts to capture the benefits of the industry's recent growth had given way, the exchange also signaled a productive point of friction between the two discourses to which the individuals involved appeal in laying claim to the knowledge entailed in Dumbara Rata weaving: that of tradition and identity on the one hand, and that of individual skill and equal opportunity on the other.

Nature, Nurture, and the Caste System

In Redigama, the conceptualization of authentic knowledge of weaving, including the manner in which it is obtained, is perhaps the fundamental point of contention between weavers who belong to the family and those who do not. To family members, knowledge regarding the local weaving industry is kept from "outsiders" such as their non-related, high-caste employees and neighbors in two primary ways. The first entails claiming an inherited or inborn ability (*pihitanawa*) held exclusively by individuals related to the family, and the second is active strategizing to withhold information from non-relative employees.[5] Both strategies involve a conviction that the authenticity of the relevant knowledge derives from its genealogical transmission and that the industry is safeguarded by this knowledge resting only with members of the family. By contrast, nonfamily members advocating for the right to weave independently of the various family-run workshops throughout Redigama stress individual talent, knowledge obtained through effort, and ensuring the perpetuation of Dumbara Rata by sharing that knowledge with anyone who desires to learn.

Dilini, a thirty-year-old mother of two, is one of the most outspoken defendants of the family's exclusive control over the Dumbara weaving industry and one of the harshest critics of those who challenge this control. Dilini began weaving in 2010, shortly after marrying the son of Bandula, a renowned weaver in Redigama and a prominent member of the extended family that controls the local industry. Two years later, when we met for the first time, she recounted how she gradually came to learn Redigama was known for the textiles produced there. Foreigners and Sri Lankans from other parts of the country would visit her father-in-law's workshop, she explained, inquiring about weaving techniques and eager to make purchases. In an early conversation at her home, Dilini noted with evident satisfaction that if a person outside her family attempted to start a Dumbara Rata business, it would fail. Initially, when I inquired as to why this might be the case, she said she was not sure. After a moment, however, she smiled and excitedly explained:

> Although others try to do it, they can't. Only members of the family inherit that ability ... Although others might invest and try to do this business, they can't do it. They can't. But if anyone in this family prepares to do it, they can go forward. It is only within this family. It's not outside.

The conviction that others "can't do it," as in, they are unable because they lack an "inherited ability," is one echoed by other family members in Redigama, but it is also one whose persuasive force is complicated by its rhetorical conflation with the idea that others "can't do it," as in, they are not permitted.

As Rukshan explained to me one afternoon in his workshop, "Whatever happens, whatever they try, we are *sure* that this business will not go outside the family." Attempts by "outsiders" to weave independently and develop their own businesses are bound to fail, he explained, because even if he and others in the family are generous with their knowledge, nonfamily members simply "don't have the talent." At the same time, Rukshan indicated there are limits to this conviction regarding others' lack in ability, recounting what happened recently when the suggestion arose that, in fact, they *can*:

> People are trying to do the business because this industry has a good market now. A few months back, there was a small issue of starting this business out in the village. We said, "if you all can, then try to do it," and we informed the Divisional Secretariat. This industry is reserved for our family. And we disagreed with it, and somehow it was stopped.

A moment later, he concluded, "Although they try to start this business, we believe that they can't carry on with it." There is an intriguing paradox in Rukshan's representation of his family's sole control over the industry—that is, this control's basis in an inherited and internal ability lacking in "outsiders" on the one hand and the felt imperative to prevent such individuals from compromising that control on the other. Relying on a notion of "inborn talent" exclusive to his relatives in order to explain and defend their domination of the industry is contradicted by a presumed need to appeal to government officials to actively prevent others from independently engaging in Dumbara Rata production. Despite the conviction that such businesses will fail because those who start them lack the proper skill, Rukshan suggests he and his family members must nonetheless actively interfere in order to ensure they do not succeed.

Rukshan thus reproduces a narrative of privileged, inherited knowledge in justifying his family's claims to Dumbara Rata weaving. Governmental and nongovernmental advocates, not to mention scholars, of Sri Lanka's "traditional arts" have long propelled the popularity of this narrative, which has also served centrally in the marketability of the textiles produced in Redigama's workshops. Today, however, Rukshan's extended family must reckon with an unexpected contender: the aforementioned government-sponsored program of rural poverty alleviation whose representatives publicly portray the family's wish to exclusively control the industry as expressive of "narrow-minded thinking" incompatible with Sri Lanka's status as a democracy. It is in meeting this challenge that Rukshan encounters the persuasive limits of the idea of an "inherited" or "inborn" ability. The inconsistency in his account is a consequence of this encounter and, as we will see, instantiates a more general pattern of ambivalence and contradiction in the accounts of both his relatives seeking to retain control over the industry and the nonrelatives seeking to weave independently.

Family members also explain their exclusive control over the local textile industry by reference to the active control of knowledge they strive to achieve in managing their businesses. Sitting alone at a loom in his empty workshop one morning, his arms and hands working furiously to complete an order, Bandula lamented to me that his former employees would prefer working in the paddy fields to weaving for him. Bemoaning the difficulty of traveling to collect materials, locating the exact color thread needed to complete a custom order, and, most importantly, setting the warp threads on the loom, he concluded the men and women who have worked for him in the past take his hard work for granted and are ungrateful of the fact that "all they have to do is sit and weave."

Bandula's narration of employer generosity sets a unique spin on a phenomenon that his relatives more commonly describe not as serving the interests of their employees but as necessary to ensuring that the industry does not "go out" from their family. If nonfamily members attempt to start a weaving business on their own, his brother later told me, "They don't know how to carry on because they don't know the basics. They just sit at the machine and do what we say, but they don't know what's really behind it . . . We tell them to sit on the machine and do something small but they don't know what's after that or before that." While more consistent with a philosophy of free and competitive production than the idea of kin-based, "inherited talent," this active control of knowledge is often explained alongside appeals to caste, a marker of difference about which weavers and others in Redigama express considerable ambivalence.

Sumal, one of the younger Berava weavers and workshop owners in the area, had been sharing his concerns about nonfamily members attempting to weave independently when I asked him whether this had been an issue in the past. He said it had not, so I asked why he thought it had recently become a point of contention. While his reply centered initially on how postwar growth in demand for Dumbara Rata textiles has driven his high-caste neighbors' desire to engage in the industry independently of is family, he dwelled at length on his perception that the desire is also motivated by a discomfort with the apparent social parity he and his family now enjoy. Whereas those who were involved in the industry were once "afraid to speak openly" when they felt slighted by their high-caste neighbors, Sumal explained, accepting "a small bribe" and keeping quiet, they are not so inhibited today. The present tension around Dumbara Rata weaving derived, in other words, from the fact that he and his relatives are neither fearful nor acquiescent in their interactions with the former. He went on to assert the industry is "inherited," which he presents as legitimation for his family's control of knowledge regarding Dumbara Rata production. While explicitly linking this mode of industry transmission to his family's caste status, and thereby demonstrating how caste difference may serve them, however, he complained to me of his former employees' problematic preoccupation with their own high caste status as driving the present threat to that control. To Sumal, this apparent preoccupation is inconsistent with their learning to weave from him and his relatives. He identified a concern with "pride" and a sense that "we are the highest caste" as underlying their increasing reluctance to work for their low-caste neighbors. Remarking that Dumbara Rata "is an inherited thing," he related, "we don't need to be at their feet to give the knowledge to them, and if they want to learn, they have to come to us."

Rather than emphasizing an "inborn ability" possessed exclusively by members of his extended family, Sumal thus centers his narrative around a tale of transformation from caste-based social vulnerability and compulsory deference to a position of advantage deriving from the exclusive possession of one critical asset: knowledge. Indeed, the imperative to withhold knowledge from employees and other "outsiders" has allowed him and his family members to benefit from the heightened postwar demand for Dumbara Rata textiles and, more generally, to achieve a social and economic position from which they may live "without fear" of their socially privileged neighbors. His account of socioeconomic improvement is common among the family members with whom I spoke. Bandula, for instance, once recounted how his ancestors would work in others' fields when they were small and that it is only because of this industry that he and his relatives have "become developed" and are now able to send their own children to good schools in Kandy. His neighbors, he explained, "are jealous of that development," thinking to themselves, "In the past, these people worked for us, so why should we now go and work under them?"

On an earlier occasion, Bandula had in fact complained that others in Redigama were not "free-minded" enough to work under individuals belonging to a lower caste. They are conservative, he reported, and thus keen to maintain a caste distinction. Yet, as we see in Sumal's words earlier, the suggestion that others are concerned about caste belies the extent to which caste-based identification also serves in the perpetuation of Bandula and his family members' control over the production of Dumbara Rata textiles in Redigama. At the same time Sumal laments, "some people here still have that caste problem," it is precisely by reiterating his own caste status that he aims to stake an unequivocal claim of ownership over the local weaving industry. When it comes to reckoning with "threats" to that industry in the form of potential competition from high-caste weavers trained, often, in their very own workshops, these men and their relatives leverage their identification as Berava. What is more, they arm themselves with a narrative in which it is precisely their overcoming a position of vulnerability imparted to them as members of a low caste that reinforces a sense that their exclusive ownership of the local textile production industry has been fairly earned.

Efforts to control or withhold knowledge and the notion of "inherited ability" are therefore central to the narratives in which family members explain and defend their control of Redigama's weaving industry. The manner in which their non-related, high-caste neighbors articulate their own claims regarding the production of Dumbara Rata is quite different, with one important qualification: in doing so, they too reinforce caste as a socially significant marker of identification. In discussions of the industry and in conversations more generally, Redigama's high-caste residents explicitly disavow the importance of caste in their own lives and are quick to lament its persistence as a carryover from an unenlightened past. Early on in my research, I naively expected nonfamily members, in their arguments for a more equitable distribution of control over the local textile industry, would affirm this position in order to explicitly undermine the family's claims of occupational exclusivity. I quickly realized, however, the purported disavowal of the contemporary relevance of caste was almost always immediately controverted by demonstrations of investment in its perpetuation.

The fortification of caste in family members' narratives of control over the local textile industry reinforces the notion of an intimate relation between a (Berava) self and a commitment to weaving that encompasses more than just the satisfaction of economic wants. To be Berava is to have an indisputable claim of ownership over the industry and, likewise, to have an indisputable claim of ownership over the industry is to be Berava. By contrast, the present reality of caste-based identification necessitates that the "highest-caste" individuals hoping to more directly reap the benefits of a growing demand for Dumbara Rata textiles couch their claims of over weaving knowledge in very different terms. In demanding the freedom to weave independently, these individuals highlight the wide and apparently "caste-blind" distribution of weaving knowledge, invoke individual skill rather than inherited ability, and insist family members are flagrantly selfish in their efforts to "keep the industry to themselves." In this circumvention of the language of tradition, heritage, and generation-to-generation transmission of knowledge, Redigama's low-income, high-caste weavers and others who sympathize with them maintain a safe distance from an industry they continue to associate with the low-caste status of their neighbors. Indeed, despite rejecting the latter's domination of that industry, they are also loath to claim the industry as their own. Doing otherwise would mean either compromising their own position as high caste or, by the same token, allowing their neighbors to forget their lowly position. Like the family members, then, these individuals come up against the uncomfortable resistance encountered in "trying to have it both ways." Whereas for the former this means facing the paradox that the growth of this "family-only" industry owes substantially to the effort of nonrelatives, for the latter, as the following shows, it has to do with keeping an arm's length between oneself and an industry over which one feels one has some claim.

Policing Dumbara Rata Production

To many of Redigama's high-caste residents, there is an indisputable contradiction in the family members' characterization of Dumbara Rata production as a "family-only" enterprise at the same time the majority (at least 60 percent) of their workforce is comprised of individuals with whom they have no kin-based relationship. In pointing out this contradiction, however, these individuals are also quick to acknowledge that, even though the family members hire "outsiders" like themselves to weave for them, they have never deliberately imparted their weaving knowledge to their employees. Yet, as the latter are often eager to point out, the family members' unwillingness to teach them has not prevented them from learning anyway, and it is precisely their experience of having learned despite this unwillingness that generates the legitimacy of the knowledge they claim as their own.

Danuka was born in 1980 and began weaving for one of the family members in Redigama when he was twenty years old. In 2007, with the assistance of his parents and siblings, he began preparing to launch his own Dumbara Rata weaving business. Members of the family reportedly responded with a heavy hand, physically confiscating looms Danuka had borrowed from one of their relatives while he was not at home and interfering in his ultimately failed attempt to secure a business loan from a local development bank collaborating with the Sri Lankan government to develop small industries. According to one rumor in circulation, family members had also used their long-standing connections with the shopkeepers from whom they purchased thread and other materials to thwart Danuka's and others' attempts at starting their own weaving businesses by interfering in sales.

Disheartened by the conflict to which his efforts had led, Danuka left Redigama and took a job in Colombo. In late 2013, however, he returned to the area to help care for his ailing mother. In the context of the recent government-sponsored effort to enable "outsiders" like him to weave independently of the family, he was reminded of the challenges he had faced earlier and was quick to highlight an incongruity he and others perceive in the family's claim of exclusive ownership over the production of Dumbara Rata textiles. He explained, "I don't know why they say that only they can do this. If only their family members can do it, then only *they* should weave! Not the others! But they hire employees." Danuka argued, even were one to set this contradiction aside, the family members' typical self-representation as the exclusive bearers of the knowledge and skill demanded of Dumbara Rata weaving is still erroneous: "When I was working there, I learned *everything* possible. Not only weaving, but also how to set the warp and how to adjust the reed. I learned all of the different thicknesses of the necessary threads and their types." Significantly, he added, "But they didn't teach me anything. I was watching."

Whereas Danuka is reluctant to involve himself in the present government-sponsored initiative to develop the local weaving industry, Uresha, a woman who reports a similar experience of learning despite not having been deliberately taught, has become one of the most outspoken critics of the family's resistance to others producing Dumbara Rata textiles. Uresha began weaving in a Redigama workshop in the early 1990s when she was twenty years old. After fifteen years, she took a position as a domestic worker in the Middle East to help pay for a surgery her husband required. In 2013, several years after returning home, she decided to begin weaving again not for the money, she stressed, her husband having by that time recovered and secured a relatively high-paying job with a foreign construction company, but for the pleasure it affords her. With money no longer being a pressing concern, Uresha took the opportunity to weave for a nearby government-owned weaving training center and workshop, which pays less for each item she weaves than do the privately owned workshops in Redigama. Despite the relatively modest pay, she reports a welcome feeling of independence and control over her own labor that was lacking in her experience as an employee of the family member for whom she wove in the past—to the dissatisfaction of the extended family of workshop-owning Berava weavers in Redigama. However, Uresha has eagerly met the government-owned workshop manager's requests for Dumbara Rata textiles.

As far as Uresha is concerned, the family's dissatisfaction with her decision to produce Dumbara Rata textiles despite not weaving in one of their workshops is unjustified. To her, the contradiction Danuka identifies in the family's claims to exclusive ownership over the industry and the fact of learning despite having not been taught provide firm justification for the rejection of any notion of "inherited skill" or commitment to a supposed generation-to-generation transmission of knowledge: "If I learned, it isn't their concern. Otherwise, they shouldn't take people from outside and teach them, right?" Later, she explained, "There is no such thing called *pihitanawa* [inherited skill]. My husband told me once, 'If you want our children to be in a good place, then we shouldn't cheat. We should teach others what we know.'" The following account of Uresha's submission of a Dumbara Rata wall hanging to a government-sponsored competition, a submission facilitated by the manager of the government-owned workshop and training center for which she now weaves, further illustrates the marked difference between this orientation to weaving knowledge and that espoused by the family members who claim exclusive authority over the production of these textiles.

In January 2014, I boarded a crowded bus in Redigama with Priyani, the manager of the small, government-owned weaving training center and workshop to which Uresha currently supplies Dumbara Rata textiles. Dressed in a crisp, cotton sari and burdened with a long reed wrapped in newspaper, Priyani carefully placed her unwieldy package on two large sacks of rice evidently headed in the same direction. Clinging to the bar above her head as the bus meandered along the winding road through the valley toward the training center, Priyani smiled and gestured toward the reed, explaining, "Uresha used it to weave a wall hanging for a recent government competition. I'm just taking it back to the workshop." Uresha's submission to the contest won the first award granted to a nonfamily member for a Dumbara Rata textile since the government competitions were introduced to the family in the mid-1970s, a fact that, while giving her great personal satisfaction, aroused the antipathy of several family members. Upon seeing Priyani, who had encouraged and arranged for Uresha's participation in the competition, walking along the main road that runs through Redigama a few days before our meeting, Himali, a member of the family, reportedly "scolded" her, shouting, "I heard what you have done. Don't weave Dumbara Rata! It is ours!"

As we exited the bus and ascended the steep, rocky path to the government-owned workshop that morning, Priyani described how this encounter had troubled her. She related that when she reported it to the Department of Textile Industries, they told her to ignore the family and to *just* weave Dumbara Rata items. While Priyani explained matter-of-factly that she would never be able to fulfill this order given the number of pieces the department actually requires each month and the relative difficulty of producing Dumbara Rata cloth, she was encouraged by the department's reaction in part because it supported her own assessment of the situation. Himali and her relatives' anger at Priyani for instructing the government-owned workshop trainees and employees to weave Dumbara Rata textiles derives, she explained, from a conviction that the industry belongs to their *paramparawa*, or lineage. Priyani argued that if their concern is truly about safeguarding the knowledge its propagation requires, as she believes it ought to be, then this fact is surely irrelevant. "Himali's reaction was unfair," she explained. "After we die, the things that we know die with us. So, to protect the things we know, we need to teach others!"

To Uresha and others in Redigama, there is an indisputable link between "development" (getting "to a good place"), generously sharing what one has mastered, and the protection of the knowledge entailed in Dumbara Rata weaving. Moreover, they suggest, to the extent that they are trained (intentionally or otherwise) in the workshops of the family members who dominate the local weaving industry, knowledge is largely indistinguishable from the skills they might acquire in any other context of instruction. As Gamini, Uresha's husband and a former employee of the family, explained to me: "If I go to an English or math class or some technical center and if I get trained in that subject and if I am really good at it, then I have a *right* to start that. The teacher can't say, 'You can't do that after I teach you this.'"

Caste, Status, and Economic Opportunity

According to this perspective, the knowledge and skill entailed in Dumbara Rata weaving may "belong" to anyone to do with as they choose. Despite this viewpoint bolstering the demands of those beyond the family to weave independently, those who advance it do tend to do so only up to a point beyond which, as suggested, they run the risk of compromising their own caste-based superiority. To make sense of this and, by extension, to better appreciate the stakes of working "under" those historically regarded as one's social inferiors or superiors, we must consider the more general contradiction that characterizes the discursive handling of caste in Redigama more generally. To offer an example, remarking on the economic success that Redigama's Berava weavers have met in recent years and on its transformation of intercaste relations in the area, Aruna, a farmer and bank employee, shared:

> Some of our [high-caste] people will go to them [a member of the family] to borrow money. They say, "Give me five hundred rupees or a thousand rupees." After that, that person will ignore the higher-caste person's status, so it's like that per-

son is at a higher status. The caste matter will be the only thing between them . . . Our people go there and do things like that [ask for money]. Not *my* family. But there are other people who do it. Because of that, caste is decreasing. They are even going and working in their fields, so no one cares about [caste] now.

While Aruna explains caste's declining importance in Redigama as stemming from the Berava weavers' new financial wherewithal vis-à-vis their high-caste neighbors, he is quick to point out that his *own* family does not engage in the small loan transactions that account for this transformation. Moreover, he suggests, even and perhaps especially when it comes to collaboration in paddy work, it is hardly the case that "no one cares" about caste.

When I interrupted to ask about the consequences he might face were he to receive food or drink from his low-caste neighbors, Aruna offered a personal anecdote remarkable for its subtle but striking inconsistency. Explaining that caste is a "culture that comes from the kings' time" and cannot be changed, he made (and in the same breath invalidated) an assertion of the irrelevance of caste in his own life:

> In this area, also, there is a lower-caste person. Their house is nearby. He had a position three grades above mine at the bank where I used to work. He retired as the area manager. He came one day and asked me, "Aruna, how can I invite you to my wedding?" We worked in the same department in the same company . . . After that, he gave me the invitation card. So, I went to the wedding. The wedding was in Colombo, and all of these [low-caste] people were also there. Our participation is a big thing for people like them. When they came back, they told the others that I was at the wedding. I don't care because I ate the hotel food. So, caste is not a problem for me.

In this conversation, Aruna reported to be pleased with his low-caste neighbors' economic success, remarking, "Now, *our* people are at the same level that we've always been at, but they have developed, and I'm proud about that." To a limited extent, this avowed pride is matched by appreciation he expressed for an apparent relaxation of the rules governing caste-based commensality in urban Colombo.

Yet the professed insignificance of caste as "not a problem" for Aruna, something he illustrates in narrating his willing attendance at his neighbor's wedding, is controverted by the qualification that he "ate the hotel food," or, in other words, upheld those very rules in order to avoid any confusion (perhaps his, perhaps others') as to his own caste status. The importance of doing so, as far as Aruna and other high-caste individuals in the area are concerned, was conveyed to me when I asked why he believes people are unable to change the caste "culture" to which he referred. In a move generally coincident with such expressions of anti-caste sentiment, Aruna attributed this inability to *others'* dominant thinking on the matter, explaining that the chief consequence of "eating and drinking with them" is the knowledge that other high-caste residents of the village will subsequently judge them for it. While stressing that the phenomenon is limited to the village so that, when elsewhere, they "go to [low-caste people's] places and... eat and drink with them without doing any bad things," he explained, "we can't do such things inside the village because of those people who think like that."

The threat of social ostracism that Aruna voices reportedly weighs heavily in the minds of many past and present high-caste weavers in Redigama. Inoka, a former employee of a family member, explained, "If I go there and drink and eat, *I'll* be neglected by *my* people. If someone sees that we are eating or drinking there, it will create problems for us. If someone from their family comes to my home, I serve them tea, but if I do the same thing at their places, it will be a problem." Uresha, Inoka's sister-in-law, conveyed the same, noting, "Normally, when we go to work under them, we're ignored [*ayin kerenewa*] by our own family members."

Tharanga, who has been weaving for the family for many years, offered a unique exception to this reported fear of derision for breaching the conventional rules of intercaste relations. Rather than lament his reliance on the family and the potential criticism he might suffer for his decision to work "under" them, he professed a disregard for caste, noting it is something he and his wife "don't think about" since, as he put it, "We are all humans, right?" As he explained one afternoon during a break from work:

> We're getting [money] from there, right? We think in terms of Buddhism; we don't think like that. People have different attitudes. Because we have our name, people have this idea that we are good [high caste]. We of course don't care about it... Others don't have my thoughts... Other people don't rely on them, right? That's what I think. It's not a problem for me.

To Tharanga, weaving for one of the workshop owners and accepting payment in return is consistent with his self-proclaimed thinking as a Buddhist. In his estimation, Buddhist thinking and the recognition that "we are all humans" run up against the notion that caste is important. Suggestions to the contrary would render his "getting something from there" unacceptable. As far as he is concerned, even his own high-caste name is irrelevant. While it may or may not fully explain Tharanga's unique adamancy about the non-importance of caste, it is worth noting he also reports feeling a significant dependence on the family for the employment they have provided him. Interestingly, his rhetorical query—"Other people don't rely on them, right?"—suggests others' relative autonomy from the family might explain their "perspective" on the matter.

While past and present workshop employees are in agreement with Tharanga that they are "getting something from there," they typically leave it at that, thus signaling the central dilemma whose resolution, from the position of non-Berava weavers, is aided most strongly by the language of competitive individualism and of skill / knowledge-based "rights" to this productive activity. In general, the fear of social ostracism by (caste-wise) equally positioned friends and relatives is prevalent and is likely why nonfamily members often emphasize their engagement in the industry as strictly "for the money."

The significance of this trend is most striking when observed alongside the manner in which members of the family who control Dumbara Rata production in Redigama explain their relationship to the industry. For them, as suggested earlier, caste is a double-edged sword, the idea that most compellingly establishes their ownership over Dumbara Rata production even as it may undercut their aspirations for social equality with their high-caste neighbors. The assumption that the industry's continuation rests in its generation-to-generation transmission is reinforced by many (but, importantly, not all) of the government officials with whom Redigama's Berava weavers interact and who encourage them to "carry on" even when demand for their textiles declines. The following excerpt from an interview with Rohan, one of the younger male weavers in the family, demonstrates this professed nonmonetary dimension of the commitment to weaving. Explaining why they "carry on" with the industry despite feeling that the profit is insufficient given how "tirelessly" they work, he related:

> Even though it's not like the other businesses, we have some status [*samanye tatweya*]. This is what we're used to. Compared to doing something new, it's our identity [*ananyataaweyak tiyenewa*]. It's the thing we desire. So, somehow we are pulling it along. Government departments and people here and there tell us not to stop doing this because it has a huge value [*loku watinakamak*]. They say, "Don't stop this. Teach this to your children." . . . So, at times when the profit isn't good, that's why we continue to do it and don't abandon it.

High-caste weavers in Redigama face something approximating the inverse of this dilemma: they must find a way to establish their own claims over the industry while keeping it "at arm's length." Many of them do so by underscoring that they weave not because of a conviction that it is their "identity" but out of sheer financial necessity.

Kamini, born in 1956, recounted the painful and somewhat desperate circumstances that once impelled her to weave for the family. Despite having passed her A-levels, an accomplishment she asserts "was really quite something" in those days, she was unable to secure a job, and the money her husband earned in the military, a job that required his absence for extended stretches at a time, was insufficient to provide for their children's education. When her children were older, it was the "caste problem" and the sense that she had failed to live up to her own potential that drove her to stop weaving. Kasun, a subsistence farmer, weaver, and father of four children, narrated his involvement in the industry in comparable but more succinct terms, exclaiming, "We are not idiots. We do this because we don't have anything else to do!" His brother, Aruna, eagerly elaborated, "It's the low-caste people who are doing that business. The upper-caste people go and weave under them, but that is to earn a living."

The claims that Redigama's high-caste residents make over the Dumbara Rata industry are qualified, then, by the assertion that one's right to weave, and the decision to do so, derives from the conviction that one's skills, however acquired, may be justifiably used to meet one's financial needs. In this respect, a vehemence about wanting to weave that might otherwise be taken as an admission of an intimacy with the industry—one comparable to that proclaimed by their Berava neighbors—is tempered by the assertion that high-caste involvement in Dumbara Rata production is, at the end of the day, "just to earn."

Importantly, government officials tasked with the promotion of the Divi Neguma program offer a powerful and public legitimation of this perspective, acknowledging the industry's apparently indisputable origins while framing the argument for a more even distribution of its economic benefits in terms of national development and democratic ideals. In a February 2014 meeting convened by such officials to discuss the program in relation to the future of the local weaving industry, for instance, one individual thus addressed the half-dozen family members in attendance:

> If the business only stays with the family—I mean, today, people's heads aren't filled with social differences between people. Today, people are struggling to do any kind of job they can . . . I appreciate the idea of not stealing others' heritage. I appreciate that idea and I think it will be there forever. Others cannot grab the craft and say that they are the ones who have inherited it. But with all of your help, and with their ability, the village will develop . . . I think we all need to get there by working together in this market as one and not thinking in a narrow-minded way.

In an oblique reference to caste ("social differences") and its popular condemnation as something with which people trying to earn a living *today* are not concerned, the officer publicly denounces the apparently anachronistic influence of a hierarchy that, as we have seen, continues to weigh on the minds of Redigama's residents.

Caste-based occupational exclusivity not only serves centrally in the family's claims of ownership over the industry but also informs the manner in which those contesting these claims articulate their own relationship to it. The officer's colleague from the local Divisional Secretariat office went somewhat further. He explicitly characterized such "narrow-minded" thinking as not only antithetical to Sri Lanka's status as a democratic country but also as suppressive of "Sinhala-ness," a quality he portrays as rooted in harmonious living and collective sacrifice for the country:

> Sri Lanka is a democratic country, and anyone can start a business if he has the potential. If someone can weave cloth, that is *their* skill ... If someone learns from your lineage [*paramparawa*], that skill belongs to him or her ... We are a great race/nation [*usas jaatiyak*]. We have to awaken our Sinhala-ness [*Sinhala kama*] and continue this. People in this village have sacrificed their lives for the nation, so we have to do these things harmoniously ... We have to forget ethnic differences and other shortcomings [*addu padu*] ... These people [referring to the family] and their forefathers have brought this industry up to the present, and they are respected for that. That won't change. [Addressing members of the family:] A new community has been formed through you and they take your advice, so you can be proud of that. If the production grows, the demand will also grow, and the market will expand. So, get rid of this narrow-minded thinking. That's what you can offer society. That is the biggest gift that your lineage can give.

Like the non-Berava weavers who hope to gain greater control over their own participation in Dumbara Rata production in Redigama, this official and his fellow officer are unequivocal about the industry being "inherited" by the family members. Taking this as a justification for the industry's control by the family, however, is not only just as quickly rejected as "narrow-minded," but also, significantly, regarded as detrimental to "the nation."

The national sacrifice to which the officer refers was an event about which many of Redigama's high caste residents had been particularly talkative in the months leading up to the meeting. In late November, the government sponsored a ceremony to commemorate the 196th death anniversary of Weera Keppetipola, leader of the ultimately unsuccessful 1817–1818 Uva-Wellassa Uprising against the British. Individuals from Redigama had reportedly participated in the rebellion, and several of their descendants, all of whom are high caste, had been invited to the recent ceremony to receive awards in their honor. The officer's timely invocation of the uprising in this context was apparently intended to remind meeting attendees, and in particular members of the family who were present, that the "nation" trumps all other kinds of social difference. Preoccupations with the latter were deemed "shortcomings" that both stand in the way of poverty alleviation and prevent the actualization of "Sinhala-ness."[6]

Concluding Remarks

Writing with respect to India, Soumhya Venkatesan laments, "the loss of traditional craft is the loss of the nation's and humankind's heritage," and suggests "development is one way to protect" it (2009: 8). As we have seen in Redigama, however, the positive trajectories of "development" and "traditional craft" are not so straightforwardly conjoined. Rather, we find something approximating the difficulty to which Lowenthal (1998: 227) refers when he notes that "too much is asked of heritage" when we attempt to balance an orientation to "national patrimony, regional and ethnic legacies," and the development and stewardship of a "global heritage shared and sheltered in common." In Redigama, a comparable tension is signaled by the assertion of the above-quoted government officers that Dumbara Rata weaving *cannot* be "grabbed" from those who claim lineage-based proprietorship over it, and at the same time that the goal is nonetheless to "spread" the industry out. This contradiction mirrors the conflict between, on the one hand, assertions on the part of high caste weavers and their sympathizers that, in order to properly steward Dumbara Rata, the knowledge and skill entailed therein must be imparted to anyone interested in learning, and, on the other, assertions on the part of the Berava family members that the industry is their "identity." While neoliberal notions of commercial freedom and competitive individualism, notions that share a certain resonance with the idea of "global heritage," arguably allow Redigama's poor, high-caste residents to claim a certain right to the industry, the avowed commitments of Berava weavers to the industry's "inherited" quality and to the "identity" that Dumbara Rata textiles reportedly mirror back at them serve centrally in their resistance to such claims.

As we have seen on both sides of this dispute, articulating a position of control with respect to the industry is also an opportunity for the reassertion of difference along caste lines. It is important to highlight, however, that only one "side" is called out, as in the meeting described earlier, for seeming to cling to caste as a category of identification, which as we'll recall is publicly disavowed in Sri Lanka. The industry's de facto owners, evoking something akin to the communalistic approach to "heritage" identified by Lowenthal, have positioned themselves in this struggle as the sole and lineage-based proprietors of an ancient and "family-only" weaving tradition. Yet the celebration that might attend "regional and ethnic legacies" elsewhere is not to be found when it comes to caste. Here, claims that manifest publicly as caste-interested are condemned as "selfish" and "narrow-minded."

Those contesting their Berava neighbors' efforts at exclusive control over Dumbara Rata are limited in the terms with which they may assert rights over the industry without compromising their privileged social position. Eschewing language suggestive of personal or collective intimacy with their livelihood, they find a certain advantage in appealing to neoliberal notions of economic freedom and competitive individualism. In thus framing the discussion of knowledge and skills entailed in Dumbara Rata, they justify their demands to weave independently while sidestepping the suggestion that their actions may be motivated by a "narrow-minded" concern with caste—even though, as we have seen, caste-based concerns *do* shape the manner in which they position themselves in relation to the industry.

Those who have historically controlled and benefited most from the industry, by contrast, are publicly portrayed as narrow-minded, anti-democratic, and generally hostile to an ostensibly common national goal of developing the *country's* "heritage" for global enjoyment and consumption. While drawing on ideas ("tradition," "heritage," "identity") central to a "discursive field of heritage" (Smith 2006: 42) out of which much of the perceived value of Dumbara Rata textiles derives, they inadvertently reiterate their ultimate disadvantage when it comes to a category of identification that, while publicly rejected, continues to shape social relations among the Sinhalese. Subject to the criticism that they have failed to "awaken" their "Sinhala-ness," they have yet to call upon an ideology that might successfully rival that upon which their high-caste neighbors draw.

There is some indication that this may change. Toward the end of my stay in Redigama, one family member told me he and his relatives had decided to form an association and, using a phrase I had not encountered in my conversations with them, perhaps consult a lawyer in the hopes of securing protection for their "intellectual property" (*buddhimaya deepala*). Deploying the legal framework of the same (idealized) neoliberal forms invoked by their neighbors, he and his relatives might thereby position themselves on the same playing field as those who have challenged their historical control over Dumbara Rata. Should they do so, one could imagine a situation in which their claims on the industry might not be disregarded so easily as demonstrative of "narrow-minded" thinking.

Aimée Douglas (PhD, Cornell University, 2017) is a sociocultural anthropologist and has been visiting and conducting anthropological research in Sri Lanka since 2005. Originally from Maryland, she completed a BA in psychology at Bowdoin College in 2005 and an MA in social sciences from the University of Chicago in 2007. Her MA thesis, "Nation-Building in Web Presentation: The Online Movement for Tamil Eelam," examined the electronically mediated strategies by which Sri Lanka's separatist Liberation Tigers of Tamil Eelam sought to garner nationalist sentiment among Sri Lankans in diaspora. Motivated by issues of difference and belonging, heritage politics, and neoliberal development processes, she examines in her more recent work the ways caste as a category of identification is reproduced among Sinhalese in Sri Lanka. At Cornell, her research and training were supported by the Foreign Language and Area Studies Fellowships Program, the Fulbright US Student Program, the American Institute for Sri Lankan Studies, and the Wenner-Gren Foundation.

NOTES

1. See, for instance, the anthropologist Soumhya Venkatesan's (2009) work on the discursive construction of "craft community" and its obfuscation of the varied interests, capacities, and projects of individual producers.
2. To preserve the anonymity of the sources, this chapter uses pseudonyms for the village (Redigama) and all individuals quoted and mentioned throughout the text.
3. Approximately 3 percent of Sri Lanka's Sinhalese population is identified as Berava (Silva et al. 2009: 32).
4. At the time, individuals earning a monthly income of less than SLR 4,000 (approximately $30) qualified as "low income."
5. In contemporary Sri Lanka, practices resembling the latter strategy are more generally referred to, and disparagingly so, as *guru musthtiya*, or the tendency for a teacher to deliberately reserve some knowledge from an apprentice or pupil.
6. The officer's stressing the importance of setting aside "ethnic differences" is of course more than a little ironic given the overall ethno-nationalist tone of his message.

REFERENCES

Andanda Pamela. 2012. "Striking a Balance between Intellectual Property Protection of Traditional Knowledge, Cultural Preservation and Access to Knowledge." *Journal of Intellectual Property Rights* 17 (6): 547–558. http://nopr.niscair.res.in/handle/123456789/15023.

Canclini, Néstor García. 1995. *Hybrid Cultures: Strategies for Entering and Leaving Modernity*. Minneapolis: University of Minnesota Press.

Coomaraswamy, Ananda K. 1908. *Mediæval Sinhalese Art*. Broad Campden: Essex House Press.

Coombe, Rosemary J., and Lindsay M. Weiss. 2015. "Neoliberalism, Heritage Regimes, and Cultural Rights." In *Global Heritage: A Reader*, ed. Lynn Meskell, 43–69. Chichester: Wiley-Blackwell.

Dowling, Ross. 2000. "Sri Lanka and the Maldives: Overview." In *Tourism in South and Southeast Asia: Issues and Cases*, ed. Colin Michael Hall and Stephen Page, 233–234. Oxford: Butterworth Heinemann.

Lowenthal, David. 1985. *The Past Is a Foreign Country*. Cambridge: Cambridge University Press.

———. 1998. *The Heritage Crusade and the Spoils of History*. Cambridge: Cambridge University Press

MED (Ministry of Economic Development). 2013. *Performance Report*. Colombo: MED. https://www.parliament.lk/uploads/documents/paperspresented/performance_report_ministry_of_economic_development_2013.pdf.

Silva, Kalinga Tudor. 2015. "Caste, Craft and Traditional Knowledge in Sri Lanka." In *Traditional Knowledge and Traditional Cultural Expressions of South Asia*, ed. Sanjay Garg, 248–257. Colombo SAARC Cultural Centre (Proceedings of the Seminar on Traditional Knowledge, Organized, 29–30 April 2013, Colombo).

Silva, Kalinga Tudor, P. P. Sivapragasam, and Paramsothy Thanges. 2009. *Casteless or Caste-Blind? Dynamics of Concealed Caste Discrimination, Social Exclusion, and Protest in Sri Lanka*. Copenhagen: International Dalit Solidarity Network.

Smith, Laurajane. 2006. *Uses of Heritage*. London: Routledge.

Venkatesan, Soumhya. 2009. *Craft Matters: Artisans, Development, and the Indian Nation*. New Delhi: Orient Blackswan.

CHAPTER 7

Heritage Activism and the Media (Framing) in Iran, 2005–2013
Ali Mozaffari

This chapter examines some of the significant themes in heritage that have emerged through interactions between various players—activists and non-activists—in Iran during Mahmoud Ahmadinejad's presidency (2005–2013). Furthering my previous work on Iranian heritage activism (Mozaffari 2015, 2016a, 2016b), here I focus on tracing recurring themes that appear in examples of written communications issued by heritage activists and their audiences, including both ordinary people and powerful officials such as politicians and heads of institutions. I examine these examples as representations of heritage activism in mass media, which form part of a repertoire of contention (Tilly and Wood 2015: 3–4). Using a theatrical metaphor, Charles Tilly (1993: 264–65) defines a repertoire as "a limited set of routines [emerging from struggles] that are learned, shared, and acted out through a relatively deliberate process of choice" and a repertoire of contention as "the established ways in which pairs of actors make and receive claims bearing on each other's interests." Repertoires change historically and from place to place (Tilly 2006: 35) and they (largely) follow established patterns and social know-how (Tilly 1993: 265).

To reveal the direction and major characteristics of Iranian heritage activism in this period, I examine the content of these examples against the context within which each is made.[1] While it is recognized that the media (as the means of communication and dissemination) itself influences the production of heritage, media representations (the symbolic content and form of the message conveyed) in their own right influence the making of heritage by virtue of the frames that emerge from them. In media jargon, "framing is a concept that refers to the selection of words, topics, and ideas in communication and the effects of these selections on public opinion" (Ben-Porath 2009).

While framing is regularly practiced in all kinds of media outlets, I will be using the concept as deployed in social movements to designate their importance to processes of making and communicating heritage through media representations. In this sense, and borrowing from movements theory, "framing" refers to the evolving process of constructing meanings and realities by activists to communicate, justify, and direct their actions (Benford and Snow 2000: 614). Framing transactions are affected by the "media norms and practices and the broader political culture in which they operate" wherein certain actors receive a higher standing and their ideas and language more readily circulated, therefore finding greater favor (Gamson and Wolfsfeld 1993: 119). Additionally, this framing and its dissemination through media suggest the locus of power is not fixed within an institution or class; rather, it is negotiated and produced through the circulation of language and "symbolic codes" that are dispersed in various social fields, as well as "forms of regulation" (Melucci 1996). From this perspective, the texts examined here are not passive products of a heritage discourse. They emerge from developments on the ground but also shape exchanges and the scope of the heritage activism that proceeds from them.

Although fragmented and multiple, culture has "an element of strategy and power" (Jasper 2010: 71). As James Jasper (2010: 72–75) points out, cultural meanings are carried through both tangible and intangible, permanent and fleeting carriers. Examples include words, speeches, jokes, images, lifestyles, music and performance, rituals and theater, people, buildings and memorials. In the following, I focus on statements as intangible carriers of culture. My starting point is that heritage is negotiated through and across boundaries of power and through the actions of multiple players. Activism is part of this negotiation process and therefore the relationship between representations of activism in the media, on the one hand, and how these representations are a part of the production of heritage, on the other, is worthy of examination. To this end, I examine the media examples from two angles: first, I establish the type of media and the representations contained, and second, I examine how these representations participate in the production and transformation of heritage.

Activism pertains to public participation, contestation of power, and, at times, contentious politics. These are present in Iranian heritage activism of this period in various forms. However, because of the circumstances of the Iranian public sphere and the presence of various and shifting state-imposed "red lines" for expression and protest, the general scope and expression of activism may take particular forms to avoid undue harm or hardship to activists (this is known in social movements research as political opportunity structures (Tarrow 1994)).² In other words, direct protest and contentious politics within the public sphere are the exception rather than the norm. Other actions, such as engaging with the media, are more often construed as a means of informing the public and directing the debate. It is precisely in this latter capacity that media pieces (the representations) actively participate in the formation of heritage. Their analysis also helps in understanding recurring themes and concerns in activism, as well as its areas of focus. Reviewing these examples, while indicating the shifting limits of the Iranian public sphere, illustrates the correlation between external events and activist responses. It can illustrate the way heritage is constructed and, more importantly, felt and experienced (and, at least publicly, performed). Additionally, this provides a perspective about the mechanisms of operation and concerns of heritage activists in Iran. It indicates how activists frame their position in relation to the political opportunities of the day and, more importantly, indicate the possible cultural tropes to which they appeal without falling foul of the state.

To conduct the analysis, I refer to publicly available (until 2018) declarations, blog entries, and news items. The focus here is not on acts of engaging and transforming the media itself, as would be the case in media democratization activism and the direct reporting of contentious politics.³ Rather, I seek to find common threads of representation, making heritage frames and similar sentiments that run across these public statements. These in turn illustrate the kinds of expressions permitted, making the media items an active participant in the process. While they reveal broad ideological inclinations or sensibilities, such as a prevalent sense of patriotism (Mozaffari 2015, 2017), they also reveal modes of legitimation, moral positioning, and the recruitment tactics utilized by activists. As pointed out, in this process, media representation is an active participant in the construction of heritage and its social workings. For the purposes of analysis, I examine the archives of two significant heritage NGOs, the Cultural and Natural Heritage Watch, based in Tehran, and Taryana, based in Khuzestan Province in southwestern Iran.⁴ The focus is around two specific construction events: a dam and metro lines. To situate the examples discussed here, I have also examined the same texts and other related material received from the archives of the secretary of Cultural and Natural Heritage Watch in Iran (in 2015), Alireza Afshari.

The following argument is organized into three parts. First, and without claiming an exhaustive review, I outline approaches to the representation of heritage contestation in the media to ascertain the state of current scholarship in this regard. This brief examination will reveal that, insofar as heritage is concerned, the topic is in its infancy, and the media has been used as raw material in discourse analysis but not sufficiently in the case of newspapers (although Smith (2006) does refer to their role), often with the assumption that the media is the mouthpiece of the establishment. Given the focus on the contentious politics of heritage, here I will also draw on the lessons learned from media and activism relationship in social movements. Second, I briefly outline the shifts between state and society in Iran. This is important for contextualizing the examples and the general environment within which Iranian heritage activism operates. Finally, I examine a select sample of declarations and media releases as examples for activism and its representations. These involve both electronic media (blogs and mailing lists) and official newspapers. In conclusion, I will offer my observations on the role of media and heritage activism in the Iranian context.

Cultural Heritage, Contestation, and the Media

The media is an important means of expression for movements and activists, but, as a review of heritage literature reveals, current heritage literature pays limited attention to heritage activism and contestation through the media and the media's role in that process.[5] To address this, I draw on developments in the field of social movements to examine the media activities of heritage activists. I posit the media representations as a manifestation of a broader frame and the media platforms (including blogs) as one of the significant arenas (see chapter 1 for this definition) in which various players engage in the process of producing and contesting heritage. Here my focus is more on one side of the media—the contests leveled by activists—as the other side (the state) was engaged less in direct media disputes and more on reactions to the media content and exercises of authoritative power.

Contested Heritage and the Media

In the existing scholarship, the emancipatory potentials of media in facilitating divergent claims to identity are recognized, yet, in the end, according to Laurajane Smith (2006: 127–278), it is authorized heritage discourse (AHD) that suppresses such potentials. Smith notes that the rise of political and environmental awareness since the 1960s was facilitated by access to, and dissemination through, a diverse range of media platforms. Heritage, she argues, is, "a useful discourse through which to make sense of, regulate and ultimately control the increasing public emergence of local and competing claims to a range of cultural, social, historical and other identities and experiences" (298). Even as the media reflects performances and encourages visitations to heritage sites, in the overall narrative of Smith's book, ultimately what is represented as heritage in the media remains in line with an expert-driven discourse, the AHD. The issue here is power asymmetries embedded in media-society relations, which is also a concern of movements scholars (e.g., Carroll and Ratner 1999). Overemphasizing the notion of an authorized discourse can lead to an assumption that people and activists are passive recipients of a given discourse and denies their agency. However, noting that a significant driver for the cultural turn in movement studies has been "inserting agency ... into models dominated by structures and functions" (Jasper 2010: 71), the examples I present here problematize this assumption.

Regarding the role of media in heritage, a growing body of scholarship focused on new technologies is beginning to address the creation, valorization, preservation or conservation, management, and dissemination of various forms of heritage.[6] While there is little focus on the contestation of heritage and its relationship with the media, the literature regarding participatory potentials of new technologies contains useful insights. Elisa Giaccardi, for example, argues social media facilitate the growth of a participatory culture, which allows for a diversity of content, affiliation, "expression, collaboration, and distribution" (2012: 27). This type of media allows for repetition (which constructs memory) and ongoing interactions that incorporate heritage processes in people's everyday lives. It can mitigate the restrictive potentials of official heritage discourses and thus problematize the assumed relationship between the AHD and the media. This mitigating potential still needs examination but from the outset appears to be related to ideas of civil society in relation to media.

While useful, the current heritage literature suffers from three shortcomings in this regard. First, analysis as to how heritage dissent and activism plays out in the media, new or old, is lacking. Second, while the mass media usually represents "the establishment," it is not totally closed to dissenters. It follows that the media itself does more than mere representation; arguably, it shapes, and thus actively participates in, the production of heritage, yet that heritage is not always "authorized." Third, while new media has significant potential, in conducting heritage research, focusing on one type of media risks producing a distorted image. However, the latter is mitigated by the increasing availability of various media across platforms. Movement theories have engaged with similar problems (media–social movements problems), and it is useful to draw on their observations in examining heritage activism in the media.[7]

Social Movements and the Media: Or, What Can We Learn from Social Movements Theory?

To mobilize, most social movements must reach their constituency, in part through some form of public discourse. While this is possible in some measure through a movement's own publications and meetings, to reach a broad audience beyond their own group, a mass media discourse is necessary. Nevertheless, "movements often have a distinctive and evolving culture that may, in various ways, conflict with media and mainstream political culture" (Gamson and Wolfsfeld 1993: 115). Smith's misgivings about mainstream media are echoed by some activists and movements theorists. The media and movements have an asymmetrical relationship: the media can choose to designate an issue as newsworthy and give voice to it and its activists through mass communication, but activists have few options beyond mass media to reach the public (Carroll and Ratner 1999). It is possible that activists within social movements often view the mainstream media as agents of the dominant groups they are challenging and not as neutral or autonomous. They see the media as maintaining and reproducing the status quo, a target for activism as much as a means of communication (Gamson and Wolfsfeld 1993: 119).

Nevertheless, media recognition can validate a movement, which will affect its standing and capacity to influence public opinion and to recruit and mobilize members (Andrews and Caren 2010; Gamson and Wolfsfeld 1993: 116). Arguably, this can influence the direction and leadership of a movement, as well as its ability to attract further resources. The media can also influence tactical and strategic choices and policy processes in a movement. The relationship between media and social movements is dynamic as they mutually, albeit unevenly, affect one another (Andrews and Caren 2010). Since mass media is not the only means of communication for activists, it is important to consider that a more comprehensive analysis would include more than one player and (as much as possible) a "repertoire of communication" (Mattoni 2013) involving various forms of mass media, blogs, and social networking (e.g., Facebook; see chapter 3).[8]

A longitudinal examination of media penetration and the importance of a movement or activism in a location is a useful means of analyzing the interplay between social movements processes to make sense of how specific combinations of the structures of the media, discourse, and organization emerge in social movements (Mattoni and Treré 2014, after Steinberg 2004: 125). The case studies presented here also show that, as in other movements, symbolic contests can be carried out within the arena of media output (Gamson and Wolfsfeld 1993: 118). However, the media structure, their inclinations, and their platform do, in turn, influence possibilities for engagement and representation, creating heritage frames. This is particularly pertinent to the Iranian example.

Heritage Activism, Negotiating Identity, and the Media in Iran

Political theory positions the media as being, ideally, distinct from the apparatuses of the state (Fraser 1997: 70, quoted in Carroll and Hackett 2006: 98). It also positions the public sphere as fragmented and resembling "a network of groups and individuals who act as citizens" (Emirbayer and Sheller 1999: 156, quoted in Carroll and Hackett 2006: 98). However, the public sphere in Iran only corresponds with this theoretical model in its fragmentation and fluidity. Instead, the state's controlling "red lines" change according to domestic and international circumstances and the balance of factional powers within state apparatuses.[9] Recent changes, especially during the past two decades, are useful considerations in a discussion on heritage activism and their expressions of collective identity.

In the early decades of the twentieth century, heritage in Iran was organized, purposive, and incorporated within the state agenda by a group of patriotic elites with a nationalist agenda suited to their time. Between the advent of the Iranian Revolution in 1979 and the early 1990s, homeland in Iran was reframed in Islamist terms, excluding pre-Islamic identities, but this had numerous contradictory strands (Mozaffari 2014). Heritage discourse in this period aimed to control emotions and engagements with the past, legitimizing hegemonic identities, focusing on Islamic sites and religious practices. The new dominant ideology reconceptualized heritage, with the Islamic taking precedence over the pre-Islamic (Mozaffari 2015, 2016b). In the atmosphere of the Iran-Iraq War (1980–1988), versions of Islamic heritage were promoted, controlled, and sanctioned by the state, leaving limited space or popular interest for heritage activism. After this period, manifest state factionalism, the need for postwar reconstruction, and a degree of economic liberalism saw an opening of the public sphere. People, especially the youth, were encouraged to engage in certain aspects of public discourse (Holliday 2013; Tazmini 2009). Arts, culture, and heritage issues became part of public discourse leading to the dichotomy between Islamic and pre-Islamic heritage being downplayed. This paved the way for citizens outside the establishment to engage in debates about history, heritage, and national identity (Mozaffari 2016b). This composite idea of collective and national identity became an accepted part of official discourse, lasting to the present. However, during Ahmadinejad's terms in office (2005–2013) the already-evolving relationship between Islamic and pre-Islamic aspects of collective identity shifted as he attempted to actively appropriate pre-Islamic heritage. This was the result of two interdependent characteristics of his administration: a hegemonic impulse seeking to dominate interpretations of heritage, and instrumental use of nationalism.

According to Ali Ansari (2007: 67), Ahmadinejad's presidency always focused on the establishment of domestic hegemony. He belonged to an official faction—known as the "Principalists"—who professed their wish to return the Islamic Revolution to its perceived original path (69). His administration expressed a repressive attitude toward his predecessors, opposing factions within the state and intellectuals. Ansari echoes the broadly accepted view that Ahmadinejad had little regard for or understanding of civil society (76). As activism had already been established, Ahmadinejad came to represent a faction that most activists opposed. His opposition was not confined to heritage and civil society activists but included establishment figures whose power networks and etiquette Ahmadinejad undermined. Significantly, his anti-establishment populist rhetoric threatened and shocked many among his own allies (71).

However, there was common ground between Ahmadinejad and heritage activists in that they both claimed ownership of patriotic and nationalist sentiments. Yet this commonality became not a site of compromise but an additional contested ground. Heritage activists challenged the legitimacy of the Ahmadinejad government's claims to patriotism and ownership of heritage as "vulgar nationalism" (77). In the volatile and delicate national and international milieu at the height of the Iran-West nuclear standoff (2005 and 2008), Ahmadinejad repeatedly used common accusations, labeling the activists "agents" of the West or "international Zionism" (78). Yet heritage activists have been genuinely concerned about preserving homeland, national unity, and territorial integrity (Mozaffari 2015). As the material covered here was produced during Ahmadinejad's administration, this background must be taken into account.

Approach to Activists and Media

Scholars describe social movements as conversations where activists engage with various audiences (Mattoni and Treré 2014: 253). Alice Mattoni and Emiliano Treré (2014: 259) also define the media practices of activists as "routinized and creative social practices" that include interactions with both "media objects," such as computers and mobile phones, and "media subjects," such as journalists and public relations managers, thus acting as both media consumers and creators. In heritage activism, media is also a means toward the politics of heritage and identity and the symbolic production of social relations. To illustrate this activism and media discourse, I have chosen examples that cover both a span of time since the inception of the movements and topics with which they are concerned at national and local scales. In my fieldwork with activists, I realized mass media, for the communication and accurate reflection of their contentions, is not their preferred outlet but is necessary to address contending claims by opposing players. In choosing my cases, I have tried—within the limits of the available data—to consider media-heritage activism diachronically so as to see if, or how, heritage activism and the media recognize each other and work together over time (Mattoni and Treré 2014: 255–256).

Media characteristics of interest to movements include whether the group is given extensive media coverage, connoting a serious reception, regardless of the context; the prominence given in the media discourse to the group's framing of issues; and the extent to which the media coverage of the group garners sympathy from the targeted public (Gamson and Wolfsfeld 1993: 121). Transactions between movements and media are characterized by "a struggle over framing" (Gamson and Wolfsfeld 1993: 118). Attaining a standing in the mainstream media, particularly including a preferred frame, is defined by William Carroll and Robert Hackett (2006) as "validation in media." Thus, the relationship between activists and the media is characterized by reciprocal considerations. This reciprocity is organized around three exchanges. First, the media provides validation for activists and movements through being a means of critiquing existing conditions, disrupting existing dominant discourses, identities or codes, and articulating and introducing selected alternatives. Second, a media presence designates activists and movements as important players, possessing claims worthy of consideration in the field, which in turn attracts the attention of their targets of influence. Indeed, a demonstration that has no media coverage is a nonevent and is unlikely to have any positive influence either on mobilizing followers or influencing the target (Carroll and Ratner 1999: 3). Finally, in terms of scope enlargement (attracting broader interest), mass media is often used by movements to disseminate their message and as a means of communicating with followers and potential recruits, as well as neutralizing, confusing, or immobilizing opponents, potential, or committed (Carroll and Ratner 1999, after Molotch 1979; Stone 1993).

Selection of Examples

Power, reach, and connections possessed by the media influence how activists frame their activism in using the media (Gamson and Wolfsfeld 1993: 123). This can depend on the organization's strength and tactics (Andrews and Caren 2010: 847), whom in the movement journalists consider serious players (Gamson and Wolfsfeld 1993: 121); how well activists engage with mainstream media framing; and to what extent the activists engage with other forms of media (see, e.g., Shamoradi and Abdollahzadeh 2016). With this in mind, I focused on case studies where the activists examined are former, current, or amateur journalists with established networks that give them additional prominence. The selection criteria used were representing the capital and a provincial location; diachronicity, meaning there must be enough items to represent a profile through time; and diversity, meaning existence of a range of representations in diverse media. As such, I have chosen a prolific heritage activist from the capital Tehran, examining five declarations, issued by his cohort of heritage activists in reaction to the inundation of the Sivand Dam,[10] and an equally significant and influential activist in Khuzestan, examining media declarations reacting to developments and archaeological discoveries arising from the building of metro stations in Ahwaz (framing two fronts simultaneously: ethnic separatists within the province, and state officials of Ahmadinejad administration). In each case, I summarize the context of the declarations and their content, as well as offering their time line, noting the interrelated context of contention over heritage and content of media communications (Mattoni 2013: 30). I then discuss the insights that could be drawn from these declarations about heritage movements in Iran, as well as their relationship to media (and their modes of using media), and reflect on the process of heritage construction and production with various forms of media as one of its actors. The first case was at a national level and contains more coherent data and is therefore given more space in this chapter.

Case Study 1: Declarations against the Sivand Dam

Twenty-first-century Iranian heritage activism came to the fore because of controversies over the construction of the Sivand Dam near the World Heritage Site of Pasargadae (inscribed in 2004) in southern Iran.[11] Historically, the site is significant, being initiated by Cyrus the Great, the founder of the Achaemenid and First Persian Empire (550–330 BCE) and is thus implicated in various identity narratives including nationalist imaginations. Its significance to recent Iranian history stems from it being heavily contested by different groups' claims to identity. Beyond domestic politics, Pasargadae also has international significance.[12] In early 2003, the Sivand Dam project began near the core zone of the site, alarming interested parties and subsequently, in 2005, triggered an almost three-year contestation. The details of activists' actions were chronicled by Afshari (2016), a central figure and organizer of activism against the dam. The bulk of dam construction activity occurred during Ahmadinejad's administration, whose views activists rejected. Part of the struggle also included Ahmadinejad's nationalist claims, from which activists had to differentiate their position. This, as well as general oppression exerted by the Ahmadinejad administration, in part determined the mode and intensity of the activism. The following, which is a summary of five declarations[13] made by interested NGOs, should be read with this context in mind. These declarations paved the way for further activism on a national scale, encapsulated the views of activists at the time, and were publicized.

The First Declaration, 4 November 2005

The first declaration was issued in Pasargadae, in conclusion to a protest visit by the core group defending the site against the dam. The program was announced in various official news outlets four days earlier (Afshari 2016: 43–49), including in *Cultural Heritage News* (*CHN*),[14] at the time a highly regarded news agency with a focus on heritage, founded and supported by groups who ended up in the faction opposing Ahmadinejad. *CHN's* reporting of protesters' intentions already validated their activism, but it would be some time before the issue gained the necessary prominence. The declaration text was prepared on site and initially bore eleven signatures, later rising to twenty-eight. It addressed "Dear readers, respected compatriots and national authorities"[15]—the public as well as the authorities—and recounted the historical, archaeological, and cultural significance of the region for Iran. Referring to possible archaeological and environmental damage caused by dam construction, the declaration called on the Iranian Cultural Heritage, Handicrafts and Tourism Organization (ICHHTO) and the Ministry for Energy join forces and dedicate the necessary funds for a rescue archaeology project, citing the example of Aswan in Egypt, and suspend dam construction until this was undertaken. It also called on authorities to find a scientific solution to the destructive effects of rising humidity levels caused by dam inundation.

The text of this declaration was circulated mainly through activists' personal blogs and other unofficial electronic media (e.g., Iran Boom 2013; Najafi Ragheb 2005). Thus, from the start, the activity leading to the declaration was buttressed by an expansive use of blogs, Facebook, and SMS by activists (Shamoradi and Abdollahzadeh 2016). However, official media was yet to lend expansive support in disseminating the declaration itself. This was a significant declaration: it formed the basis for the movement's agenda and articulated a sense of urgency and concern for heritage on the part of the signatories. It also reported the unusual step of the first ever protest visitation to Pasargadae. This was a novel and symbolic use of space for protest purposes. Between this and the next declaration, more activities, gatherings, individual newspaper articles, and protests took place and were reported through various media. Such a presence would maintain momentum and raise the profile of activists. Activists also started to regroup, recruit, and establish their own website and means of communication such as dedicated mailing lists.

The Second Declaration, 20 January 2007

The second declaration came after a period of hiatus in activities due to internal conflicts within the movement (Afshari 2016: 18–218). However, despite this hiatus, developments on the ground—dedicated symposia, news items about archaeological rescue activities, foreign media coverage—elevated the issue of the dam in the public discourse. This declaration was signed initially by forty-seven NGOs, but the numbers later grew to fifty-nine (176–181). It was published by *CHN*, which bestowed a considerable amount of prominence to the movement and its contents. By 14 February 2007, the declaration was covered by other national media. Afshari (2016: 166–69) describes the context of this declaration as a developed version of the previous one, which suggests both the focus and framing remained constant. It was published in the "reformist" newspaper *Kargozaran* (representing the views of the faction opposing Ahmadinejad) under the Society section. The paper did not have a dedicated heritage section at the time, but the framing under Society elevated the issue from a purely technical conversation to a social issue. The second rendition of the declaration was published in other "reformist" daily papers: *Poul* and *Hambastegi*, and later in *Hamshahri* (under the guise of an essay, as the paper was warned not to publish declarations; see Afshari 2016: 181).

Referring to developments on the ground (a symposium held discussing rescue archaeology in Pasargadae; Afshari 2016: 176), this declaration disputes the official interpretation suggesting a consensus among archaeological experts regarding the inundation. Here the framing of claims was intended to garner sympathy with a broader audience and prompt the ICHHTO into action; first, by emphasizing a sense of urgency and alarm in relation to the dam inundation, and second, by rejecting claims by Hassan Fazeli, Head of the Iranian Archaeological Institute, that the rescue archaeology mission was concluded. By bringing disputes into the public sphere through the media, the pronouncement highlighted the politics behind the dam construction. It also encouraged sympathy from the public and thus operated as a public recruiting tool by emphasizing the cultural and natural significance of the area and its monuments. Concurrently, the declaration linked the issue surrounding the dam to various other contemporary issues, suggesting there are larger concerns, beyond the preservation of historic relics, at stake. This was a strategy for broadening the audience and gaining support and momentum. Dissemination through media assisted this, thus broadening the scope of the contest. At the same time, the declaration implored the ICHHTO to use public opinion—which the NGOs were building up—to its advantage to delay the inundation of the dam for another year so that all concerns could be addressed.

The Third Declaration, 6 February 2007

As the atmosphere of protest and contention intensified, the third declaration was issued on 6 February 2007 and signed by seventy-four NGOs (from both natural and cultural heritage groups) (Afshari 2016: 189–93).[16] In drafting this declaration, Afshari got feedback from a more experienced journalist (and former colleague) and an older political activist, a former minister for culture. This was an opportunity to address the criticism of some other groups, possibly ethnonationalist and separatist activists, against activism for preserving Pasargadae.

This declaration also received important media coverage, including in the *CHN*. The content suggested an escalation in claims against heritage officials, pointing out neglect and possibly active mismanagement of the heritage of all periods by the authorities, providing examples of endangering significant monuments by various development projects around the country, and their silence in the face of environmental damage and the neglect of handicrafts. The declaration also referred to the symbolic and cultural significance of the site as a place of national origin, thus emphasizing the emotional value of the site to all its readers to garner sympathy. It addressed the "bystanders," as well as those active in the arena of heritage. Activists used the declaration to outline their past activities, including letters to the president (Ahmadinejad, 20 February 2006) and a complaint to the Parliamentary Committee in charge of overseeing executive power (known as the Point 90 Commission), threatening further escalation by complaining to UNESCO. This threat, while illustrating their resolve in pursuing and escalating the protest, suggested the activists would seek to articulate a scale that engaged international players. Such mentions further raised the profile of the movement in the eyes of the media as a newsworthy item.

The Fourth Declaration, 25 February 2007

This declaration was signed by eighty NGOs.[17] Here, the frame for activism began to be consolidated: the declaration emphasized the national, technical, and cultural character of the Sivand Dam debate and that this debate could be pursued through existing mechanisms within the public sphere, thus distancing activists from charges of sedition. Following this frame, the declaration engaged in refuting official claims through technical counterclaims. According to Afshari (2016: 294), this declaration was prompted by two unnamed government experts in archaeology and dam building. The declaration itself notes a group of experts in the construction industry—from the Fars Province Chapter of the Institute of Engineers—who had inspected and documented the state of the construction works (296). It also responded to a protest held by a group of approximately four hundred farmers from Arsanjan County (Keshvari 2007)—the apparent beneficiaries of the dam—before the regional Water Corp of Fars Province (17 February 2007). The farmers' protest may have been organized by the provincial government of Fars and factions within the Parliament aligned with Ahmadinejad. In that protest, activists were labeled as stooges of foreign governments and their media.

The text emphasized three issues: sustainable development, the financial viability and feasibility of the dam, and the need for transparency in the Ministry for Energy by way of sharing its expert assessments with the public. In a respectful and sympathetic tone, the declaration asserted the dam could not resolve the drought problems faced by farmers. Instead, it pointed to the adverse effects of the dam—which it deemed unfeasible—on the farmers' livelihoods and that unsustainable agricultural development ultimately damages farmers' livelihoods. Listing the actions of activists, it noted the spontaneous protest that had erupted a week before in front of the ICHHTO's office in Tehran against the dam and demanded the calling of expert reviews of its planning and construction, demanded the public release of the rescue archaeology funds, and summarized activist engagement with other state factions in the Point 90 Commission.

The Fifth Declaration, 3 March 2007

This declaration contained eighty-four signatures from both NGOs and individuals. The declaration was long and detailed, benefitting from supportive expert opinions—a sign that the movement was gaining a broader audience and stronger momentum. This was triggered by escalating action by farmers from Shiraz who staged a two-day sit-in before the Parliament in Tehran and were received favorably by some parliamentarians. While supporting the legitimate claims of farmers for a better life, the declaration suggested this could be realized through tourism development in the region. It cited an expert opinion from Chahryar Adle, who managed the registration of Pasargadae as a World Heritage Site, that the deposits behind the dam would be detrimental for future archaeological work in the region and pointed to historical precedents of quakes resulting from pressure behind dam reservoirs. Additionally, it demanded the Research Centre for Conservation and Restoration within the ICHHTO comment on the possible effects of humidity on the structures. It pointed to unfinished archaeological works in the area and the imminent danger the dam posed to the archaeology of the region. It did all this with considerable detail, suggesting input from experts in relevant fields. In the end, it invited all interested people to join them (activists) in visiting Pasargadae on the fifth day of the Iranian New Year holidays (21 March–4 April).

Case Study 2: The Ahwaz Urban Train (Metro) and the Discovery of the Ancient City of Hormoz Ardeshir

The second case study is located in Khuzestan Province in southern Iran. The province has two major ethnicities, Persian-speaking Lurs and Arabs who have historically co-occupied this region, where ethnic tensions have traditionally occurred. As the selected examples suggest, activism in the provinces has a local focus, but even that is defined within a national—or national interest—frame. The protagonist in these media pieces was Mojtaba Gahestouni, an ethnic Lur from the city of Shushtar in Khuzestan. Gahestouni is a respected freelance journalist and leading figure in heritage activism whose interest in cultural heritage was instigated by his journalistic activity taking him to different sites and locations in the province. This prompted him to establish the Society of the Friends of Cultural Heritage of Khuzestan (known as Taryana), which was officially registered on 26 July 2008 and is arguably the most high-profile heritage NGO in the region. During Ahmadinejad's terms in office, Gahestouni was banned from entering the ICHHTO, and their relationship became increasingly confrontational. The Taryana website contains twenty-three items related to the Ahwaz metro. Of these, eight are directly related to the Archaeological Research Institute or the ICHHTO.

The examples presented cover the period between 2008 and 2011 (but continuing piecemeal even until 2019). They were reactions to both official heritage policies and ethnic tensions in the area that categorized ethnic Arabs as native to the region and others as "settlers." As I have argued elsewhere (Mozaffari 2015), there is an irredentist line of argument that suggests the city of Ahwaz was an Arab town with a very short history of Persian (non-Arab) occupation.[18] It is in this context that the ancient Persian archaeological evidence gains significance. The specific trigger for these was the discovery of archaeological remains of the ancient city within Ahwaz during excavations for a metro station, resulting in confrontations between activists, authorities from the ICHHTO, and metro employees. The exchanges focused on several issues, including the prevention of access to sites for activists; charges, claims, and counterclaims in the media and the activist website, as well as during speeches; and disputes over where the ancient city was and if the metro passed through it at all. Unlike the previous case, they are not all "declarations" but exchanges that have occurred in various forms in different types of media. Some have appeared in local or even national papers. However, the media of choice has generally been virtual, such as the blogosphere and mailing lists.

Preliminary studies commissioned by the Urban and Suburban Railway Organization in 2002 had located a metro station—which would become the center of controversy in 2007—on Line 1 of the city of Ahwaz (AUSRO 2016). The proposed metro line ran through pre-Islamic and contemporary heritage sites (the city of Hormoz Ardeshir, discovered by André Godard and registered as National Heritage in 1931; the Four Lions Square, a twentieth-century urban space registered on the national heritage list on 31 December 2002; and the remains of a Parthian city adjacent to this square, registered in 1932) (Keshvari 2007). The works began in March 2007. From April 2007, possibly with the help of NGOs, news was published that the ancient city of Hormoz Ardeshir would be damaged by metro works (Kianpour 2008). The impending destruction of the Four Lions Square triggered the controversy, causing concern among local heritage activists and subsequently, the formal objection of Ahwaz MP Hamid Zangeneh. Activists such as Gahestouni were at the forefront of objection to the destruction the metro would cause to the square and the remains of the pre-Islamic cities.

On 18 December 2007, Gahestouni learned the metro excavation had unearthed some historic relics within this location and publicized the documentation while informing the province's ICHHTO (interview, April 2014; see also Taryana 2008a). The project was suspended because of this pressure but then restarted. In November 2007, construction works at the square damaged ancient column bases at the depth of twelve meters, and this time, the Research Centre for the Cultural Heritage Organization also demanded and succeeded in suspending the works pending archaeological investigations for ten days starting from January 2008 (Asr Iran 2008). It was at this point that the existence of pre-Islamic remains, and the danger posed by construction, became public knowledge and caused further uproar. The Head of the Khuzestan Heritage Organization, however, did not issue a full suspension order. In February 2008, an article appeared on the popular news website *Tabnak* arguing for the significance of ancient archaeological remains over and above the metro (Mahmoudi 2008). His ethnocentric tone notwithstanding, he attempted to count the historic, strategic, economic, and national significance of these remains. On the International Day of Historic Monuments (18 April), Taryana published a speech by another activist, Muna Kianpour (2008), about the location of Hormoz Ardeshir. Then, in May 2008, the website published a long article (possibly by Gahestouni) about the problems of transport in Ahwaz and the specific pitfalls faced by the planned metro lines and the damage that would cause to cultural heritage (Taryana 2008b).

The dispute between activists such as Gahestouni and cultural heritage and metro officials ran for more than three years. To reconstruct this picture, I have referred to the Taryana website for their news items. These are a combination of declarations and essays involving Gahestouni or Taryana, and there are news items by other news agencies related to the controversy and disseminated through the Taryana website. Recounting the history of the city and drawing on the audiences' patriotic sentiments, the speech invited all to be "good guardians for the valuable cultural heritage of this domain and of our own national identity" and concluded by saying the metro works have damaged parts of the periphery of the ancient city, and Taryana is "relentlessly following up the issue as a matter of first priority" (Kianpour 2008).

This came in the context of a dispute over the very existence of an ancient city in the area.

By 4 August 2008, the website alleged ICHHTO experts were stalling the works (Taryana 2008c, 2008d) and by October, they claimed archaeologists sent to the field were there to expedite the metro works (Taryana 2008a). By November 2008, claims and counterclaims intensified leading to Gahestouni (2008) referring to authorities in ICHHTO and the Archaeological Research Institute as "betrayers" of cultural heritage for reasons including rejecting the existence of Hormoz Ardeshir. In the same month, two city council members criticized the ICHHTO for its lack of care toward Hormoz Ardeshir (Taryana 2008e). On 1 December 2008, Gahestouni announced to the Khuzestan Chapter of the Iranian Students' News Agency that within a fortnight Taryana would send a request for the original documentation related to the registration of Hormoz Ardeshir to the French Archaeological Service. This was in response to ICHHTO's reluctance to cooperate in releasing relevant documents after a dispute involving the Metro authorities and ICHHTO on one side and the NGOs on the other.

This scenario of claims and counterclaims, raising the stakes and following through with a frame—here, as in previous cases—references collective local and national identity. Based on available evidence online, from 2009 to 2014, the controversy over the metro and Hormoz Ardeshir was reflected in various media (as direct interviews or news items) including national media *Mehr News* (Taryana 2009), *Fars News* (aligned with the Principalist or hardliner faction of the state), and *CHN* and local media such as *Khuzestan Khabar*. Arguably, it took a few years for the news of this work to attain the necessary momentum and gain the status of national news item. This may in part be ascribed to the gradual shift in official postings within the ICHHTO. Toward the end of Ahmadinejad's term and with the election of Hassan Rouhani, there were changes in ICHHTO local chapter as a new administration was appointed to the Khuzestan Chapter (in 2013). With this change, Gahestouni acquired a desk within an office in the provincial offices of the ICHHTO. Although the relationship between Gahestouni and the ICHHTO had somewhat improved, the critical exchanges and objections continued well into the latter parts of 2014 as evidenced in newspapers and other media.

Observations and Concluding Remarks

It is possible to draw several observations from the two case studies presented here. The first relates to the common ground among activists and several precepts that frame this common ground. Signatories to declarations in the first case study and activists in the second case seem to share a kind of patriotic impulse communicated through, among other things, frequent references to patrimony, history, homeland, national unity, and terms that refer to guardianship. All such notions transcend the immediate case in hand, framing it in the larger picture in relation to the nation and its history. At times, this impulse uses the same expressions used in nationalist tendencies. Few, if any of these expressions appear to be from what would be traditionally identified as the "left" side of politics (although it may come close to ethnocentric claims favored by sections among the traditional "left"). The framing of issues and the use of language suggest and advocate a concept of a continuous historical heritage that informs contemporary identity. These declarations and their framing also played a part in directing the debate over national heritage as, once in the media, and given the emotionally charged concepts they signified (history, homeland, territorial integrity, etc.), they could not be ignored by authorities who were in turn and ultimately forced to defend their own credentials.[19] This demonstrates the content of these texts were an important facet of media as well. Thus, the text contains the contest and at times, the battle.

Leadership in movement-media engagement and their production of media items was also a significant issue. There were interesting commonalities between the leaders of the two cases, in terms of both their journalism experience and their personal contacts with professional journalists within media outlets. Additionally, from my fieldwork, Afshari seems to have influenced the tone and thrust of these declarations in response to external events. He has contributed significantly to formulating the ideas and, in some instances, has been the sole author of the declaration text. In other instances, he drafted the declarations by gathering other people's ideas, sending these drafts to them for feedback. When there was little time for feedback, signatories contributed their endorsement before the fact, based on the trust they had in Afshari's character. Gahestouni enjoys a similar standing: a senior journalist with *CHN* told me he was "honored to know and work with" him. Given this standing, he could readily access media people and publish in their outlets.

In both cases, activists used concrete issues that were then framed as tropes through which the state was critiqued on multiple grounds. These cases reveal activist critiques of the management of heritage in the country, the ideology of the political system and its version of national identity. However, despite their forcefulness, they work within, or at the permissible boundaries of, public discourse in Iran. This is achieved by referring back to concrete "technical" issues, such as humidity in the Sivan Dam and archaeological evidence in Ahwaz. Activists' focus on specific issues diffused the state's charges of political motivation. Further, as the example with the Point 90 Commission in the first case study and the change of official attitude toward Gahestouni in the second case suggested, activists are not just acting as critics from the sidelines but are prepared to engage with authorities and express willingness to be of help to them in protecting and advancing cultural heritage. This somewhat blurs the lines between dominant and subaltern divisions of heritage (Chong presents a parallel example of such blurring in chapter 4).

All these texts should be seen in the context of other activities organized by the NGOs. Some of these activities, such as protests, symposia, media engagements, and the publication of essays in newspapers, made it to the news. In some instances, the news item was prepared by them and then published (e.g., the case of the Symposium for Protection of Cultural Heritage, which was published in *Sarmayeh*; see Afshari 2016: 242). Various modes of communication reinforced one another. Thus, for example, the general framing of the issue was reinforced in Kianpour's public speech and then published online and amplified with other material by Gahestouni. These various players and modes of communication served to keep the issue "alive." Given the circumstances surrounding the limits of expression in the country, activists have used the objective nature of the debate above anything else. Thus, while there is constant reference in media statements to ideas of homeland and national identity, the contest is focused on concrete, local issues. Even in personal attacks (in the case of Gahestouni), the opposing party was called a "traitor" to cultural heritage.

The cases presented in this chapter provide examples of the unfolding of heritage contests through various media platforms. In both cases, forms of new media (including but not limited to blogs and websites) have been major vehicles for communication among activists. The dynamics between media and heritage activism are also clear through the case studies: once a movement has gained traction, the media gets involved and this becomes a cycle whereby further coverage increases the momentum of activism, as is suggested by the evidence in social movements research. Both cases contain an observable (and predictable) time lag between the events on the ground (activism) and the uptake of the issue as a newsworthy topic by relevant national media such as *CHN* or other daily newspapers. There appears to be a cycle of reinforcement according to which activism occurs on the ground and then is represented and disseminated through various media items leading to attention being attracted and sympathies garnered among bystanders, which in turn leads to further action on the ground. The media and activism on the ground are thus mutually reinforcing and legitimizing. William Gamson and Gadi Wolsfeld's astute observation that "movements need the media to broaden the scope of the conflict" applies here, but the scope frequently changes during its course. They add: "The introduction and subtraction of players alters the power relations between the contestants. Where the scope is narrow, the weaker party has much to gain and little to lose by broadening the scope, drawing third parties into the conflict as mediators or partisans" (1993: 116).

Debates surrounding this topic, and broader ideas of social movements, tend to focus on whether the existence of formal organizations and resources heightens media attention and whether there are relative advantages and disadvantages in having "routine, insider tactics versus more disruptive outsider tactics" (Andrews and Caren 2010: 845). The two cases discussed provide an interesting insight in this regard. In Pasargadae, several disruptive tactics—protests on the ground—were directly related to the declarations. In Ahwaz, actions on the ground were less disruptive, and activists used insider media tactics, with which they were familiar, in their representations. We may attribute this in part to the nature and limits of expression within the public sphere in the two cases; activists I interviewed noted that disruptive expressions were more tolerated in the capital than in the provinces.

In understanding why activists communicate through the mass media, it is useful to recognize and talk about the frames in the formation of the discourse of letters in the media. In line with this, the varying elements found within social practices, which are not merely single interactions, include the forms of both physical and mental activities, the use of objects, how forms of understanding are developed through background knowledge, the know-how of the group, emotional states, and the knowledge that provides motivation (Mattoni and Treré 2014: 258). The framing was substantiated through repetition (activist media being a significant facilitating element) and public events and speeches. Once substantiated, the issue was more likely to be taken up by national and official media. Arguably, the numerous claims, counterclaims, engagements, and rejoinders that appear on the Taryana website, for example, suggest various media representations contributed to constructing and advancing the discourse of heritage and its related activism. Often representing the particular framing advanced by activists, these representations influenced the terms and type of engagement by opposing sides. I mentioned in the introduction that framing transactions are affected by "media norms" and that the locus of power shifts through the production of "symbolic codes" through various social fields. These fields are susceptible to collective action, in this instance heritage activism, which can affect the flow of information and therefore the operation of power. While acknowledging the main difference between the two cases—one being a series of declarations and the other one an ongoing dispute—they both, more or less, followed the same pattern articulated in this chapter, from which it is possible to speculate about the characteristics and direction of heritage in Iran. This speculation suggests the growing significance of heritage in political disputes and cooperations at international, national, and subnational levels.

In summary, it is apparent that many ideas in social movements studies are applicable to heritage contests through the media. The capacity to create and distribute through multiple media platforms is essential for the recruitment of others into the contest, a cooption that needs to be backed up and complemented by actions on the ground. More importantly perhaps, this shows that media itself is not uniform, and it is through these fractures that activists can further their issues. This brings me back to my opening argument that heritage is negotiated through and across boundaries of power and through the actions of multiple players. From this perspective, understanding the production and the cultural and social work of heritage requires a detailed examination of various engagements between groups of actors over time. The methodological implications of this realization call for critical and nuanced application of the potentially rigid binaries, propositions embedded in some postcolonial approaches, or other theoretical formulations such as the AHD.

Acknowledgments

I wish to acknowledge the generous support given through research grants from the Australian Research Council (grant no. DE170100104), Curtin University's Australia-Asia-Pacific Institute, and Deakin University's Alfred Deakin Institute. I am also grateful to my Iranian friends and colleagues for their time and generous contribution of information as well as Freyja Bottrell and Bakhtyar Lotfi for their assistance. I especially wish to acknowledge my collaborator Tod Jones, whose critical engagement has been a source of intellectual stimulation and a lot of fun throughout the years. All shortcomings, of course, are mine.

Ali Mozaffari is a fellow of the Australian Research Council with the Alfred Deakin Institute at Deakin University. Through his research, he seeks to understand the uses of the past in contemporary discourses of heritage and built environment in Iran and West Asia. His areas of interest include heritage and social movements, liminality and heritage, and development and heritage in late-twentieth century Iranian architecture. His publications include *Forming National Identity in Iran: The Idea of Homeland Derived from Ancient Persian and Islamic Imaginations of Place* (2014) and *World Heritage in Iran: Perspectives on Pasargadae* (2016), and "Picturing Pasargadae: Visual Representation and the Ambiguities of Heritage in Iran" (*Iranian Studies*, 2017).

NOTES

1. As defined by the Dictionary of Sociology, activism is, "the involvement of individuals and groups in a number of electoral situations and organizations concerned with power. The level of participation is said to be lower among women and the young, as measured by the propensity to vote, join, be active in political organizations, and stand for election."
2. Various scholars recognize the peculiarity of the public sphere and civil society in the Middle East and Iran. For observations on the Middle East and Iran, see Kienle (2011). For different insights into the Iranian condition, see Amir Arjomand (2000); Boroumand and Boroumand (2000); Khiabani and Sreberny (2001); Rivetti and Cavatorta (2013, 2014).
3. For some examples of the scholarship in this type of activism, see Carroll and Hackett (2006); Couldry and Curran (2003); Napoli (2007); Shade (2011).
4. While the website of the Cultural and Natural Heritage Watch is available at the time of writing (http://www.irandidehban.ir), the Taryana website has been unavailable since early 2019. The weblinks provided in references are therefore extracted from the Internet Archive (https://web.archive.org/).
5. For examples of literature, regarding contestation and the media in the field of social movements, see Loader (2008); Schachtner (2012); Van De Donk et al. (2004).
6. See, e.g., Addison (2000); Affleck and Kvan (2005, 2008); Cameron and Kenderdine (2007); Christou et al. (2006); Fairclough (2012); Giaccardi (2012); Giaccardi and Palen (2008); Kalay et al. (2007); Malpas (2008); Petrelli et al. (2013). Topics are as diverse as virtual reality, virtual reconstruction, collective or social media curation and creation of heritage, serious gaming and heritage, technological reproduction and its effect upon the experience and preservation of heritage.
7. Two specific biases can be observed in relation to the study of media for social movements which Mattoni and Treré (2014: 254) term "one-medium bias and the technological-fascination bias." They further state that overall the fragmentation linked to the one-medium bias still remains a trait of media and social movements literature.
8. Mattoni (2013: 47) defines a communication repertoire as: "The entire set of activist media practices that social movement actors might conceive as possible and then develop in both the latent and visible stages of mobilization, to reach social actors positioned both within and beyond the social movement *milieu*."
9. For further reading on factionalism in the Iranian state, see Moslem (2002). For the effects of this on the media landscape (the heritage activists' outlet), see Khiabany 2007; Khiabany and Sreberny 2001).
10. For a comprehensive diary of events in relation to this controversy, see Afshari (2016); Jones et al. (2018).
11. For a fuller discussion of this site, see Mozaffari (2016b), esp. chap. 1, by Remy Boucharlat.
12. The details are beyond the scope of this chapter and are discussed in Afshari (2016); Jones et al. (2018).
13. They used the term declaration, and they were each issued with a number, from 1 to 5.
14. This respected news agency was annulled in 2016 and the domain subsequently made available for sale.

15. This was also published in CHN as a news item.
16. The full text is available in Afshari (2016: 236–242).
17. The full text is available in Afshari (2016: 294–299).
18. Such ideas are expressed by proxies of countries around the Persian Gulf (e.g., Al Habtoor 2015).
19. An example of this was apparent in the defensive position of the head of Dr. Fazeli, Head of the Iranian Archaeological Institute in the case of the Sivand dispute (for more on this, see Afshari 2016; Jones et al. 2018).

REFERENCES

Addison, A. C. 2000. "Emerging Trends in Virtual Heritage." *IEEE MultiMedia* 7 (2): 22–25. https://doi.org/10.1109/93.848421.

Affleck, Janice, and Thomas Kvan. 2005. "Reinterpreting Virtual Heritage." *Digital Opportunities: Proceedings of the 10th International Conference on Computer Aided Architectural Design Research in Asia*, vol. 11, 169–178. New Delhi: Architexturez Imprints.

———. 2008. "A Virtual Community as the Context for Discursive Interpretation: A Role in Cultural Heritage Engagement." *International Journal of Heritage Studies* 14 (3): 268–280.

Afshari, Alireza. 2016. *Defending History*. Tehran: Shurafarin.

Amir Arjomand, Saïd. 2000. "Civil Society and the Rule of Law in the Constitutional Politics of Iran Under Khatami." *Social Research* 67 (2): 283–301. http://www.jstor.org/stable/40971474.

Al Habtoor, Khalaf Ahmad. 2015. "Arab Ahwaz Must Be Liberated from Iran." *Alarabyia*, 29 March. http://ara.tv/v524b.

Andrews, Kenneth T., and Neal Caren. 2010. "Making the News: Movement Organizations, Media Attention, and the Public Agenda." *American Sociological Review* 75 (6): 841–866. https://doi.org/10.1177/0003122410386689.

Ansari, Ali M. 2007. "Chapter Four: The Ahmadinejad Presidency—Domestic Policy." *The Adelphi Papers* 47 (393): 67–90. https://doi.org/10.1080/05679320701868177.

Asr Iran. 2008. "Ghatar-e shahriye Ahwaz ham be tarikh bar khord/takhrib shahr-e 1700-saleh." 8 January. http://bit.ly/2jimPy0.

AUSRO (Ahwaz Urban and Suburban Rail Organization). 2016. "Sima-ye Tarh." Last accessed 23 March 2017. http://www.ahwazmetro.org/Default.aspx?tabid=63 (website no longer available).

Benford, Robert D., and David A. Snow. 2000. "Framing Processes and Social Movements: An Overview and Assessment." *Annual Review of Sociology* 26: 611–39. https://doi.org/10.1146/annurev.soc.26.1.611.

Ben-Porath, Eran N. 2009. "Framing." In *Encyclopedia of Journalism*, ed. Christopher H. Sterling. Thousand Oaks, CA: Sage. http://dx.doi.org/10.4135/9781412972048.n161.

Boroumand, Laden, and Roya Boroumand. 2000. "Illusion and Reality of Civil Society in Iran: An Ideological Debate." *Social Research* 67 (2): 303–344. http://www.jstor.org/stable/40971482.

Cameron, Fiona, and Sarah Kenderdine, eds. 2007. *Theorizing Digital Cultural Heritage: A Critical Discourse*. Cambridge, MA: MIT Press.

Carroll, William K., and Robert A. Hackett. 2006. "Democratic Media Activism through the Lens of Social Movement Theory." *Media, Culture & Society* 28 (1): 83–104. https://doi.org/10.1177/0163443706059289.

Carroll, William K., and R. S. Ratner. 1999. "Media Strategies and Political Projects: A Comparative Study of Social Movements." *Canadian Journal of Sociology / Cahiers Canadiens De Sociologie* 24 (1): 1–34. https://doi.org/10.2307/3341476.

Christou, Chris, Cameron Angus, Celine Loscos, Andrea Dettori, and Maria Roussou. 2006. "A Versatile Large-Scale Multimodal VR System for Cultural Heritage Visualization." In *VRST '06: Proceedings of the ACM Symposium on Virtual Reality Software and Technology*, 133–140. New York: ACM. https://doi.org/10.1145/1180495.1180523.

Couldry, Nick, and James Curran. 2003. *Contesting Media Power: Alternative Media in a Networked World*. Lanham, MD: Rowman & Littlefield.

Emirbayer, Mustafa, and Mimi Sheller. 1999. "Publics in History." *Theory and Society* 28 (1): 143–197. https://doi.org/10.1023/A:1006921411329.

Fairclough, Graham. 2012. "Others: A Prologue." In Giaccardi 2012: xiv–xxiii.

Fraser, Nancy. 1997. Justice Interruptus: Critical Reflections on the "Postsocialist" Condition. New York: Routledge.

Gahestouni, Mojtaba. 2008. "Pasokh anjoman doostdaran miras-e farhangi Khuzestan be ezharat modir amel ghatar shahri Ahwaz." *Taryana*, November 8. http://bit.ly/22JDCdz (website no longer available).

Gamson, William A., and Gadi Wolfsfeld. 1993. "Movements and Media as Interacting Systems." *Annals of the American Academy of Political and Social Science* 528: 114–25. https://doi.org/10.1177/0002716293528001009.

Giaccardi, Elisa. 2012. *Heritage and Social Media: Understanding Heritage in a Participatory Culture*. London: Routledge.

Giaccardi, Elisa, and Leysia Palen. 2008. "The Social Production of Heritage through Cross-Media Interaction: Making Place for Place-Making." *International Journal of Heritage Studies* 14 (3): 281–297. https://doi.org/10.1080/13527250801953827.

Holliday, Shabnam J. 2013. *Defining Iran: Politics of Resistance*. Farnham: Ashgate.

Iran Boom. 2015. "A Request from a Group of NGOs to Dismantle the Sivand Dam." [In Persian.] 7 November. http://www.iranboom.ir/didehban/30vand/10660-darkhast-gorohi-az-anjoman-ha-sivand.html.

Jasper, James M. 2010. "Cultural Approaches in the Sociology of Social Movements." In *Handbook of Social Movements across Disciplines*, ed. Bert Klandermans and Conny Roggeband, 59–109. Boston: Springer.

———. 2015. "Introduction: Playing the Game." In *Players and Arenas: The Interactive Dynamics of Protest*, ed. James M. Jasper and Jan Willem Duyvendak, 1–33. Amsterdam: Amsterdam University Press.

Kalay, Yehuda E., Thomas Kvan, and Janice Affleck. eds., 2007. *New Heritage: New Media and Cultural Heritage*. Routledge.

Keshvari, Zahra. 2007. "Ghatar-e shahri-e Ahwaz asar-e tarikhi-ye in shahr ra neshaneh rafteh." *Cultural Heritage News (CHN)*, 7 March. http://www.chn.ir/NSite/FullStory/News/?Id=56548&Serv=0&SGr=0.

Khiabany, Gholam. 2007. "The Iranian Press, State, and Civil Society." In *Media, Culture and Society in Iran: Living with Globalization and the Islamic State*, ed. Mehdi Semati, 17–36. London: Routledge.

Khiabany, Gholam, and Annabelle Sreberny. 2001. "The Iranian Press and the Continuing Struggle over Civil Society 1998–2000." *International Communication Gazette* 63 (2–3): 203–223. https://doi.org/10.1177/0016549201063002007.

Kianpour, Mona. 2008. "Shahr-e tarikhi-ye Hormoz Ardeshir dar kodam noghteye Ahwaz gharar darad?" Taryana, 23 April. http://bit.ly/2jir6BM.

Kienle, Eberhard. 2011. "Civil Society in the Middle East." In *The Oxford Handbook of Civil Society*, ed. Michael Edwards, 146–158. Oxford: Oxford University Press.

Loader, Brian D. 2008. "Social Movements and New Media." *Sociology Compass* 2 (6): 1920–1933. https://doi.org/10.1111/j.1751-9020.2008.00145.x.

Mahmoudi, Jahangir. 2008. "'Hormoza Ardeshi' mohemtar az ghatar shahri Ahwaz." *Tabnak*, 10 February. http://bit.ly/2jioEem.

Malpas, Jeff. 2008. "New Media, Cultural Heritage and the Sense of Place: Mapping the Conceptual Ground." *International Journal of Heritage Studies* 14 (3): 197–209. https://doi.org/10.1080/13527250801953652.

Mattoni, Alice. 2013. "Repertoires of Communication in Social Movement Processes." In *Mediation and Protest Movements*, ed. Bart Cammaerts, Alice Mattoni, and Patrick McCurdy, 39–56. Bristol: Intellect Books.

Mattoni, Alice, and Emiliano Treré. 2014. "Media Practices, Mediation Processes, and Mediatization in the Study of Social Movements." *Communication Theory* 24 (3): 252–271. https://doi.org/10.1111/comt.12038.

Melucci, Alberto. 1996. *Challenging Codes: Collective Action in the Information Age*. Cambridge: Cambridge University Press.

Molotch, Harvey. 1979. "Media and Movements." In *The Dynamics of Social Movements: Resource Mobilization, Social Control, and Tactics*, ed. Mayer N. Zald and John D. McCarthy, 71–93. Boston: Little Brown & Co.

Moslem, Medhi. 2002. *Factional Politics in Post-Khomeini Iran*. Syracuse, NY: Syracuse University Press.

Mozaffari, Ali. 2014. *Forming National Identity in Iran: The Idea of Homeland Derived from Ancient Persian and Islamic Imaginations of Place*. London: I.B. Tauris.

———. 2015. "The Heritage 'NGO': A Case Study on the Role of Grass Roots Heritage Societies in Iran and Their Perception of Cultural Heritage." *International Journal of Heritage Studies* 21 (9): 845–861. https://doi.org/10.1080/13527258.2015.1028961.

———. 2016a. "Open Letter to the President Elect: An Example of Heritage Activism through the Media in Iran." In *Indian Ocean Futures: Communities, Sustainability and Security*, ed. Thor Kerr and John Stephens, 15–33. Newcastle: Cambridge Scholars Publishing.

———. 2016b. *World Heritage in Iran: Perspectives on Pasargadae*. New York: Routledge.

———. 2017. "Picturing Pasargadae: Visual Representation and the Ambiguities of Heritage in Iran." *Iranian Studies* 50 (4): 601–634.

Najafi Ragheb, Mehrnoush. 2005. "Final Statement of the NGO's Gathering in Pasargad and Protest against the Depletion of the Sivand Dam." [In Persian.] Blog entry, 2 December. http://www.najafiragheb.blogsky.com/1384/09/02/post-12.

Napoli, Philip M. 2007. "Public Interest Media Activism and Advocacy as a Social Movement: A Review of the Literature." McGannon Center Working Paper Series no. 21. http://fordham.bepress.com/mcgannon_working_papers/21.

Petrelli, Daniela, Luigina Ciolfi, Dick van Dijk, Eva Hornecker, Elena Not, and Albrecht Schmidt. 2013. "Integrating Material and Digital: A New Way for Cultural Heritage." *Interactions* 20 (4): 58–63.
Rivetti, Paola, and Francesco Cavatorta. 2013. "'The Importance of Being Civil Society': Student Politics and the Reformist Movement in Khatami's Iran." *Middle Eastern Studies* 49 (4): 645–660. https://doi.org/10.1080/00263206.2013.798311.
———. 2014. "Iranian Student Activism between Authoritarianism and Democratization: Patterns of Conflict and Cooperation between the Office for the Strengthening of Unity and the Regime." *Democratization* 21 (2): 289–310. https://doi.org/10.1080/13510347.2012.732067.
Schachtner, Christina. 2012. "Social Movements and Digital Media." Paper presented at the Second ISA Forum of Sociology, ISA Conference, Buenos Aires, 3 August. https://isaconf.confex.com/isaconf/forum2012/webprogram/Paper13579.html.
Shade, Leslie Regan. 2011. "Media Reform in the United States and Canada: Activism and Advocacy for Media Policies in the Public Interest." In *The Handbook of Global Media and Communication Policy*, ed. Robin Mansell and Marc Raboy, 147–164. Hoboken, NJ: Wiley-Blackwell.
Shamoradi, Elham, and Ebrahim Abdollahzadeh. 2016. "Antinomies of Development: Heritage, Media and the Sivand Dam Controversy." In Mozaffari 2016: 225–254.
Smith, Laurajane. 2006. *Uses of Heritage*. London: Routledge.
Steinberg, Marc W. 2004. "The Intellectual Challenges of Toiling in the Vineyard." In *Rethinking Social Movements: Structure, Meaning, and Emotion*, ed. J. Goodwin and James M. Jasper, 121–134. Lanham, MD: Rowman & Littlefield.
Stone, Sharon D. 1993. "Getting the Message out: Feminists, the Press and Violence against Women." *Canadian Review of Sociology / Revue Canadienne de Sociologie* 30 (3): 377–400. https://doi.org/10.1111/j.1755-618X.1993.tb00943.x.
Tarrow, Sidney G. 1994. *Power in Movement: Collective Action, Social Movements and Politics*. Cambridge: Cambridge University Press.
Taryana (Society of the Friends of Cultural Heritage of Khuzestan). 2008a. "Aya bastanshenasan baraye nejat shahr Hormoz Ardeshir be Ahwaz amadehand?" 25 October. http://bit.ly/2Z0teCk.
———. 2008b. "Dast-andazhaye ghatar-e shahri-e Ahwaz." 12 May. http://bit.ly/2Z3YRuL.
———. 2008c. "Kavosh shahr Hormoz Ardeshir ba etebarat shahdari Ahwaz aghaz mishavad." 4 August. http://bit.ly/2Z2RyTW.
———. 2008d. "Pajooheshkadeye bastanshenasi-e keshvarr baraye gamaneh-zani dar masir ghatar-e shahrio Ahwaz vaght koshi mikonad." 4 August. http://bit.ly/2Z3YVuv.
———. 2008e. "Takid do tan az azaye shoraye shahr-e Ahwaz be kashf-e Hormoz Ardeshir." 25 November. http://taryana.ir/node/174 (website no longer available).
———. 2009. "Sazman miras-e farhangi Khuseztan Hormoz Ardeshir ra zir rail rah ahan shahri leh mikonad." 24 August. http://bit.ly/1UPMPyh (website no longer available).
Tazmini, Ghoncheh. 2009. *Khatami's Iran: The Islamic Republic and the Turbulent Path to Reform*. London: I.B.Tauris.
Tilly, Charles. 1993. "Contentious Repertoires in Great Britain, 1758–1834." *Social Science History* 17 (2): 253–80. https://doi.org/10.2307/1171282.

———. 2006. *Regimes and Repertoires*. Chicago: University of Chicago Press.
Tilly, Charles, and Lesley J. Wood. 2015. *Social Movements 1768–2012*. London: Routledge.
Van De Donk, Wilm, Brian D. Loader, Paul G. Nixon, and Dieter Rucht. 2004. *Cyberprotest: New Media, Citizens and Social Movements*. London: Routledge.

Index

Note: Page numbers in italics refer to illustrations; *n* refers to a note number.

A

activism, 20, 24, 107, 108–109, 171
  art and, 49
  backroom, 119–20
  cause-specific, 117–18
  in China, 81, 87–88, 103*n*5
  defined, 81, 191*n*1
  demographics of, 64–65
  environmental, 64–65
  food rights, 133
  in Indonesia, 64–65, 66–68
  intellectual, 113–17
  in Iran, 171–72, 179–88
  media and, 174–75, 177–78, 187–88
  nationalism and, 95, 107–108
  in Nepal, 131–36, 141–42
  in Singapore, 108–13, 116–20
  as transnational, 109, 117, 141, 142
  types, 117–18, 119
  vandalism and, 43, 49
  See also arenas; protest; social movements
actor-network theory (ANT), 36
Adle, Chahryar, 183
Afshari, Alireza, 172, 179, 181, 187
agency, 3, 44
  in activism, 2, 35, 174
  in China, 84, 87, 89–90

Ahmadinejad, Mahmoud, 170, 176–77, 179
Ahwaz metro project, 184–86, 187
archaeology, 14, 15, 182
  colonialism and in Indonesia, 65, 72–73
  rescue in Iran, 180, 181, 184
architecture (as heritage), 87, 100
arenas, 40–42
  in China, 82
  defined, 34–35, 36, 42, 81–82
  emotion and, 44, 182
  international heritage, 182
  See also media; social media
art, 49
  See also Dumbara Rata (weaving)
Asia, 17–19
  See also specific countries
assemblages, 15, 16, 36
authenticity, 112, 152
authorized heritage discourse (AHD), 14, 173–74

B

Bai (ethnic group), 92, 93, 97
Bardiya (Bardia) National Park, Nepal, *125*
  access to, 132, 134
  fishing rights and, 134–35, 136–37
  management of, 130, 137
  Sonaha rights and, 131–36, 141–42
Beijing, 87
Beijing Cultural Heritage Protection Center (CHP), 91

Berava (caste), 148–49, 168n3
  identity and, 163, 166
  See also Dumbara Rata (weaving)
biocultural heritage, 22, 124, 127
  Indigenous peoples and, 127, 141
  of Sonaha, 129–31, 140–42
Bol Brutu (Facebook group), 20–21, 45, 57, 63–64, 72–73
  identity of, 69, 70
  membership of, 67–68
  study of, 65–66
Brady, Anne-Marie, 83
Brown, David, 111
Buffer Zone Management Council (BZMC), 134, 135, 143n8
Bukit Brown Cemetery, Singapore, 45, 116–18, 120
BZMC (Buffer Zone Management Council), 134, 135, 143n8

C
Canclini, Néstor García, 147, 148
caste, 47, 148, 162
  Berava, 148–49, 156–57
  Dumbara Rata and, 149–50, 152, 154–57, 160–65
  labor and, 149–57, 166
CDO (Community Development Organization), 133, 137
cemeteries and tombs, 46, 116
  See also Bukit Brown Cemetery, Singapore
China, 6, 80, 81
  activism in, 21
  Belt and Road Initiative, 19
  business partnerships in, 86
  contested heritage in, 80–81
  history of heritage in, 84–87
  Maoist, 84, 87
  NGOs in, 90–91
  scenic zones in, 86, 90
  tourism and, 21, 81, 85–86, 88–89, 92–94
  tradition and, 85
China Principles, 89
Chinatown, Singapore, 112, 114–15

CHN (*Cultural Heritage News*), 180, 182, 186, 188
Christian socialism, 38
civil society, 5–7, 8
  in Iran, 191n2
  See also activism; social movements
class, 35, 84
  middle, 22, 24, 45, 113
  See also caste; elites
colonialism, 65, 111
commodification, 86, 88, 112
  See also tourism
community, 88–90, 101
Community Development Organization (CDO), 133, 137
competition
  caste and, 160–65
  industry control and, 157–60, 166–67
  labor, 149–57
conservation
  heritage and, 127–28
  Indigenous peoples and, 128–29, 141–42
Convention Concerning the Protection of the World Cultural and Natural Heritage, 85
corporatism, 111
cosmopolitanism, 72–73, 74
craft, 80, 166
  globalization and, 22–23, 47
  identity and, 163, 166
  in Sri Lanka, 149–52
  See also Dumbara Rata (weaving)
Crete, 12
Cultural and Natural Heritage Watch, 172
cultural heritage. *See* heritage
Cultural Heritage News (*CHN*), 180, 182, 186, 188
Cyrus the Great, 46, 179

D
Dali, China, 82–83, 92–93, 99, 103n11
dams, 179–83
destruction (of heritage)
  in China, 84–85, 87, 91, 100–101
  by dam in Iran, 180

by metro in Iran, 184–86
See also vandalism
development (economic)
  in China, 81, 85, 88–89, 92–93
  consultation and, 112, 115
  craft and, 148, 149–50, 164–65
  heritage and, 9, 109, 147–48
  Indonesia, 64
  in Singapore, 110
  in Sri Lanka, 150–52, 160
  See also modernization; urbanization
discourse analysis, 172
dissonance, 13, 46
diversity (biocultural), 128
Divi Neguma (development initiative), 151
Dumbara Rata (weaving), 22, 47, 148–50
  caste and, 149–50, 152, 154–57, 160–65
  control over, 151–60, 166–67
  demand for, 149–50
  as heritage, 148, 166–67
  knowledge of, 148, 152–54, 155–57, 160
  learning, 157–59

E
elites, 35–36
  activism and, 108–109
  in Singapore, 109, 111
emotion, 43–46
  site visits and, 45, 72
  social media and, 62
  social movements and, 34, 43–46
empowerment (of Sonaha), 132, 140
Enlightenment, 7–8
Environment Conservation Society (ECOS), 131
ethnicity and ethnic groups
  in China, 85, 92
  Chinese in Singapore, 47, 112, 116
  legal recognition of, 139, 141
  in Singapore, 109–110, 111
  See also Bai (ethnic group); Sonaha (Indigenous people)
ethnography, 12, 14, 15, 50

experts and expertise
  heritage management and, 14, 65, 88
  in Iran, 182–83
  in Singapore, 119

F
Facebook, 62, 117
  administrators and, 68–69
  social movements and, 59, 73
  use in Indonesia, 63, 68–69
  See also Bol Brutu (Facebook group)
FIAN (Food-First Information and Action Network), 133, 139
fishing rights, 134–35, 136–38
Food-First Information and Action Network (FIAN), 133, 139
foreigners (in China), 83, 95–100
Foucault, Michel, 5–6
frames and framing, 170–71, 184, 187

G
Gahestouni, Mojtaba, 184, 185–88
gender, 90, 103n6
genealogies (lineage), 89–90, 103n6
geography, 17–19
globalization, 2–4
  craft and, 22–23, 47
Godard, André, 8, 184
GONGOs (government nongovernment organizations), 81, 90
Govigama (caste), 149
Graddy, T. Garrett, 128
Gregory, Jenny, 62

H
handicraft. *See* craft; Dumbara Rata (weaving)
Harrison, Rodney, 7, 15–16, 36
heritage, 3, 4, 7–15, 32, 109
  architecture as, 87, 100
  biocultural, 22, 124, 127
  class and, 10, 11, 111
  commodification of, 86, 112, 147
  contested in China, 96, 100, 102
  craft as, 80
  defined, 13, 32, 35
  digital, 61

history of in China, 84–87
homogenized, 3, 100, 108
intangible in China, 80, 85, 90
intangible in Japan, 9, 19
international standards of, 117
knowledge as, 130, 147–48, 152
narratives, 46–47
nationalism and, 6, 64, 95–96, 167
nostalgia and, 7, 46, 108
occupation as, 140
ownership of, 96
politics and, 10–11, 12, 147
as resistance, 48
song as, 90
heritage activism. *See* activism; social movements
heritage legislation. *See* legislation (heritage)
heritage movements. *See* social movements
heritage organizations, 3, 7, 11
See also NGOs
heritage studies, 10–15
Herzfeld, Michael, 6, 12–13
history (discipline), 11, 12
Hormoz Ardeshir (ancient city), 184, 185, 186
hotels, 93, 94
See also Linden Centre
Human, Helen, 15
Human Rights and Environment Concern Centre (HURECOC), 133, 137
Hunter, Robert, 38
HURECOC (Human Rights and Environment Concern Centre), 133, 137

I
ICHHTO (Iranian Cultural Heritage, Handicrafts and Tourism Organization), 180, 181, 183, 184, 186
identity, 43, 46, 48
architecture and, 100
in China, 81, 100
collective, 47–48, 59

commodified, 115
craft and, 163, 166
in Iran, 176, 187
Islamic, 176
Janajati in Nepal, 139–41
as performance, 50
in Singapore, 120
Sinhala in Sri Lanka, 165, 167
technology and, 58, 59
See also caste; ethnicity and ethnic groups
ideology, 102*n*2, 109, 110–11
Indigenous peoples. *See* Sonaha (Indigenous people)
individuals, 88
emotion and, 43–44
foreign in China, 83, 95–100
as stakeholders, 37–40, 81
Indonesia, 63–65
nationalism in, 39, 64
political reform of, 66–67
social media and, 63–64, 76*n*6
See also Bol Brutu (Facebook group)
industry. *See* Dumbara Rata (weaving)
instrumentalism, 35
intangible heritage. *See under* heritage
International Centre for the Study of Preservation and Restoration of Cultural Property (ICCROM), 40, 41
interviews (method), 66
Iran, 8, 23, 48, 176–77
activism in, 171–72, 179–88
Iranian Cultural Heritage, Handicrafts and Tourism Organization (ICHHTO), 180, 181, 183, 184, 186
Islam, 46, 176

J
Japan, 9
journalists
in Iran, 178, 181, 187
Sonaha activism and, 132, 138

K
Karnali River, 130, 136
Keppetipola, Weera, 165

Kianpour, Muna, 185, 188
knowledge, 130, 147–48, 152

L
labor, 149–50
Land Transport Authority (LTA), 120
Latour, Bruno, 36
Leatherman, Thomas, 128
Lee Hsien Loong, 111
Lefebvre, Henri, 130
legislation (heritage), 8
 in China, 91, 100–101
Liang, Kenneth, 115
Lijiang, China, 86
Lim, Kim San, 110
Lim, Merlyna, 58
Lim, William, 113
Linden, Brian, 83, 94, 95–101, 102
Linden, Jeanee, 83
Linden Centre, 83, 84, 93–94, 97, 102
Loong, Lee Hsien, 111
Lowenthal, David, 11, 147, 148, 166

M
management (of heritage), 13–14, 65, 88
material culture, 88
 in China, 80, 84–85, 93
 ethnicity and, 110–11, 100
Maxwele, Chumani, 43
McGregor, Katharine, 39
media, 24, 42, 173–74
 coverage of metro dispute, 185, 186, 187, 189
 framing and, 170–71, 175, 178, 187–90
 in Iran, 171, 172, 179–83, 187, 189
 limits on, 110
 mass, 170, 174, 175, 178, 189
 National Trust and, 38
 news, 180, 181
 social movements and, 174–75, 177–79
 validation by, 175, 178, 180
 visual, 58, 62, 69
 See also social media
memory, 61
 See also nostalgia

methods (research), 50, 65–66
microfinance, 131, 151
middle class, 22, 24, 45, 113
migration, 90, 93, 99
modernization, 24
 in China, 92–93
 See also development (economic)
Monas Museum (National Monument History Museum), 39

N
Napoleon, 8
narratives, 46–47, 88
National Foundation for the Development of Indigenous Nationalities (NFDIN), 139, 143*n*9
nationalism, 116
 activism and, 95, 107–108
 in China, 81, 87, 88
 Chinese Dream and, 98
 heritage and, 6, 64, 95–96, 167
 in Indonesia, 39, 64
 in Iran, 176–77, 185, 186–87
 in Sri Lanka, 165
National Library, Singapore, 114
National Monument History Museum (Monas Museum), 39
National Museum of Iran, 8, 46
National Park Victims Struggle Committee (SCJAM), 132–34, 135
National Trust, 10, 25*n*3, 38
nation-state. *See* state
neighborhoods. *See* Chinatown, Singapore; Queenstown, Singapore
neoliberalism, 35, 148, 167
Nepal, 124, 142
 activism in, 131–36, 141–42
 ethnic groups in, 124, 126, 139–41
 See also Sonaha (Indigenous group)
Nepal Sonaha Sangh (NSS), 132, 134, 135, 136, 141–42
 conflict within, 137–38
 ethnicity and, 139–41
news media, 180, 181
NFDIN (National Foundation for the Development of Indigenous Nationalities), 139, 143*n*9

NGOs, 48
  in China, 90–91, 103n9
  in Iran, 172, 180–81, 182
  in Nepal, 131–34, 137
  See also Nepal Sonaha Sangh (NSS); Singapore Heritage Society (SHS)
Ningaloo Coast, 41–42
nostalgia, 7, 46, 72, 108
NSS. See Nepal Sonaha Sangh (NSS)

O
ownership, 94, 96

P
Panama, 41
Pancasila, 39
Pasargadae, Iran, 44, 46, 179, 183, 189
patriotism. See nationalism
PCDF (People-Centered Development Forum), 133, 134
People-Centered Development Forum (PCDF), 133, 134
People's Action Party (PAP), Singapore, 109–10
permits. See fishing rights
persuasion, 33, 34
Perth, Australia, 62
photos and photography, 64–65, 69
players, ix–x, 20, 81
  See also individuals; stakeholders
poaching, 136
politics, 10–11, 12, 147
  in China, 80, 100–101
  in Indonesia, 63, 64–65
political ecology, 128–29
power, 35–36, 128, 171
preservation, 11
profit motive, 97–98
progress. See development; modernization
protest
  in Indonesia, 63–64
  in Iran, 49, 171–72, 179–83, 189
  in Nepal, 134, 135, 137

Q
Queenstown, Singapore, 118

R
race, 110–11
Rajipur Declaration (2006), 132, 139
rally. See protest
Rawnsley, Canon, 38
Redigama, Sri Lanka, 148
religion, 46, 138, 176
research. See heritage studies
resistance, 48
  in China, 84, 102n2
  Indigenous, 129, 141
  Sonaha, 131–36
Rhodes, Cecil, 38
Rhodes Must Fall (movement), 38, 43, 47, 48–49
rights, 141
  Sonaha fishing, 134–35, 136–38
Riomandha, Transpiosa, 57, 67
rivers, 129, 141–42
  See also Karnali River
Robertson, Iain, 35, 43
romanticism. See nostalgia
Ruskin, John, 38

S
Samrachit Chetra Jana Adhikar Magasangh (SCJAM), 132–34, 135
Samuel, Raphael, 2, 11–12, 38, 73
scale, 4–5
scholarship. See heritage studies
SCJAM (Samrachit Chetra Jana Adhikar Magasangh), 132–34, 135
Scotland, 43
Shiism, 46
Singapore, 21–22
  activism in, 108–13, 116–20
  heritage of, 114, 115, 116–17
  politics in, 109–11
  tourism, 111–12, 114–15
Singapore Heritage Society (SHS), 45, 111, 113, 114, 115–18
Singapore Tourist Promotion Board, 112, 114–15
site visits, 45, 72, 183
Sivand Dam, 179–83, 192n19
Smith, Laurajane, 14, 173
social media, 20–21, 24, 42, 62–63

defined, 57
　as heritage arena, 42, 61–62, 73–74, 174
　humor and, 70, 71
　identity and, 58
　in Indonesia, 63–64, 76n6
　in Iran, 180
　in Singapore, 62
　social movements and, 56–58, 59–62, 73–74
　success of, 58, 59–60
　visual content and, 58, 62
　See also Bol Brutu (Facebook group)
social movements, 10–12, 16, 49, 57, 60
　conflict and, 48–49
　defined, 16, 32–33, 83, 128, 177
　emotion and, 34, 43–46
　identity and, 140–41
　Indigenous, 128
　media and, 174–75, 177–79
　political ecology and, 128–29
　social media and, 56–58, 59–62, 73–74
　Sonaha Indigenous, 131–38, 141–42
　study of, 33–37
　theory of, 33–34
　See also activism
Society of the Friends of Cultural Heritage of Khuzestan (Taryana; NGO), 172, 184, 185–86, 189
Sonaha (Indigenous people), 22, 123–24, 129–31
　as ethnic group, 138–41
　settlements of, 124, 126
　social movement of, 131–38, 141–42
song, 90
South Africa, 43
Sri Lanka, 147, 165
Srinivasan, Ramesh, 60
stakeholders, 9, 34, 36–37, 50
　in China, 88–91
　in Indonesia, 63–64
　in Iran, 182
　resources of, 37–38
　types of, 37–40
　urban, 64, 67–68, 72–73, 74
　See also elites; individuals; NGOs

state, 6–7, 9, 107–108
　See also nationalism; and specific countries
status. See caste; class; elites
structure, 35, 50, 62
Suharto, 39, 64
Sukarno (Soekarno), 39, 52n3
survey (method), 66

T
Tan, Kevin, 119
Taryana (NGO), 172, 184, 185–86, 189
technology, 59
　See also media; social media
textiles. See Dumbara Rata (weaving)
Tharu (Indigenous group), 126, 129, 132, 140
things, 37–38
thinking-feeling processes. See emotion
Tilly, Charles, 170
tombs and cemeteries, 46, 116
　See also Bukit Brown Cemetery, Singapore
Touraine, Alain, 83
tourism, 3, 112
　in China, 21, 81, 85–86, 88–89, 92–94
　community participation and, 89
　critique of in China, 99–100
　ethnicity and, 110–11
　luxury, 94, 98, 99
　sexualization and, 99, 104n16
　in Singapore, 111–12, 114–15
tradition. See heritage
trespassing, 131
trips. See site visits
Tsing, Anna, 3, 60, 64–65, 73

U
UNESCO, 15, 40
　See also World Heritage Committee (WHC)
urbanization, 6
　in China, 86–87, 89–90
　in Iran, 183–85
　in Singapore, 109, 111, 114–15, 116–17
Urban Redevelopment Authority (URA), Singapore, 111, 114, 116

V

vandalism, 43, 49
  See also destruction
village development committee (VDC), 126, 143*n*2

W

Walzer, Michael, 5
Waters, Malcolm, 2
weaving. *See* Dumbara Rata (weaving)
Weera Keppetipola, 165
Weiss, Meredith, 59–60
Wijoyono, Elanto, 56
World Heritage, 3–4, 8, 86
  See also Pasargadae, Iran
World Heritage Committee (WHC), 40–41
World Heritage in Danger, 41
World Heritage List, 40, 41–42
World Monuments Watch List, 117

X

Xizhou, China, 82, 93

Y

Yang, Mayfair, 103*n*7
Yogyakarta, Indonesia, 64, 67
Yunnan Province, China, 82

www.ingramcontent.com/pod-product-compliance
Lightning Source LLC
Chambersburg PA
CBHW072153100526
44589CB00015B/2213